GUARDED BY THE GOALIE

WITTMORE U HOCKEY BOOK 2

ANGEL LAWSON

FOREWORD

Readers!

Dropping in my little pre-book note to give you a heads up about my new hockey romance, Guarded By The Goalie. These books are written between the ROFU books and are my "palate cleanser." I decided to stop writing dark romance outside of the Forsyth Universe because I like to save all of that dark depravity for our Royals. But I also need a moment to get my sweeter romance on, which sure, is still sexy and angsty, just... toned down a notch.

This is the second book in the Wittmore U Hockey standalone series. That means, each book is a different m/f coupling with a complete story and HEA in their book. Characters and small themes do cross over from book to book so if you worried about missing out on some context, start with book 1, Faking It with the Forward.

Now, many of you know me from my darker worlds, like the Royals of Forsyth U or The Cult of Serendee. My hockey romances are not dark. They are not RH. They are strictly m/f. Do they have angst? Of course. What am I? A monster? How could I deprive you of angst? This is an Angel Lawson book after all. Also? There will be trauma. Angst smothered trauma. But most of all this is a love story about two hot people looking to reform their ways.

Heat level: slow burn to spicy heat. Lots of unresolved sexual tension (UST) and build up while these two try to get their lives—and Axel's dirty mouth—in check.

What you can find is the following:

- College/Hockey Romance
- M/F pairings
- Past Trauma
- Reformed Playboy
- Blacklisted Jersey Chaser
- Secret Relationship
- Slow-ish Burn to Spicy Heat

Enjoy!
Angel

1

Nadia

College parties suck.

Not that anyone would admit it, or that people would ever stop going to them, but it's true. Everything from the thumping, ear splitting music, to the shitty, watery, lukewarm beer. Or, God, worse, the mystery fruit punch served to all the girls the instant we walk through the door. What I hate most of all is the couples, paired off, with their tongues thrust down one another's throats, with zero regard to anyone else in the room.

"Hey, you look like you could use another drink." The statement comes from the guy standing next to me; Jacob. Cute. *Ish*. A sophomore. Baseball player for Wittmore U. Third baseman. He adds a wink that's not as sexy as he thinks it is.

He was also the one that offered me the first drink, the one that is still full, that I'm currently clutching to my chest.

"I'm fine, thanks." I give him a smile and take a fake sip.

I don't take drinks from guys I don't know at parties. I don't even take drinks from guys I *do* know at parties. Not anymore.

This party is more annoying than most. It's game day and everyone started partying early. I mean–*early*. When I walked into the coffee shop after my 6 AM shift at the gym, the three sorority girls in line in front of me were already dressed for the game. It's November, and the cool air did nothing to deter them from being out in short sequined dresses, designed to look like the Wittmore football jersey. The number '04' stamped on the back in a shimmery black. Beneath the short hem, their long, slim legs were bare, only covered in identical white cowgirl boots. One girl had a button pinned to the front, a photo of a tough looking face of one of the players. Her boyfriend, I presumed.

I stood behind them in my campus gym work shirt and leggings feeling self-conscious, jealous, and for the fiftieth time that week, reconsidering my new haircut which includes bangs. I thought I'd be one of those girls when I got to Wittmore. Sorority sister. The quarterback's girlfriend.

God, I was a fool.

Hours later, the game is over and everyone is here for the afterparty. Those girls all look a little more haggard. Makeup smeared and messy, fueled on energy drinks, loud music, and the excitement of a Wittmore win.

Jacob presses his hand against the wall behind me and leans close, giving me a whiff of cologne as he peers into my drink. Or maybe my cleavage? Either way, when he notices the cup is still full, a flicker of annoyance crosses his face. He does have the good sense to shake it off and gives me what he thinks is a charming smile. "I'm here to serve when you're ready."

"When I get thirsty, I'll let you know."

Poor kid. He's been on me since I walked in the room, his intentions clear. His gaze familiar. He knows me even if I don't know him. I've got a reputation, one I helped build. Nadia Beckwith: jersey chaser. He's convinced, rightly, that if he plays his cards right, I'll be an easy lay.

Every varsity athlete on campus knows me. Over the past few years, my number has been passed between them as a sure bet.

Too bad for the third baseman I'm reformed. No more athletes.

And to be fair, baseball players have never been my interest. I do have *some* standards.

I like my men big. Rough. The kind of guy that can pick me up and carry me to bed. One-hundred-percent alphahole. Football players, preferably. Maybe the occasional starter on the basketball team.

Or at least I did.

"Nadia!" I turn at my name and see Twyler wave from across the room. My roommate is at a table set up for a game of Quarters and is sitting on her boyfriend's lap. Reese, captain of the Wittmore hockey team, has one hand on her thigh and another wrapped around her waist. It's as much affection as these two will commit to in public, well at least Twyler. She tilts her head and calls out, "Come play with us!"

"In a minute," I lie. As much as I don't want to be over here with the baseball player while he plots ways to get under my skirt, the idea of being a third-wheel with Twyler and Reese is worse. They're the most unlikely pairing. The quirky sports trainer and the captain of the hockey team. They started off with some fake dating scheme to get his ex off his back, but Reese fell hard and fast. Nothing about those two has been fake since the first time he kissed her in the coffee shop. I would know. We share a bedroom wall.

Anyway, being fake isn't Twyler's style. That girl is as real as it gets.

But me? It's where I'm most comfortable. I excel at pretending to be something I'm not.

Across the room, my best friend closes one eye and lines up the quarter, making her toss. The quarter lands, dropping into the cup with a *plop*.

"Take that!" she cries, her grin wide with victory.

Across the table, her opponent, Axel Rakestraw glares at her. "Are you fucking kidding me?" he groans, running his tattooed hand through his platinum blonde hair. It's spiky on top, short on the sides. "How is she this good? You barely even go out."

Twyler shrugs and gives him an evil grin. "It's a gift."

"It's bullshit." He narrows his eyes at Reese and I see a shadow under his nose. Is that a mustache? Lord. Well, at least his shirt is still on, although the night is young. "She has to be cheating. No one hits it every time."

"My girl does," Reese replies to his teammate with a smirk. "Undefeated."

Axel frowns, his teeth worrying the ring in his lip. He's annoyed. Not at Twyler, but his competitive edge boils under the surface. He hates losing. I feel the tiniest flicker in my gut because, yep. Axel Rakestraw *is* my type. But even if I wasn't reformed, Axel is off limits for two reasons.

One, I promised Twyler I wouldn't chase any of the guys on the hockey team. Initially because she was working with the team, but even after she stopped she didn't want to risk any upheaval between us. Fair.

Two, Axel had seen me at my lowest, most humiliating, moment. He knows my secret, and I can barely stand to face him, much less have sex with him.

"You know, if it's too loud in here we can go somewhere more quiet. My buddy Rich lives here. We can head up to his room."

"Huh?" I turn, forgetting Jacob is still here. I look at his face, well, I try to, because this time he's definitely staring at my cleavage. Eyes nowhere near my face. I can't blame him. My tits *are* pretty spectacular. But from the glazed over glint in his eye, I can tell it's time to cut this kid loose. "Listen, Jacob–"

"Oh shit, they came." He straightens, gaze leaving my tits to peer over my shoulder.

"Who came?" I ask, looking behind me, but I already know. The tingling in my spine– a warning signal.

It's impossible not to see them, based on size alone. The guys walking in the front door are massive, each one bigger than the last. They have to duck their heads as they enter and they barely make it into the living room before the crowd swarms, each wanting a piece of our local celebrity football players.

I keep track of two of the players: Brent Reynolds and CJ McMichael. Brent's hair is damp, fresh from his postgame shower. He's surrounded instantly, by girls and guys, happily accepting the bottle of whiskey thrust in his hand. Next to him CJ wraps his good arm around one of the girls in the jersey dress. Even off the field, nursing an injury, it doesn't seem to lessen his status. A wave of nausea builds in my gut.

I look across the room to the Quarters game, but Twyler and Reese have vanished. Another one of Reese's teammates, Reid, has taken their place, and Axel looks much happier about it. His green eyes flick up, meeting mine, and he gives me a friendly smile and wink.

"I have to go," I blurt.

"Are you serious?"

Without an apology, I leave the baseball player, and go the opposite way from the front door. The last thing I want to do is to run into either Brent or CJ. This is their territory, not mine, and I don't want to do anything to provoke either of them.

My heart pounds as I make my way through the kitchen toward the back of the house. I used to think Brent was the one. He's handsome. Strong. Popular and skilled. He's headed to the NFL draft and it's predicted he'll get picked in an early round.

I was willing to do anything for him.

And a few months ago, when I'd been lucky enough to catch his eye, I had. Back then those feelings felt like butterflies. Nervous excitement. Like maybe what we had between us could be real. But the churning in my gut that I'm currently experiencing? That's not excitement. It's fear. Even I can't pretend otherwise.

"Excuse me," I say, squeezing past two girls leaning against the refrigerator, lips locked. They shift, never leaving their embrace, and I squeeze past, ducking into the hall that I know leads to the back deck.

I'm not sure why I'm scared–I barely remember that night. I've never even seen the video, but it's like my body knows something my mind can't–or *won't*–recall. I just have flashes of Axel barging in the room and getting me out of there. Of the weight of his jacket being thrown over my bare shoulders, and the slap of cool air on my bare legs as Twyler met me outside. What isn't blurry is the aftermath. How she wanted me to report what happened to the police. How she and Reese almost broke up over Brent's threats. How Axel's gaze went from flirty to sympathetic.

That was the night I became a victim.

"Leaving so soon?"

The voice I'd been avoiding for weeks comes from behind. Heart pounding, I swallow and turn. Brent stands in the hallway, his shoulders broad enough to almost go wall to wall.

"Brent..." I peer behind him, looking for CJ, but he's alone. "Hi."

"Hi." He leans a shoulder against the wall, effectively blocking me in. "It's been a while."

"Yeah," I nervously reach for my hair, but the length is no longer there. "It has been."

His eyes track my fingers. "You cut your hair. I almost didn't recognize you."

Almost.

"I was looking for a change," I shrug. "Something different."

"I like it," he says, reaching for a strand to tug between his fingers. "It's sexy."

A month ago I would have been thrilled for Brent to track me down at a party and call me sexy. Even though we're in a back hallway, it's still more public than he's been willing to commit to.

"Thanks." With my drink still clutched in my hand, I take a step back. "I was just going to find Twyler and Reese. We're about to leave."

I don't miss the flicker of irritation cross his face when he hears the name of the two people that know about our history. He catches himself, smoothing out his expression and letting his mouth curve up.

"Sure you don't want to stay?" His tone is casual. Easy. "I thought maybe we could talk. Catch up."

"I don't think that's a good idea, Brent."

The deal Twyler and Reese made with Brent was clear. He and CJ would not only remove the video of me that they put up on Lonely-Cams without my permission, they'd destroy it. They'll also leave me alone. Otherwise, I file a report.

That was the deal *they* made. I just want to forget the whole thing happened.

Brent takes a step closer, out of the shadows, close enough for me to smell the whiskey on his breath. The bottle hangs loose in his fingers down by his side. "Now that everyone has cooled off, I thought maybe we could reassess."

"Reassess?" I ask, not following.

"Our relationship."

That one gets me. "We didn't have a relationship. We had an arrangement. You called. I came over. We fucked." Until he got tired of me and decided to get a 'real' girlfriend. Someone that looks good on his arm. *Not* a jersey chaser. "You handed me over to CJ."

He takes a deep breath. "In hindsight, I can admit that trying to look out for CJ wasn't a great idea. He was just in such a low place and I wanted to help him out. I thought that's what you wanted too?"

That's the problem. I had willingly hooked up with his best friend. Why? One reason. He asked me to. "Yeah, well... he took it too far."

It's an understatement.

"I regret it." Brent's eyes drag down my body, lingering over my chest and down to my hips. That look used to give me hope, make me willing to do whatever he asked, but I know better. He reaches out and I feel the firm press of his fingers grazing down my neck. "Seeing you with him–seeing what you did with him on camera. It made me realize what I was giving up."

I try to process what he's saying. He regrets giving me up? Does he actually want me back? I close my eyes and ask, "What about Shanna?"

He doesn't even blink at his girlfriend's name. "Our relationship has nothing to do with Shanna, and you know that." His thumb strokes the divot at the base of my throat. "I need her for certain, official, roles." His tongue darts out and wets his bottom lip. "I need you for entirely different reasons, Nadia."

Heat creeps across my skin at the implication. Brent is insatiable in bed and I was willing to do whatever he wanted. Even things I wasn't always comfortable with. I was certain–*desperate*–that I could convince him I could fulfill all the roles in his life; a partner in and out of the bedroom. He disagreed, and when Reese and his long time girlfriend, Shanna, broke up, Brent had swooped in to claim the girl who spent her life preparing to be an athlete's wife. Basically, Shanna's good enough to be seen with in public.

I'm not.

"Come on, babe," he says, leaning in, breath hot by my ear, "let's give this another shot."

I tense. "You know that can't happen."

"Why?" He jerks back, glaring at me. "Because you don't want it to happen or because you're afraid of Cain and his girlfriend knowing you want it?"

"It's not about them," I say, knowing it's only half true. "It's about me having some self-respect for once in my life. I'm better than just being some booty call, or worse, the girl you get tired of and hand off to your friend." I swallow. "Once you're ready to be seen with me in public, and not including a dark hallway at the back of a frat party, maybe we can talk."

His jaw tenses. "I knew you were a slut, Nadia, but I had no idea you were so fucking stupid."

And there he is. The Brent I knew was hiding under the surface. The mean, petty, entitled, athlete that wants what he wants, *when* he wants it.

"Fuck you, Brent."

I step away, not wanting this to escalate, but his hand snaps back out and his fingers tighten around my throat. "I'd watch your mouth or you're about to see the other side of this, the one where I'm not so nice. I'll put the word out to every athlete at Wittmore that you're toxic. That baseball player out there, the one trying so hard to get in your pants? He won't even look your way. You'll be blacklisted. Every girl down on sorority row, everyone that you so desperately want approval from, will see you for what you are; trash." There's no mistaking the ferocity behind his threat. In the hierarchy of Wittmore, the captain and quarterback of the football team, is always going to outrank a jersey chaser. But to get one last dig in, he adds, "You'll be less than nothing when I'm through with you."

"I'll go to the police," I whisper.

He cocks his head. "I don't think you will."

One thing that I hate most of all, is how well Brent knows me. He knows all the buttons to press. What gets me out of bed at 3 AM to go over to his house for a booty call. What my goals and aspirations are. How desperate I am for approval–for the life he dangles in front of me like a carrot. And in this moment, with his smell all around me, and his fingers on my throat, all I want is for everything to go back to normal. Just accept who I am. Even without him spreading the word around campus that I'm blacklisted, what do I have? A crappy reputation. A best friend who is currently living my dream life. The fear of everything in my life falling apart even more than it already is.

"Hey," an upbeat voice carries down the hall, "you guys having your own party back here?"

Brent glances over his shoulder and grunts, fingers loosening. "Rakestraw. Nadia and I were just catching up."

Axel strolls up, eyebrow piercing glinting in the overhead light, and slaps Brent on the shoulder. "Reynolds," he says, in greeting. "Ran for three touchdowns. Who even needs the rest of the team, amirite?"

Brent crosses his arms over his chest. "Sometimes you gotta take matters into your own hands."

"Maybe I need to leave the goal more and get some glory." Axel looks at me for the first time and nods at my drink. "You gonna finish that?"

"Uh–" He grabs it before I can reply, tipping it to his lips. I stare at his Adam's apple, bobbing as he swallows. "Sure, go ahead."

He finishes, licking the corners of his mouth and wrinkles his nose at the empty cup. "Jesus, that's some shitty punch."

Brent doesn't look amused, but he's also not dumb enough to start something up with Axel. He's a notorious, no-fucks-to-give, wild card, with his tattoos, piercings, and love of partying. He's also one of the few on campus unafraid of the Wittmore quarterback. Unfortunately for me and Brent, he knows everything that went down that night.

"Twyler was looking for you," he says, crushing the cup in his inked fingers. I try to make out the letters across the knuckles but can't. "I think they're ready to go."

"Oh, great." I feel a sense of relief. "I was looking for them too."

"Cool. I'll walk you out." He places a wide, steady hand on my lower back.

"Thanks."

I don't give Brent another look, but I only take a step before I feel the quarterback's hand wrap around my bicep, holding me back. "Think about what I said, Nadia."

Axel doesn't give me an opportunity to answer, placing his body between me and Brent, forcing him to release me.

"God, he's a self-absorbed douche," he says once we step into the cloud of smoke on the deck. "Was he bothering you? Do I need to go back in there and break some knuckles?"

"No knuckle breaking, please." I intentionally don't answer the other part of the question. I hate that Axel was there the night Twyler and Reese dragged me out of Brent and CJ's house. This makes the second time he's been witness to my messy life. "Oh, there's Twyler and Reese."

I see our friends down in the yard, and push through the smokers to reach them. Twyler is looking down at her phone, fingers flying over the screen.

Reese squeezes her shoulder and lifts his chin in our direction. "Sunshine."

Her eyes meet mine and she shoves her phone in her pocket. "There you are! We were looking all over."

"Reynolds had her cornered in the back hall," Axel says with the slightest slur of his words. I jab him with my elbow and he grunts. "What?"

"You were talking to Brent?" Twyler shouts. "He's not allowed to even look at you, much less talk to you!"

"Shhh," I tell her, while shooting Axel a dirty look. Narc. "It wasn't a big deal."

"Nadia," Reese starts, "we made a deal with him. No contact."

They made a deal. They moved on. *My* life imploded.

"I promise it was nothing." I give her a reassuring smile. "He just wanted to brag about the game."

"He ran for three touchdowns," Axel adds, stumbling over a few syllables. He rolls his eyes at Reese. "Marshall was wide open in the end-zone the entire time."

"Prick," Reese agrees, then lifts an eyebrow at his teammate. "How much have you had to drink?"

"Just a few beers–oh and Nadia's drink." He makes a displeased face at the memory. "It was terrible."

"That's all?"

"Yes." He shrugs. "Unless you're counting the joint I shared with the rowing team before we got here."

"Jesus, Axel," Reese mutters. "We have morning practice."

"It's Sss-unday," he slurs. "Not until ten. I'll be there, Cap. No worries."

Reese exhales a frustrated sigh. "You better be."

"Y'all be safe," he says, before spinning around and ambling back toward the party.

"Is he going to be okay?" I ask, watching as he climbs the deck stairs and slides his arm around a girl's waist. She nuzzles affectionately against his side.

"Probably," Reese says, taking Twyler's hand. "He'll feel like shit in the morning, but that's his problem."

"How about you?" Twyler asks, waiting for me to fall in line with them as we head down the road toward our house. "Are you okay?"

Other than being a third wheel of a couple who are so perfect together I can't be mad about it? Jealous, totally. Mad, not a bit.

"I'm fine, Twy. It was no big deal. Brent was just flexing, like always."

She doesn't seem convinced, but Reese distracts her with a kiss on the cheek. She blushes, embarrassed at his affection. I smile encouragingly, pretending like everything's okay.

Because that's what I do best.

2

Axel

Thud, thud, thud.

The pounding outside my room sounds like a herd of cattle running down the hall.

This is what it's like living with three other hockey players.

"Reid! Shut the hell up!" I shout, face pressed into my pillow. "It's the goddamn middle of the night!" Even though the words come out in a rasp, the sound of my voice reverberates back, shuddering against my temple.

Thud, thud, thud.

I blink, or try. My eyelids are heavy.

Jesus.

That's not cattle. Or my roommates.

That pounding is coming from inside my head.

"What's wrong, baby?"

The voice drags me out of sleep. The *female* voice or rather, the hand of the female under the sheets wrapped around my–

Holy boner!

I force my eyes open, the glare of the sunlight harsh and painfully bright coming from my bedroom window. It shouldn't be this hard to look over at the girl holding onto me like a hockey stick. When I finally peel them open, a blonde is grinning back. "Morning."

Even with the bedsheet crease on her cheek and bedhead, she's cute. I can see why I brought her home, but I also have no freaking idea who she is. No memory of... fuck, much of anything. I drop my eyes to her chest. How the hell did I forget those tits?

She frowns, her lips parting downward. "You okay?"

I rub my face. It feels numb, like I'm still wasted. "Yeah, sorry. My head is killing me."

How much did I have to drink?

She licks her bottom lip and I see the glint of gold on her throat. Squinting, I make out the name Chantelle etched across a flat disk. "How about we do what we didn't get to last night because you passed out and then we can head over to the dining hall for Sunday brunch. They have the best waffles and it's still open for another hour."

The mention of food makes my stomach roll, and not in a hungry sort of way. I fight back a gag, and blink again, trying to clear the cobwebs in my head. "Sunday?"

"Yeah, Sunday." The look Chantelle gives me makes it pretty clear she thinks I'm a total dumbass.

Which I am, but not for the reason she thinks.

I take her hand off my cock and look around for my phone. "I gotta go."

"Now?"

"I'm late." Not sure how much, but from the brightness of the room and the quiet of the house, it's too late.

"For what?"

"Practice." Hopping out of bed, I spot my phone sticking out of my jeans pocket. I pull it out. *Fuck fuck fuck*. Thirty minutes.

"So after passing out on me half-limp last night, you're not even up for morning sex?"

That doesn't sound like me–the limp part. I mean whiskey-dick is a real thing, but in general, my cock is always ready to please and *to be* pleased. And if not that, I'm happy to eat pussy and show my partner a good time. A tiny part of me wants to tell her to wait for me to get back and I'll make it up to the both of us, but another part knows I'm not going to be in the mood for it. Or maybe even *alive* for it.

Reese is gonna kill me.

After Coach Bryant makes me suffer.

Fucking great. My last act in this world will be having a limp-dick and passing out with a hot chick in my bed. That's what finally gets me moving, my reputation, despite the impending berating and punishment from my coach.

"Sorry, babe," I tell her, rushing toward the bathroom, "but I'm late."

Woah. I sway, catching myself on the sink counter and close my eyes, counting to ten to keep the contents of my stomach inside my body. When I think I can manage it, I look up, catching my reflection in the mirror. I'm still getting used to the 'stache. Every time I see my reflection it takes me by surprise, but today that's not what catches me off guard. It's the half moon of dark shadows under my eyes, and the dry and chapped lips. My skin, under the tattoos, is pale. I tilt my head and frown, thumbing at the red spot on my neck.

"You gave me a fucking hickey?" I glance over my shoulder and see her still sitting in the middle of the bed, scrolling on her phone. She shrugs, like it's no big deal.

Jesus, the guys will never let me live this down.

Splashing water on my face, I try to wake up, but this is worse than any other hangover I've had. If I can call it a hangover. I think I'm still drunk. I've got a pretty hardcore reputation as a partier–I won't deny it–but getting blackout isn't my thing.

Maybe it was the weed?

Or maybe, like Reese keeps telling me, I've got to slow down.

That's easy for him to say. He's got this master plan and has been pushing towards it his entire life. He knows what he wants, and his goals align with his family, our coach, and his girl.

But I'm running out of time. Once these four years are up, the party ends. My fate is sealed. So I may as well have fun while I can.

No regrets, right?

Quickly, I brush my teeth, trying to remove the taste of cotton and death out of my mouth, then grab my Wittmore hockey hoodie and pull it over my head. My laundry is in a pile on the floor and I rummage around for a semi-clean pair of sweats. Chantelle watches me cram my feet into running shoes and shove my phone in my pocket.

"When will you be back?"

"Uh," I turn the doorknob. "A while. Pretty sure, I'm gonna be paying for being late."

"I can wait."

Oh, Chantelle. Pretty, perky-tits, Chantelle. Whatever happened the night before, and from everything I can tell, it was a big nothing, is definitely not happening again. "Sleep in," I tell her. "Or go get those waffles, but don't wait."

Her jaw drops, but I'm out of the room before she responds further. There's no time. I head down the stairs and sure enough, the house is empty. The kitchen table cluttered with the remains of a hasty breakfast.

They could have at least woken me up.

I start down the street toward the arena. It's walking distance, thank god, because I'm pretty sure if I drove right now, I'd get pulled over for a DUI.

One of the perks of living in Shotgun, the community just on the edge of campus, is its proximity not only to the university, but to the ice arena. It's a former mill town, the majority of the houses 'shotgun' style. Rooms stacked one behind the other, so that you can see from the front door straight through to the back. Our house is bigger–The Manor–the former home of the mill owner.

My stomach surges right when I'm outside the Teal House–the

brightly painted, skinny house Twyler and Nadia live in. "Oh shit," I mutter, glancing around. It's quiet out, everyone still recovering from the night before. I lurch toward a small bush in the corner of the yard and heave.

Sorry, girls.

Emptying my stomach makes me feel slightly better. I'm sweating, a cold, uncomfortable sensation as the toxins weep out of my skin. Swiping my access card in the arena door, I step inside and let the cool air wash over me, providing a hint of sweet relief.

I made it.

If I played a line, it's possible I'd be able to just slip in with the others, mixing in with the pads and helmets swarming around the ice, but I'm a goalie–the *starting* goalie. Not only is my uniform different, I practice different, and there's no fucking way Coach isn't going to notice. My plan is to suit up, get my ass on the ice, and beg for forgiveness.

I'm not above groveling.

Turning the corner to the locker room, I stop short, confused because everyone is still here. And not even dressed out. They're all still in sweats, standing around–no–standing in a line.

I wrack my brain trying to remember if something special was scheduled for today.

Jefferson, my third roommate, sees me and shakes his head. "About time you showed up."

Jeff is on the starting line, a kick ass defender. Not quite as uptight as Captain America over there, but he's not a slacker, that's for sure.

"A wake up call would've been nice." I open my locker and shoving my bag inside.

"Dude, we tried to wake you up. Banged on your door for five minutes."

"Bullshit." There's no way I slept through that.

"Reid even went inside."

Reid is three people down the line. I grab his shoulder and spin him around. "You came in my room?"

"To wake you up!" He holds up his hands. "I swear I didn't see anything."

"What the hell are you talking about?"

"The girl. As soon as I saw you weren't alone I backed out. Figured you didn't want to be interrupted." His eyes dart to my throat. "Guess she was too busy leaving a mark."

Ah, Chantelle strikes again. I rub the spot where I saw the hickey in the mirror.

"Next time, wake me up. Chick or no chick." I exhale, realizing it's pointless to be upset at them. I'm the one that fucked up. I nod to the line. "What's this about anyway?"

Jefferson jerks his chin toward Green's office and the two guys wearing white lab coats. "The NCAA showed up this morning."

A sinking feeling fills my gut. "The committee?"

"Random drug tests," Reid says. "Bryant's pissed about not getting any notice."

"They always pull this shit when a team starts doing well," Jefferson adds.

We're not just doing well, we're killing it. Undefeated and on track to finish up what we started last year–winning the Frozen Four.

And I just fucked it up for everyone.

∽

"Rakestraw! Get your ass in here."

After pissing into a cup and handing over a vial of blood to the drug tester, Coach Bryant does his best to kill us.

You'd never know we're undefeated.

But that's the kind of coach Bryant is. That's why he's a legend, with more Frozen Four wins than any other coach in the league. When we're winning that's when he steps on the gas. Pushes us harder. More time on the ice, reps in the gym, hours watching film. He doesn't slack off and neither do we.

Which is one reason I feel sick standing outside his office. I'd barely taken off my pads, when my name was called out with two others–freshmen. Every eye in the locker room was filled with both pity and irritation. Reese didn't even look at me, just tossed his dirty practice uniform in the bin and stalked into the showers.

You'd think my seniority would give me the perk of going in first, of ripping off this Band-Aid, but that's not how Bryant works. He's going to make me stand out here in the hallway and suffer.

The door opens and Craddock and Moriano, the freshmen, step out, both pale and quiet. I raise my eyebrows, hoping to get some kind of idea of how bad it's going to be. Suspended? Kicked off?

"Rakestraw," Coach Green says, "you're up."

"Yes, sir."

The good news, I think, as I step in the room, is that the workout forced the toxins out of my system. I'm exhausted, but awake, the nausea not completely gone, but less of an imminent threat. Coach Green shuts the door behind me, and takes the only available seat, leaving me to stand in front of the desk. It's impossible not to remember the long dormant memories of similarly standing in front of my father in his office, waiting for a similar ax to fall.

"As I'm sure isn't a surprise, your urine test came back positive for cannabis," Coach Bryant says, looking from the sheet with the test results to meet my eye. "The blood results won't get here until next Monday."

He's right, it isn't a surprise. I'd smoked up with the rowing guys before the party last night.

"I'm sorry, Coach. I fu–," I swallow, "screwed up."

"You sure the fuck did, Axel," he says, apparently not worried about cursing. "You're not one of these green freshmen like Craddock and Moriano coming in here learning the ropes and figuring out how to balance college life and D1 hockey. You're a senior. An adult. And you know the expectations I have on players on this team and the rules you have to follow to stay on it."

I know better than to respond. When Coach strings together more than six words, it's best to let him get it out of his system.

"You know that when a team has a run as good as we are on, others are going to do anything to slow us down, including sending in reports to the committee that suggests there may be drug use on the team." His jaw sets. "Catching a few starters in a sweep is a dream come true, which is why we have to be better, more diligent, than everyone else in all areas."

"I know," I say, when it seems like he's taking a break. "I do, sir. I know."

"Do you?" he asks, sighing and resting his forearms on the desk. "I won't bullshit you, Axel. You're our starting goalie. An integral part of the team and even with that, I'd be willing to toss your ass out on the street today and pull up one of those younger kids to take your place."

I tilt my head. There's a 'but' coming. Please let there be a but coming.

"But you lucked out. The NCAA has loosened its policy on cannabis use. You get a one time pass." He looks a little disappointed. "Although there will be a probationary period and mandatory education."

I'd heard something about this, but wasn't sure how the policy shook out inside an organization. "Whatever is needed, I'll do it. I don't want to let you or the team down."

"I hope you mean that, because with your seniority, you're on the hook. Cutting the freshman would be easy, but you're the example here. A leader on the team, if you like it or not. I need you to step up for them as much as the men out there looking to go all the way to the finals."

I rankle at the term leader. That's not something I've ever aspired to be. I'm not Reese, who was born to wear the captain badge. I'm just here to live my best life, play some kick-ass hockey, until I get called back home–back to my true calling.

Coach Bryant studies me for a moment. The man was an All-American back in his day. His instincts are top notch and he must sense something because he sets the report aside and says, "You're a good player, son. You can have a career if you want it, you know that right?"

Ah, but that's the question. What do I want? Fuck if I know. Fuck if it even matters. I can say what I *don't* want, which is the life expected from me by my family. Taking over my father's legacy. Becoming a leader in a whole different world, one I don't even respect. I've been given a reprieve. Four years to escape life in Texas, time away from my family, and the obligation that comes with my last name. I'm here to have fun, to do all the things that won't be allowed of me once I graduate. My father views it all as a rebellion: tattoos, women, hockey, excess. But it's just me trying to live my life while I can, pretending like the future isn't coming for me.

"The league is showing interest, but taking the path toward the draft is hard work. It requires absolute dedication and focus, and I don't always get that drive from you." Coach leans back in his seat, his thumb spinning the heavy gold ring on his finger. "Whether you realize it or not, your teammates look up to you. Those two knuckle-heads that just walked out of here think you're a fucking god. They rely on you, and in general, you pull through."

In general, but not this time.

"Tell me something, Axel." He levels me with one last hard look. "I'm not going to be surprised by anything on the blood test, am I?"

"No, sir. It was just a joint at a post game party. Nothing else."

That, at the very least, I'm sure of.

"In three weeks, you'll be retested, per NCAA rules. If you're clean, we can put this behind us and move forward." He frowns. "If not, well, the rules aren't as lenient the second time."

"Understood."

He jerks his chin at the door. "Now get the hell out of here, you smell like a locked up boot bin."

"Yes, sir."

Coach Green opens the door for me and rests a hand on my shoulder. He leans in and says, "If you're just partying, that's one thing, but if this is something else, like you're struggling with something, I'm here if you need me."

"I'm not, but thanks," I say, stepping into the hall and taking a deep breath. At twenty-two years old I still hate getting called to the mat by authority figures. Makes me feel like a little kid again. I do my best to avoid it, but I have no one else to blame for this one but myself.

It's obvious from the lack of noise coming from the locker room that the rest of the team has already left. There's no post practice music or loud trash talk. I'm relieved, definitely not in the mood to rehash what just went down. I feel like such a fuck up. Weed? I'm smarter than this.

I walk in and immediately realize that someone is waiting for me. Reese.

He's sitting on the bench, a skate between his thighs, adding a fresh pair of laces. My shoulders tighten at what I know is going to be my second lecture of the day. So, I decide to get ahead of it. "Probation," I tell him, reaching my locker and opening the door. "I'll probably have to go to a health seminar or watch some of those godforsaken videos the conference puts out. But I'm still on the ice."

I hear a grunt, but nothing else, as he fusses with his skate.

I strip, yanking off my practice jersey and pants. I ball them up and toss them in the bin across the room. Resting my hands on my hips, I look at him. "Just say it."

"Say what?"

"Whatever you obviously hung around after practice to tell me."

"I'm not waiting to talk to you." He looks up for the first time. "My fucking lace snapped during practice."

"Good, because Bryant already did the job of informing me that I need to get my shit together and stop letting the team down." I turn back to my locker and grab my bag. "I don't need to hear it from you too."

I just need to get out of here. Get some food in my belly and take a long nap. I've just pulled my sweats up to my hips when he says, "He's right."

Jesus Christ.

I slam my fist into the metal door. "I knew you couldn't let it go."

"Dude, I think I've earned the right to say something right now. Not just as your captain, but as your friend."

I spin and spread my arms. "Go ahead then, take your best shot."

He's standing now, and Reese is a big mother fucker. At least three inches taller than I am. "It's not a shot, Ax, it's the goddamn truth. I've been watching you party harder and harder as the years go by. Every day we get closer to winning this thing, you amp it up another notch. You know I don't have a problem blowing off steam. You can drink whatever you want, fuck whoever you want, go on a three day bender. I don't give a shit."

He takes a breath, and I sense him trying to maintain control.

"But what you're doing now is looking a lot more like sabotage every day, which if it was just you, then I'd say go for it. But the problem is that it's not just you. It's the team. It's me, Jefferson, and Reid. It's those freshmen who are relying on us to leave them with a legacy. It's Coach Bryant. We've all worked too fucking hard to get to this place, but without you in the net there's no fucking way we can win this thing." He swallows. "And to be honest, I don't want to win it without you. We got here together. We're going to finish this together."

Well damn.

This is why Reese is the captain. It's not just because he's the best on the ice. He's the best off too.

I thrust my hand in my hair and say, "I told coach I'll do better, and I will. You have my word."

"Thank you." He reaches out, fingers curled. "It'll be worth it. We can walk out of Wittmore with the trophy and all the opportunities it will afford us."

I nod, linking my hand with his and clutching it tight. The tension between us smooths, although the tight ball in my chest doesn't. Winning that trophy will change nothing about my future. It'll just be another reminder of how much I have to give up.

3

Nadia

After three years, you'd think I'd be used to the sharp feel of cold wind as I walk across campus, but it still surprises me every time. Ducking my head, I hurry to the front doors of the business school and rush inside. It's hard to believe that I only have the final month of fall semester and then the spring left before I'll graduate and leave Wittmore behind.

I feel like I've barely accomplished any of the goals that I set out when I arrived from Florida. I'd picked a school so far away, because other than an education, I came here with the grand plan of reinventing myself. I wanted nothing more than to be a different person than I was back home, where I'd wrapped up my high school career with drama and bad decisions. I'd hoped for a fresh start in a new town, a new school, with new friends, but whatever I thought was going to change my life for the better, didn't. I guess in eight months, I'll have the opportunity to do it again.

I enter the room late, and take an open chair on the edge of the room, unwrapping the scarf my aunt knitted for me from around my neck. I hang it and my hat on the back of my chair. It's the layers that I hate. Scarves, hats, gloves, coats. I still prefer the shorts and crop tops I can wear year round in my home state. Peeling off the rest of the layers, I get out my laptop while the professor continues with his lecture.

I've seen the looks people give me when I say that communications is my minor. They think it's an intentional, desperate move to be around the varsity athletes at Wittmore. It's well known that it's a common degree for athletes–a backup plan if their sports career doesn't take off. But it was my mother that suggested it. She thought it would give my business degree a boost when I look for a job after graduation. The fact that my classes are filled with hot athletes? Originally, that had just been a bonus.

After years of hook-up apps and trying to meet men at parties, I had an all organic opportunity to meet the guys that I was interested in. For once, I wasn't just a jersey chaser. I was a classmate. A peer.

Hopefully, I was girlfriend material.

Until everything with Brent and CJ blew up, and if I'd hoped that Brent was just throwing around idle threats about having me blacklisted, I can sense the shift already.

Things had been tense and awkward for a few weeks–ever since that night at Brent and CJ's house. The football players that I'd been talking to all semester, the same guys I'd been texting and hanging out with at parties, suddenly grew cold. Even the ones that I'd been intimate with, like Rocky and Austin, stopped acknowledging me.

I'm more embarrassed by how hurt I feel, than the actual fact Brent carried through with his promise.

Opening my computer, I try to orient myself to the professor's lesson. Behind me, Rocky, all two-hundred-and-twenty-five pounds of him, taps his foot to the beat of whatever song is playing on his headphones. At least he's not singing this time. His voice is *not* good. Not that anyone would ever tell him that.

Turns out that the special privilege everyone thinks student athletes get on campus is real. They're loud and entitled. Showing up when they feel like it and when they do, barely paying attention. I'm sure it's not every player, but this class? With these particular guys? It's obvious they're used to being the center of attention and the professor has been told to cut them slack. He never skips a beat when Darius, the six-foot-seven starting basketball player, leaves the room, grabs a snack from the shop on the first floor of the building, and returns, loudly eating a bag of chips. Or when the entire defensive line naps in the back row.

It's surreal watching people get away with so much just because of their status.

They have power that I don't understand, but I'm unrelentingly attracted to.

No.

The word echoes in my head.

Not anymore.

I've sworn them off. No more athletes. No more trouble. No more jersey chasing.

"Hey."

The whispered voice comes from the seat next to mine and I look over at Eric, the only other non-athlete in the class. Really, he's the only person in here that doesn't look at me like I'm a piece of trash stuck to the bottom of their shoe. He tilts his laptop in my direction so I can see his notes.

I smile gratefully. "Thanks."

"No problem."

Eric's a normal guy and the only friendly face in the group. Quickly, I take down the notes and manage to ignore the distractions in the room. The class moves swiftly–which happens when I'm interested in a topic. Even with all the hostility around me, I get into the lecture, taking notes until the professor wraps up, and I quickly start to pack my things.

"One last thing before you go," the professor says from the front of the room. "If you looked at your syllabus, you'll know there's an end of semester project that will count as your final grade. You'll do them in pairs and I'll be assigning you randomly to a partner."

My stomach sinks. Projects in this class suck for two reasons. One, these guys don't want to do any of the heavy lifting on classwork. Two, none of them will even acknowledge me. So how the hell is that going to work?

Anxiety crawls up my spine as he starts calling the pairs: Rodriguez and Smith. Davenport and Lane. Beckwith and Lassiter.

I look over at Eric with my eyebrow raised. Well, that's convenient.

"Looks like we're partners," he says, as our professor continues to rattle out names.

"Sorry." I feel the need to apologize. "I'm sure you'd rather work with someone else."

"Why would you say that?" he asks, tucking his laptop into his backpack.

I make a face. Eric, like the rest of the guys on campus, is a Wittmore football fanboy. He loves being in this class with the players, always stopping them to talk about the game. There's an expression of innocence on his face–like he maybe actually doesn't know about my reputation. I slide my laptop in my bag and zip it up. "Don't worry. I'll do my part."

"I'm not worried about it," he says with an easy shrug, while pulling out his phone. "It'll be fun. Can I get your number?"

"Sure."

Quickly, we exchange and set up a time to text about specifics later. I've put on my coat and have my bag over my shoulder when I hear him say, "Congrats on the game, man. You guys killed it."

See? Fanboy.

I don't even look to see who he's talking to, I'm just ready to get out of here. Unfortunately, I'm barely ten feet away when I realize I left my scarf in the room. Crap.

My aunt knitted the scarf for me when she heard I was coming up north for college. It's yellow and black, Wittmore colors, and made of the softest yarn. I'll slip in and out. No big deal.

I hear the voices before I step back in the room.

"Congrats to you too, brother."

"What do you mean?" Eric asks.

"She's a jersey chaser, but with the freeze out, she'll probably happily fuck you." I recognize this voice too. Austin–Wittmore's superstar tight end–we hooked up for a few weeks in September. Right before Brent started texting me.

"Just make sure you wrap it up," Rocky adds. I can hear the smugness in his voice. "That cunt has taken a lot of dick."

"At least get a blow job," Austin adds. "Her tits look fantastic when she's on her knees."

Not wanting to hear another word, I turn on my heel and rush out, leaving my scarf and dignity behind. Whatever hope I had about moving on with my life vanishes in a heartbeat, and I only have myself to blame.

∼

"Just stay for an hour, then we can go home," Twyler says, pushing open the door to the Badger Den, Wittmore's popular hockey bar. "Please?"

I'm not sure when Twyler and I swapped lives. I guess around the time Reese Cain kissed her in the coffee shop and swept her off her dirty sneakered feet. I've always been the one up for a party or closing out one of the off campus bars, but in the last month it's been hard for me to get the energy up for socializing. It all seems so pointless.

But I also know I dragged her out countless times when she didn't want to go, and even with the captain at her side, she still feels socially awkward in bars and at parties. I owe her for having my back all those times she just wanted to stay home and binge true crime documentaries.

Tonight, the bar is crowded, mostly filled with guys from the team. As captain, Reese plans these bonding nights, where they all hang out after practice to chill out and build relationships. After a few hours, girlfriends and puck bunnies show up to join in.

"Twy!" Reid calls out, grinning as we approach the bar. "You made it."

Reese hears his girlfriend's name and turns, his eyes sweeping over her. God, to have a man look at me the way Reese Cain looks at Twyler. He pulls her close and drops a kiss on her mouth.

"Hey, Nadia," Reid says, leaning against the bar.

"Reid, how are you?"

"Not as good as those two," he says, eyes darting back to the couple. Reese's hand slides down Twyler's back, never quite going into PDA territory. She'd cut his balls off. "But otherwise I can't complain. Still undefeated."

Hockey. The only barometer that really matters. Once upon a time, I'd been interested in Reid. He's a year younger, but he's hot, with the most adorable dimples. I'd asked Twyler to give her permission for me to pursue him earlier in the fall. My one-time hockey player pass. She'd agreed, but only if we went on a real date. We did–sort of–and it was fine, but the sparks weren't there.

It's okay. It's kind of nice having a group that's off limits for me. I know it. They know it. It's a safe place and right now I need more of those.

"You want a drink?" he asks, holding his hand up to get the bartender's attention.

"Nah," I say. "I'm good."

His eyebrows raise but he shrugs. "Water? Soda?"

"Yeah, sure, water with lemon would be great."

He leans over the bar and orders the drink from the bartender, before turning back to me.

"Undefeated, huh?" I ask. It's a big deal. They narrowly lost the championship last year and the guys are incredibly focused. "Sounds like you're a lock for the finals."

"If we can keep our shit together," Jefferson says, turning away from the game playing on the big screen over the bar. He and Reid exchange a look.

Sensing a vibe, I ask, "Something happen?"

"Someone made a report to the NCAA and they did a surprise drug testing. A few guys got busted," Jefferson says.

"Probation," Reid adds quickly. "But it's not the kind of drama we need right now."

"That really sucks," I say, taking the water from Reid. "I bet Coach Bryant is furious."

"Livid." Reid takes a swallow of his beer. "But there's no such thing as an obstacle free season. We'll pull through."

On the screen over the bar, the game comes back on and both guys are drawn back in. Twyler and Reese are still engrossed with one another and I let my gaze travel over the room. That's when I notice Axel sitting at a high top table, alone, a plate of hot wings in front of him. He's got his own glass of clear liquid in front of him. Unless it's straight vodka, I'm pretty sure he's drinking water too.

He notices me watching him and his lips quirk. "See something you like, T?"

I have no idea what 'T' stands for, and after the last month, I don't really want to know. Axel is notorious for handing out nicknames like candy.

"Want a fry?" He holds up the basket. Needing something to do with my hands other than hold this glass of lame water, I take one. The salty goodness is perfection on my tongue.

"Thanks."

Now that I'm closer, I notice he looks different. And not just that godforsaken caterpillar under his nose. Even with it, he's hot as fuck. All those dark tattoos peeking out from under the collar of his shirt and down his hands. The silver hoop in his lip draws my eyes to his sexy mouth, but his trademark easiness seems replaced by something that looks like exhaustion.

"What?" he asks, tearing the meat off a wing.

"You look miserable."

He snorts and tosses the bone in the pile, then his tongue darts out, licking sauce off his fingers. "What gave it away?"

"Well, for one, your shirt's on–"

He holds up his hand. "Mike has a rule about the shirt at the Den. He'll kick me out if I take it off."

"Huh." If I've learned one thing, it's that if there's a rule specifically created for you, it's for a reason. "I also don't think I've ever seen you drink water outside of a game."

"You keeping tabs on me, T?"

I shrug. "I'm just observant."

His clear green eyes draw away from the TV overhead and over to mine. "I'm guessing Twy didn't tell you."

"Tell me what?"

The green in his eyes darken. "That I failed a drug test and Coach put me on probation for the next three weeks."

"Fuck. No! Seriously?" I drop to the stool next to his. "You're the one that got busted?"

"So, she did tell you."

"No." I tilt my head over to the bar. "Reid and Jeff mentioned that a couple of guys got busted. No wonder they're worried. I don't know much about hockey, but I do know that the goalie is a pretty integral part of the team."

He picks up the glass of water and takes a drink. "I'm not sure about worried. Pissed is more like it, especially Reese."

I look over at the captain who is drinking a soda by the bar with his arm wrapped around Twyler. I know he keeps pretty clean during the season–only drinking occasionally and only when they've got a break in the schedule. He's not letting anything get in the way of his goals.

"So, you're sober now?" I ask.

He shrugs and nudges the basket of fries toward me. "Until I earn Cap's trust back."

I grab another. "Wow."

"Epic fuck up, huh?"

"Pretty spectacular." Not like I can judge fuck ups. I'm the reigning queen.

"What about you?" he says. "Haven't seen you out in a while."

I frown. "Dude, we talked the other day." His expression is blank, like he's got no clue what I'm talking about. I sigh. "When you saved me from Brent at the party?"

"Shit. You were there?" A line creases his forehead, like he's searching his memory, but then his expression clouds. "What the hell were you doing with Brent?"

"You seriously don't remember?"

I sure as hell wish I didn't.

"Not a fucking thing. I got blackout. Which believe it or not, isn't like me."

Axel is fun at a party. No, he's the *life* of the party. The kind of guy everyone, male or female, wants a little piece of. He's fun, good looking, talented... and there's definitely a dangerous vibe going on with the tattoos and piercings. I can't help but think that if he's partying enough to black out his memories, it's probably a good idea to slow down.

He picks up a drumstick and asks, "So what did you need saving from this time, T?"

"Myself, mostly." I shrug. "He was just being a dick."

"So nothing new." He takes another bite and chews, before asking, "So how's all that going?" He gestures with his hands. "You know, everything with Brent and CJ?"

I take a deep breath, weighing how much to tell him. If he doesn't remember anything from the party, I'm not going to remind him. "Fine, I guess. I think the video is still down, but it seems like he's spread word to the rest of the football team and maybe a few others not to talk to me."

"Good." He scowls. "You don't need to talk to any of those pricks."

"It doesn't feel good to be ignored and ostracized," I admit, the shame from hearing the guys talking to Eric about me after class resurfacing. "They won't even look at me in the class we have together, and I'm pretty sure they orchestrated it so that I'm not paired with any of them in a group project."

"Why would you want to be?" He shakes his head. "You're better than these fuck-head, abusive, entitled assholes. Don't look to them for validation. You're never going to get it."

In a moment of pure honesty, I blurt, "This is my identity, Rakestraw. I'm a jersey chaser. If I'm not on the arm, or in the bed, of a varsity athlete, who am I?"

Axel looks at me like he wants to tell me exactly what he thinks, his teeth pulling at that silver hoop, but instead he reaches for his water. "Hold up your glass."

"My glass?"

"I'm making a toast, T, humor me."

I shake my head, but lift the water glass into the air. "What are we toasting?"

"To new identities," he declares. "To no more epic fuck ups. No more partying for me. No more athletes for you. Not until we get our shit together."

I laugh, but he looks dead serious. "Okay." Yeah, I can get behind this one. I clink my glass to his and repeat the mantra. "No more epic fuck-ups."

Maybe it'll be easier if we do it together.

4

Axel

I'VE WALKED HOME from the bar district with a hot girl more times than I can count, but this may be the first time I'm stone-cold sober, *and* there's zero chance of a hook-up at the end of it.

"Thanks again for offering to walk with me."

Nadia's a good foot and a half away, her hands shoved into the pockets of her jacket.

I repeat: Zero-chance.

"No problem," I tell her truthfully, "hanging out at the bar and drinking water is exactly as lame as it sounds. You gave me an excuse to be a gentleman *and* save face with my teammates."

"I wasn't always paranoid about walking around campus by myself, but Twyler keeps making me watch those murder shows and now I'm convinced a psycho clown murderer is behind every tree."

"You too?" My laugh is followed by a cloud of cold air. It's still an adjustment getting used to how early winter comes here. "Every time

I come downstairs, TG and Reid are obsessing over some crime scene. I keep waiting to find a bulletin board in the kitchen with strings connecting all the suspects."

My roommate already had a strange interest in true crime, but when Reese started dating Twyler he found a partner in sleuthing.

"Better your house than mine." She gives me a quick grin, stopping at the split off where the sidewalk leads to the Manor. "I can probably survive getting between here and there without some stranger kidnapping me."

The last few weeks have been rough on Nadia. Not that she says anything about it. In fact, I get the idea she'd rather not talk about that night we found her at Brent's place, but I can sense the change in her. She's not just scared of making an epic fuck-up. She's just scared.

"Eh," I say, noticing the way she constantly looks over her shoulder, like she's either worried about being followed or being seen with me. My ego is secure enough to assume it's the former. "What if there's someone waiting in the bushes by your house?"

"Well, then they're going to be knee deep in some frat-boy's vomit."

Oops.

"Came out of the house the other day," she continues, "and the whole plant was dying from toxic poisoning."

"Yikes," I say, not even thinking about confessing. "People are assholes."

"Tell me about it," she mutters, turning down the path that leads to the porch of the Teal House. I follow her up to the door and watch as she gets her key out.

"I really do appreciate it," she says quietly. "I hate feeling like this."

I frown. "Like what?"

"Like I have no control anymore. Paranoid and suspicious."

"Because of Brent and CJ," I venture.

"I can't tell you how many times I've checked every room in the house for cameras since then." She wraps her arms around her upper body and I get a flash of her from that night, my jacket hanging over her frame.

"You shouldn't have to live like this," I tell her, wishing I could take it all back–to have gotten to the house sooner that night and stopped it from happening at all. I'd been the one to find her back in CJ's room, stripped down to her panties, completely unaware of the camera recording her. I'd gotten her out of there and wrapped her in my coat, but it's obvious it still haunts her.

She shrugs, sliding the key into the lock. "They're not the only ones to blame. I went over there. I partied with them. I'm the jersey chaser, Axel. I'm aware of the expectations that come with the title."

She's right. There's a certain expectation to the girls that hang around athletes. The jersey chasers, or for us, puck bunnies. They're an easy lay–fun, sexy, ready to party, and best of all, no commitment required.

But there's a line, and those two crossed it.

"T," I say, shoving a hand in my hair, "don't even *think* about blaming yourself for those assholes' behavior. Just because a woman enjoys sex doesn't mean she's open to exploitation."

She narrows her eyes at me. "Are you trying to get in my pants?"

"What? No? Why would you ask that?"

"Why else would you be so nice to me?"

Fuck. Those guys really are assholes.

"Darlin'," I rest my hand on the door jamb, "I won't pretend that I don't understand why CJ thought he could make money off of you. You're gorgeous. Sexy as fuck. But consent means something, and they took that choice away from you." She blinks, tears hot in her eyes. I reach out and swipe one away with my thumb. "But I also understand the desire to be something that you're not–to want more out of life than what you've been given. It can lead to desperate and stupid decisions."

"Epic fuck-ups."

"Exactly."

"I just want to get some control back," she says, after taking a deep breath. "Get my footing where I don't feel so unsure and scared all the time."

"Scared of what?" I ask, needing to hear it.

"Men like Brent and CJ." Her gaze flits down to my hand clutching the edge of the door, then straight ahead, at my chest. "Men like you."

"You're scared of *me*? You think I'll hurt you?"

Her eyes finally meet mine when she says, "Every other man in my life that looks, and acts like you, has."

Well, damn.

I take a deep breath and look out to the street. It's quiet, but the sound of my heartbeat rushes in my ears. It covers up the warning bells, the one I should have listened to before I smoked that joint. But I don't like to see this girl question herself. It makes me fucking furious.

"How about you give me a chance to prove to you otherwise."

With her hands behind her back, she braces herself on the door frame across from me. Interest flickers in her expression. "And exactly how do you propose that?"

It's not a no, but this girl deserves more than me reading signals, which is why my next move is slow, and I lean across the small space, trying my best not to crowd her in. Using my fingers, I brush the hair off her cheek, tucking it behind her ear.

"Can I kiss you?"

I wait for the rejection. I'm expecting it. But her chin lifts, and she says the words that will change everything, "Yes."

5

Nadia

OH FUCK.

What have you done?

That's the first thought when I wake up to the weight of an arm circling my waist. A *male* arm. He's warm. Comfortable. And, well, from the steel rod stabbing into my backside, hard as fuck.

And big. Really big.

I don't have to look to see who's got me tucked into his body. Yet, I carefully lift the sheets and peek underneath to confirm. Yep, no doubt about it. The tattoos are a dead giveaway. No mistaking the owner of the dark ink that covers his muscular forearm all the way down to his hand. From this angle, it's a jumble of designs and symbols, but it's the letters on the knuckles that turn my gut to stone: YOLO.

Axel.

His fingers graze my lower belly, right at the edge of the elastic band of my panties. Butterflies swirl in my gut as the morning fog clears and the memory of the night before comes rushing back. Last night was...

An epic fuck-up.

Jesus, we didn't even last two hours.

"Axel," I whisper, shifting to get his hand to a less dangerous spot. Unfortunately, he shifts with me, sliding his hand to my breast and cupping it.

"Five more minutes." He buries his face in the back of my neck. "No morning skate today."

I roll my eyes, because of course this guy has my tit in his hand and all he can think about is sports. I definitely have a type. A type I swore off, yet here we are.

I'd love to say I didn't know how it happened, but that would be an outright lie. Axel and I were at the Badger Den, toasting with water about how we were going to get our shit together. Unfortunately, once the hot wings and fries were gone, sitting around the bar while everyone else partied and partnered up was lame. Which is why when he offered to walk me back to the house, it seemed like a good plan. The smart, *responsible,* plan.

I start to rise, but he holds me tight, and I sigh.

"You need to get up," I start, but outside my room, I hear footsteps on the hardwood and the bathroom door open and close, followed by the hum of the fan turning on. Damn it. Twyler must have slept here last night, which means–

"Axel," I whisper more urgently, pushing at his handsy hands, "*get up now.*"

He groans, but rolls away, rubbing a wide hand over his face. "What's wrong?"

"Shhh!" I sit, pulling my tank down from where it had pushed up over my tits. His sleepy eyes track my moves. "And what do you mean what's wrong? You're in my bed. Half-naked!"

He lifts the sheet, which is already tented, and looks underneath. A smirk lifting the corner of his mouth. "More than half, T."

"Oh my god." I drop my face to my hands. "What the hell have I done?"

Next to me, Axel's hand shifts beneath the sheet, clearly adjusting himself, and then he stretches back, propping an elbow behind his head. I peek over at him and get an eyeful of the ridiculously hard-packed muscle that makes up his upper body. Last night wasn't the first time I've seen him shirtless, but it was the first time I knew what all that smooth skin felt like under my hands. What it tasted like.

No.

"Are you talking about us fucking?" he asks, drawing that hand out from under the sheet and resting it on the tattooless spot on his lower abdomen.

"Don't say that." I wince and hop out of the bed. "Please don't say that ever again."

"That we fucked? How come?" His eyes roam over my body and I get the distinct feeling he's remembering what I looked like bare as much as I am about him. I lunge for a pair of flannel pants on the floor and tug them on quickly. "It was pretty awesome, right?"

"Wrong," I say, keeping my voice low. If Twyler finds us…

Epically fucked, times a million.

"It was a mistake, that's all. A complete lapse in judgment." He's been sweet. I was vulnerable. And yes, I agreed to it. I wanted it, but… I grab his jeans off the floor and toss them to him. "Get dressed. *Quietly.*"

"It didn't feel like a mistake when you were getting a mustache ride last night, T."

My lady parts tingle at the memory and I really wish the flare of heat didn't rush to my cheeks, but my mind isn't in control of my body right now. Obviously. "Can you just not? And get up. You *have* to go."

He shrugs, but he's wearing that smug expression that says he knows I think he's hot. And dammit. Of course I think he's hot. Who wouldn't? I throw his T-shirt at him as he slings his bare legs over the side of the bed and stands. I turn away, but not before I catch sight of his rock-hard ass. Damn. I bet I could bounce a quarter off those cheeks.

"Why are you freaking out?" he asks, fumbling with fabric. "We're two extremely hot, completely sober, consenting adults that had a little bit of fun." I hear his zipper and determine it's safe to turn around. I was half right. His pants are on, but he's got his shirt in his hand, and my knees wobble. I grip the back of the desk chair as he lifts the shirt over his head and continues. "I asked for a chance to prove myself to you and I think I did a pretty damn good job of it."

Too good of a job, I think, but don't say.

"I don't get what's the big deal," he continues, "I mean, if anything, we should get back in bed and do it again."

"It's a big deal because last night I–no, *we*–toasted to not fucking up anymore. And part of not fucking up for me, is doing this." I wave my hand in a vague motion between us. "Chasing jerseys. Sleeping with athletes I barely know."

Betraying a promise to my best, and only, friend.

"You didn't chase me, T." He lowers the shirt down his body, covering up the tats and muscle. I toss him his shoes, one after the other and he deftly catches them mid air, before sitting on the end of the bed to put them on. "You wanted to take back a little control and I gave you that opportunity." He wedges his foot into one shoe. "And we know each other a hell of a lot more than anyone would realize."

"Which makes it worse for me," I blurt. "If I could make you black that out, I'd be good with it."

"Why?" He ties the second shoe and stands.

"Because it's humiliating," I admit, picking up his hockey jacket from off the messy pile of clothes on the pink chair in the corner of the room. "You've seen me at rock bottom. You're a witness to the lowest, most embarrassing moment of my life. Every time you look at me, it's filled with pity, and it makes me feel like shit all over again."

Before he can respond, I hear the fan shut off, and the bathroom door open. I hold up my hand and give Axel a pleading look. His mouth forms a thin, hard, line but he stays quiet.

"Nadia, you here?" Twyler's voice is followed by a soft tap on the door. The handle turns, but it catches. Thank god I had the awareness to lock the door.

"Yeah, I'm up," I call, stomach twisting with the fear of being caught.

"Oh good, I'm out of the shower."

Her shadow shifts under the door and this is just too awkward. Twyler asked one thing of me when she started working with the hockey team–to leave the guys alone so it wouldn't make it awkward for her. Although she isn't working with them anymore, she is dating the captain, and the rule still applies.

I give Axel a hard look and gesture for him to be quiet, then unlock the door and crack it open, filling the space with my body. She's in Reese's team hoodie, with her hair wrapped up in a towel.

"Reese and I are meeting at the dining hall for breakfast, if you want to come join us."

"Yeah, that sounds good. Let me get ready."

"Twenty minutes?" her head tilts in question. We both know it'll be thirty, but I nod in agreement and shut the door. I exhale, and turn, pressing my back to the door. When I look back at Axel his arms are crossed over his chest and he's staring at me.

"What?" I say. "She'll flip out if she finds out about you."

His teeth run over that piercing in his lip and he says, "You think I pity you?"

I blink and push off the door. "I know you do." Why wouldn't he? "Look, I don't blame you for what happened last night. You're right. We both consented. But I have to stop hooking up with guys–athletes–because it's easy and makes me feel good for a few minutes."

His eyebrow lifts. "So you admit it was good."

Better than good. I'm not used to the men I'm with making me feel like that.

"I admit it was a mistake. One I'd like to forget and one we never, ever, tell anyone, especially Twyler and Reese, that it happened."

His jaw sets and there's a dark flicker in those green eyes. He walks over to me and the room suddenly feels too tight–too small. My body reacts instantly to his proximity, because he's right, even if I won't admit it to him, the sex was fantastic. His mouth and hands, and fuck, his cock, were all way better than any of my other hook-ups lately. He was confident and respectful and made sure I came before him.

Both times.

"Let me make one thing clear," he says, sliding his hands into his pockets. "Again. That shit that went down with Reynolds and McMichael? That's reflective of them. Not you." The muscle in the back of his jaw tics. "When I look at you, it's sure as fuck not with pity. All I see is a ballsy, sexy, kickass woman, who's fun to hang out with and also makes my dick hard. You're Twyler's best friend and she's dating *my* best friend, which means you've got to be pretty fucking awesome." He eyes me carefully. "But if you want to forget this, we can forget it."

"I want to forget it."

He swallows, Adam's apple bobbing. "Done."

"Thank you."

He starts toward the door. "Axel," I grab him by the arm, "wait."

He looks at me, eyebrow raised and I swear I see a glimmer of interest in his eyes. "Yeah?"

"You can't go out there. If Twyler or Reese see you…"

"Oh."

I turn and lean over the pink chair, flipping the latch on the bedroom window. "It's a short drop."

He laughs, but crosses the room, leaning down into the open space. "I haven't had to sneak out of a girl's room in a long time, T."

"Tell me something," I say, once he's worked his body through the opening and he's standing on the other side. He leans back in, his shoulders nearly as wide as the frame. "What's the 'T' for?"

"It stands for what I think of every time you walk in the room."

"What's that?"

He smiles, that one that I know he uses to get what he wants and winks. "Trouble."

6

Axel

I can't forget it.

Despite every effort. Every cold shower. Every other girl that I smile and wink at around campus, I can't get Nadia Beckwith out of my head.

Even now, three days later, I'm standing in the net, taking warm-up shots before the game, and all I'm thinking of is Trouble.

Nadia Beckwith.

That night had started out innocently enough. Hanging out at the Badger Den, drinking water, and feeling the weight of my probation. We'd commiserated over stupid decisions. Taking a shot of water in solidarity. Later, I offered to walk her home. There were no intentions. I just needed to get out of the bar where my teammates were drinking and having a good time, and she wanted to go home.

It was on my way.

I was being a gentleman.

Even without her regular energy, Nadia is an easy girl to talk to. Fun. How we went from her asking if I wanted to come in to watch some TV to the two of us fucking–*twice*–I'm still not sure.

Don't get me wrong, Nadia is hot. All curves and a bright, welcoming smile. I've flirted with her before, but she's never been interested in anything but some light flirting. Not enough of a meat-head, I imagine, or plans of being drafted to the NFL. If her type is Brent Reynolds, then no wonder she's not into me. Even though we know he's a class-A douche, on the outside he's got that Tom Brady, All-American good guy vibe that pro-teams eat up.

The way she reacted to waking up in bed together? Embarrassed and secretive–she definitely didn't want Twyler and Reese to find out about us–that isn't a response I'm used to.

I'm chalking the whole thing up to hormones and stress release. That's it.

Except I don't feel less stressed. I'm horny as fuck just thinking about her.

My teammates criss cross around the ice, passing the puck in sharp, zinging snaps. Despite the distraction, I do my best to stay alert and ready, catching Reese's shot in my gloved hand.

"Nice," Jefferson says, skating past. "Good catch."

He takes the puck from me and tosses it on the ice. Another shot is fired my way, this time by Kirby. I bend, blocking it with the long pads that cover my knee, and it bounces back in play. He and Emerson circle one another in a quick, choreographed dance. They've come a long way in the last few weeks, finally gelling with one another. That cooperation is one reason we're undefeated.

Snap!

Reese gets off another shot, I move to block it, but the biscuit soars past my shoulder, hitting the back of the net.

"Fucking hell," I mutter. "Nice one, brother."

"Don't take it the wrong way," Reese skates up, a cocky grin on his face. "If anyone is going to get one past you, I want it to be me."

We bump fists, and I grab my water bottle out of the pouch on the back of the goal. The refs blow their warning whistle—signaling the end of warmups. Following my teammates off the ice, I see Reese wave to someone up in the stands. I follow his gaze and spot Twyler dressed in a Wittmore jersey. She smiles down at her man, and I instantly look next to her, for Nadia, but she's not there.

Jesus, what's my problem?

One night and I can't get this girl off my mind. Was the sex that good or was it because for the first time, in a long while, I was fully sober while doing it?

Whichever it is, now isn't the time. We file into the locker room for a last minute pregame talk. The room is busy–hot. We're all fully suited up. Coach Green and the new intern that took Twyler's position are busy working with the guys that need extra support. I spot a familiar face by the door–Pete– his leg in a brace.

"Hey man," I say, "how's the leg?"

"Good. The surgery went well. I just have to let it heal up and keep up with PT."

"Awesome," I tell him. Pete's a good guy, and an excellent player, but he fucked up his ankle by not listening to Twyler's advice. "You do what they tell you and I'm sure you'll be back on the ice soon. We need you out there."

"I don't know, man, you guys are killing it out there this season. Although," he says, tilting his head, and looking at me thoughtfully, "I'm thinking maybe you guys should throw a game."

"Why the hell would we do that?" Reese asks, offended at the idea of losing on purpose.

"To get Rakestraw to shave that caterpillar off his upper lip."

I crack a smile and smooth out the fuzzy strip of hair with my fingers. "Jealous you can't grow one of your own, baby face?"

"*Don't* even think about getting rid of it," Reid snaps. He's the most superstitious of us all with an entire series of pre-and-post game rituals. "It's our good luck charm."

"Eh." Jeff shrugs. "I've noticed a definite lack of puck bunnies around you the last week." His eyebrow raises. "It's the 'stache isn't it? It repels hockey pucks *and* pussy."

"Just because I don't announce my every hook up on the group chat like you do, doesn't mean I'm not getting laid."

"He did come in before dawn the other day wearing the same clothes as the night before," Reid says. "That 'stache may work the magic on and off the ice."

I'd like to think I worked my magic with Nadia, but I haven't heard a word from her since I crawled out her bedroom window. Not that I expected to, because frankly, after that fully sober one-night-stand, she made it perfectly clear she wanted to pretend the whole thing never happened. Nadia's got a reputation as a jersey chaser, but I have my own as a fuck-boy. Neither of us are strangers to a one time hook-up, but there was something different. Maybe because it wasn't fueled by our usual bad habits.

Or maybe it's because it felt incredible being inside of her.

It's like I told her, we were two sober, horny, consensual adults looking to get off.

And damn, if all I want is to do it again.

"Men!" Coach Bryant's voice booms over the room. "Stop talking about Rakestraw's facial hair and get focused on the game." He shoots me a glare. "But if you shave that off without permission, the whole team is doing bag skates after practice for a month."

～

"Good game, Rakestraw."

I wasn't just good. I killed it. A shut out, and against a team like Northridge that's no easy feat.

"Thanks," I say, knocking fists with one of the coaching staff on the way out. The post game energy is high with Reid playing DJ and getting everyone worked up for the afterparty. Down the hall, Reese waits by the entrance, adjusting his tie. Coach has a rule about leaving a game dressed up–he likes us to look like winners, regardless of the results. Reid walked out of here in a bright red suit, looking like a clown, although Darla doesn't seem to mind. I'm used to suits–growing up formal wear was pretty standard for special events. Part of me wants to push back but on a night like this, I look *and* feel like a badass. "What's wrong?" I ask Reese as I get closer and see the weird expression on his face. "Tie too tight?"

"No." He makes a face and releases the tie.

"Then what's with the constipated look on your face?"

My phone buzzes in my back pocket and I check it for the first time since the game ended. There's a series of 'congratulations' texts from friends that saw the game and a few offers from puck bunnies to celebrate, including one threesome.

Look, I promised to get my shit together. I didn't promise to go celibate.

I scroll down to the final text, quickly realizing it's one I don't want to read: My father's.

"You really dominated out there tonight," Reese says, giving me an excuse to put the phone away and deal with those messages later.

"Yeah, well, contrary to popular belief, I like to win as much as everyone else on the team."

"I never said that." He pushes open the door. "You just seem different. Like you were two steps ahead of everyone else out there."

"Just my same old awesomeness, bro, accept it." I refuse to admit it, but even though I've been bored as hell, physically and mentally, I feel better. Other than waking up to Nadia induced hard-on's every morning, my sleep is great. I'm less tired when I get up. Better hydrated. My cravings for all that shit have diminished, replaced with one other desire–getting in between the thighs of a girl that's not interested. "Your game was on point too, don't forget that."

"Are you fishing for compliments, Cain?" Twyler steps out from the crowd waiting for the players outside. The group is filled with girlfriends, friends, and family hanging around after the game to congratulate the team. The group is bigger than normal, which is pretty common when the team is doing well. People want to be a part of the energy of a winning team. I don't even look to see if anyone is waiting for me. My parents haven't even been to one of my games since high school.

"I don't need to fish, Sunshine," Reese says, sliding his arm around Twyler's waist. "My two goals speak for themselves."

She rolls her eyes, and shifts her attention to me. "That last save was amazing, Axel. I thought maybe that kid was going to get it past you, but you were so quick."

"You know me," I wink, "I'm good with my hands."

Reese punches me in the arm. "Don't flirt with my girlfriend, dumbass."

Behind Twyler, I hear a loud choking cough. Craning my neck, I see her. Nadia. Huh. She did come to the game, afterall.

Twyler shifts and places her hand on her friend's shoulder. "You okay?" She holds up a bottle. "Need some water?"

"Sure, thanks." Nadia's voice is husky and brown eyes flick to mine as she takes it, unscrewing the cap. Her cheeks have a faint pink tint, and I watch as she wraps her lips around the mouth of the bottle, then takes a big swig.

My cock twitches under my pressed suit pants.

Before I can figure out how to respond to her being here, a kid in a Badger jersey rushes over, program in his hands.

"Reese! Can I get your autograph?"

"Sure," Reese says with a friendly smile, taking the marker out of the kid's hand. "What's your name?"

"Walker."

A moment later it's clear that Walker was the Trojan horse, because a heartbeat later, an entire team of U12s swarms toward him. Twyler and Nadia step back as the kids push forward to get to us.

"One at a time," Reese laughs, signing his name. "What's your position?"

He's so good at this, making small talk with the kids, being a superstar. After he signs the program, Twyler offers to take a photo of Reese with the kids.

I start to step away, letting Reese have his moment, when Walker turns to me. "You too, Axel?" he asks, grinning up at me.

"Yeah." I take the program and flip to my photo inside, scratching my name next to it. Handing it back, I'm surprised to see the line behind him has grown. Fuck. My eyes dart toward the parking lot, the route to my escape.

As much as it seems like I enjoy being the center of attention–and I do, when it's chicks in tight skirts and fans offering to buy me a free drink–being a role model, or someone to look up to? That's where I draw the line.

"Don't even think about it," Reese says over the kids' heads, giving me a pointed look. I catch the meaning behind it instantly; if I walk away from these kids, I'm walking away from my obligation to the team.

"Who's next?" I ask, ignoring the uncomfortable feeling in my chest.

"Me!" The next kid pushes forward and I can't help but notice the pink jacket and a knit hat with a sparkly pom pom on top.

I raise an eyebrow. "What's your name?"

"Greta."

"You play hockey?" I flip open her program and she nods. "What position?"

"Goalie, like you."

"You must be pretty tough to play goalie." I sign my name, and hand her back the program.

"More than my brother," her chin lifts. "He plays forward."

"He's about the glory, huh?" I laugh, taking a little stab at Reese. "I have a little sister, she's pretty tough, too."

"Does she play hockey?"

"Nah. She's not interested in sports." Although I have no idea if that's true. I'm pretty sure no one has ever asked Shelby her opinion on anything in her life. Father tells her what to do and she's always done it. That didn't mean she was weak. Hell no, she's the toughest person I know to be able to put up with all of that.

I ran halfway across the country to escape it. She never had that choice.

"Too bad," Greta says, smiling down at the signature. "She's missing out."

"Smile!" Twyler calls, and next thing I know I'm caught up in taking photos. "Make sure you tag the team!"

"I thought you were studying to be a sports trainer," I accuse once all the programs are signed and the crowd disperses, "not a marketing major."

"Oh, that was Nadia's idea," she says. "Business, communications, marketing..."

Nadia smiles and shrugs. "Never waste an opportunity."

"But now that you mention it," Twyler says, focusing on Reese. "You took a pretty nasty hit in the third. Let me see it."

He rolls his eyes, but when Twyler lifts up his shirt to inspect it, I can tell he loves having someone take care of him.

I flex my hand, then shake it out.

"Hand cramp?" Nadia asks.

"I'm not used to signing that many autographs."

"Those kids love you."

"They wouldn't if they knew about my probation." I doubt Coach Bryant will be happy to see my face plastered all over social media. So far we've kept the violation out of the media, but there's no need to give someone the opportunity to call me out. "I'm not cut out for being the face of the team." I hold up my tattooed hands. "They prefer clean cut, pretty boys like Cain over there."

"That's not how it looked to me."

"Yeah?" I ask, eyebrow raised. "How do I look to you?"

Because I really, really, want to know.

When she doesn't answer, I add quietly, "Come on, tell me you haven't thought about me since the other night?"

She swallows. "I haven't thought about you. Not once."

The pink on her cheeks tells me that we both know that's a lie.

I worry my teeth over the piercing in my lip. "Maybe you just need a reminder."

Her hand flies up, palm flat. "Nope."

I blink at her hand. "Why?"

"Because," she looks over her shoulder to where Twyler is feeling up Reese's ribs, "we agreed to forget it ever happened."

"Yeah, well I'm having a hard time with that because I keep thinking about how fucking hot you look when you come." Her pupils dilate and her mouth parts. "Don't tell me you're not doing the same thing. Thinking about my mouth on your–"

"Oh my God," she cuts me off with a grimace and whispers, "Do you ever give up?"

"Not when it's something I want, T." I hold her eye. "And right now, you're what I want."

"You're ridiculous."

I shrug. "Some people find my perseverance an attractive quality."

"Well, I'm not one of them." Again, her gaze lingers on the happy couple.

I frown. "If you're really worried about them, they don't have to know. I've got no problem with discretion."

Her eyes sweep over me, traveling from my inked hands to the piercing on my lip, to the platinum hair on my head. "Nothing about you says discrete, Axel."

I reach a hand out, placing it on her hip. "Then what does it say?"

Her hip eases forward, reservations slipping, but she recovers quickly, and eases back toward her friend. "Everything about you says that I'm not the only one that should be called trouble."

∽

"Dude," Reese says, once we're in my truck. With the crowds after the game, it's best to have a car to make a quick exit instead of walking.

"What?" I adjust the heat, blasting it from the vents to cut the chill of the night.

"Stay away from her."

I'm not sure I heard him right.

"Stay away from who?"

He stares at me for a moment, then rolls his eyes. "Nadia."

"What about her?" I ask, shifting the vehicle into gear.

"Don't pretend you weren't hitting on her."

I snort. "You mean you noticed something while you were mining for gold down your girl's throat?"

"I noticed. You're just lucky Twyler didn't."

"Even if she had, all she would have seen was two people talking after a game while their friends were making out across the parking lot." I turn onto the road that leads to Shotgun. "What am I supposed to do while you two tongue fuck? Ignore her?"

"You know she's vulnerable after the shit that went down with Reynolds and McMichael." My hands tighten around the steering wheel at their names. They both deserve an ass kicking for what they did to her. Reese continues, "She acts like everything is fine, but Twyler noticed she's going out a lot less. Like she's avoiding it or maybe scared."

No more epic fuck-ups.

"Do you blame her?" I ask.

"No." He sighs. "Twy's still hoping she decides to report it, but regardless, she doesn't need anyone sniffing around her while she's figuring things out."

As we talk about them, I pass the Teal House. The soft blue light flickers inside and a small sedan sits in the driveway, indicating the girls made it back home. I don't look at the bush I poisoned on the way to practice the other day.

"I'm not sniffing around her. We happen to be the best friends of two people that are dating. We're going to get tossed together and you need to chill out." The tense expression on his face doesn't ease so I add, "She's not my type anyway."

"Bullshit." He laughs. "She's hot, fun to be around, and loves a cocky athlete. She's *exactly* your type."

"Yeah," I say, pulling into the driveway of the Manor. "Except for the fact that I agree with you. She's vulnerable and I'm not looking for that right now. I need to get off probation, focus on hockey, and figure out what I'm going to do after graduation. Would I fuck her? *Hell yes.* "Sure. Am I going to? That's not something you need to worry about."

Because even if he's right, and she is my type, Nadia has made it infinitely clear she wants nothing to do with me.

∽

TWO HOURS LATER, after refueling on the food Jefferson's mom had sent to the house, and kicking Reid's ass, twice, gaming, the post-game energy finally wanes enough to head to bed. It's hard to settle down after going hard for two hours on the ice. Our bodies may be tired, but that's when the adrenaline kicks in. On the weekends, we'll blow off steam at one of the parties on Greek row, or host one of our own, but on weeknights, we take it easier. Our schedule is rough, we've got two more games this week before Thanksgiving break, then we'll get a couple of days off before games resume.

Lying on my bed, I torture myself by scrolling through Nadia's photos on ChattySnap. I hate to admit it, but CJ knew what he was doing when he came up with the LonelyFans scheme. Although she's gorgeous, with big brown eyes and plump lips, he hadn't shown her face while he was secretly recording her. No need to. Nadia's a sexpot. Curvy hips and big tits. She flaunts it on her own account, taking selfies with the camera angled straight down her cleavage, while wearing tiny shorts that show a smidge of ass cheek, just enough to make you want to sink your teeth in. I scroll back, past the newer photos of her up at Wittmore, down to the ones from high school where her skin is a warm brown and she's wearing even less clothing on the beaches in Florida. My cock thickens when I pause on one of her in a white string bikini, sunkissed and eye-fucking the camera.

Pushing my hand down the front of my shorts, I'm prepared to take the low road, when I hear the creak of the top stair and a soft, feminine giggle. It could be anyone. Reid is on-again-off-again with his girl, Darla, and it's entirely possible he sweet-talked her into coming over. Jefferson and I usually slip out to sorority row, and me hanging back won't keep him from going. He's been making his way down the alphabet and currently is fucking around in the P's.

But when I hear the soft snick of the bedroom door across from mine, I know exactly who's sneaking around; Reese and Twyler.

Now I just feel like a pervert, pulling my hand out of my shorts, and tossing the phone across the bed.

That'll be the last we hear from them, even though I know they'll be fucking like rabbits in a few minutes. Twyler is quiet, the opposite of his ex, Shanna, who's the type to let her presence be known. My boy's always been the monogamous type. He dated the same girl all through high school and most of college. Sure, he had a post break up wild streak, where he made his way through his share of puck bunnies, but all that stopped when he noticed Twyler. I'm pretty sure their sex is vanilla as hell.

Me? I'm definitely more of an exhibitionist. The thrill of getting caught is part of the fun, but all I can think right now is that sex is still sex, and those two are about to have more of it than I am.

My phone buzzes and I lean across the bed, picking it up.

Chantelle: You out celebrating after the game?

Huh. Figured my early morning brush off would have waned her interest. I type out a reply.

Me: Eh, not tonight. We're taking it easy.

Chantelle: I could come over, pick things up where we left it off.

It's tempting, but before I can respond, a close up photo of a pair of lace covered tits fills my screen. At the top I see the edge of that gold necklace.

Jesus. This girl is definitely not about the chase.

Even so, I'm not one to say no to a willing partner, and I'm about to give her the go ahead when the next text comes through, displaying across those pretty tits.

Shelby: Did you get dad's text? You need to respond.

My hard-on instantly deflates and I quickly swipe the image away. I can ignore my dad, but my sister? I try not to mess around.

Me: Had a game. I'll reply now.

The phone rings before I can open another text box.

"Axel," my dad says, my name pronounced with a sharp, Texan twang. "You're still up."

"Hey, Dad, sorry. We had a late game. Just got home a little while ago." I slide my legs over the side of the bed, needing to move. "Did you catch it?"

It's a trick question, that I already know the answer to. "Sorry, Son. Not this one."

Right. *This one.* He hasn't watched a single game since I got to Wittmore.

"Too bad," I say, proud of the team. "It was a good one."

"Maybe the next one won't be on during bible study."

Unlikely. The man never leaves the church. One activity after the other, anything to keep the parishioners busy. Reverend Nolen Rakestraw may not be there for his son, but he's always there for his flock.

"I called to talk about preparations for the holidays," he says, moving on to the real motive for the call. "Have you practiced the piece I sent you?"

"A little."

Not at all.

"I wanted to give you plenty of time before Christmas to learn the material and if you need any assistance over Thanksgiving, Reverend Boyce will be happy to help."

"I'm only going to be there for two days, Dad, one of those Thanksgiving Day. Reverend Boyce doesn't want to spend his day with me instead of his family."

"I'm sure you two can make something work." When I don't instantly agree, he adds, "The congregation is expecting you to speak. It's tradition."

"I know. I'll get it done. I always do, don't I?"

"Not without testing my patience first," he says. "How are your public speaking classes?"

"Good," I lie. "You know, talk-y."

My father thinks I'm majoring in communications with a focus on public speaking, but I switched to sports management after Freshman year. I *do* have a minor in communications, which keeps me in enough classes for him not to fully notice.

"I hope you're gaining a good knowledge base for when you return to Kingdom's Reign." His tone lightens. "Only seven more months and you'll be back."

"Yep, seven months."

Fuck my life.

"I just wanted to check in. Make sure we were on the same page."

That'd be a first. "Sure, Dad."

"Next time, try to respond faster. Your mother and sister worry when you don't."

"I will," I reply, pissed he dragged Shelby and my mom into this. They aren't worried about me. He's just obsessed with controlling all of us.

"Night, Son." I brace myself for the next part. "To the Kingdom."

I swallow and force out the words, "To the Kingdom."

I don't breathe for a full thirty-seconds after the call ends, until another text comes through.

Shelby: Thanks

Me: Sorry I missed it. Be Safe.

I stare at the text for a long time, hating that he still has this control over me, two-thousand miles away. But that's how my father works, with leverage. If I won't do what he wants out of an obligation to him, he knows I'll do it to protect my sister.

The call leaves me rattled–pissed and frustrated–and I want nothing more than to blur the lines of reality right now to try to go back to that feeling from before, of hopped up adrenaline. I want to chill out, to have a drink. Take a hit. Lose myself in pussy.

I thrust my hand in my hair. Fuck the promise I made with Nadia. Fuck Cain and his easy road to the future and his perfect girlfriend he's going down on across the hall.

I don't owe them, or anyone else, anything.

Hopping off my bed, I fling open my closet door and reach for the top shelf. My fingers brush over the hard wood and I grab the box I'd stashed up there months ago, before the season started. I'd been saving it for a special occasion.

My fingers wrap around the box, the ink on my knuckles taunting me.

YOLO. That's the motto I've held since I walked out of my father's house.

You only live once, and I plan to live it to the fullest.

7

Nadia

Swipe.

Swipe.

Swipe.

With the TV as background noise, I flip through the guys on BadgerUp, a Wittmore athlete dating app. Even though I'm not swiping right on anyone, that doesn't mean I can't look, does it? It's habit, mostly. A thing to do when you're at home by yourself, bored, and rewatching the same rom-com for the fifteenth time.

That's the justification I'm giving myself as my thumb lingers over Caleb, a sophomore on the water polo team with abs made of steel. I checked him in at the gym a few weeks ago. His face is cute enough, but who cares about his face when he's got a body like that? I zoom in, able to actually count the ladder of muscle.

"What the hell, Caleb?" I say out loud. "Were you made in some kind of laboratory?"

I flip through his photos, landing on another shirtless picture, this time he's slick with water on a dock by the lake. Normally, I wouldn't be interested in someone that plays on a non-varsity sport like water polo, but the urge to feel something—someone—is getting harder and harder to resist.

Especially when they look like a Greek god.

"Fuck it," I say, thumb hovered over the screen. So I'll swipe right. See how this goes—

The sound of a loud thump against the front door makes me pause. I hold still, waiting to see if that was a knock or something else. We live on a busy street. It's mostly foot traffic, but more than once a random, drunk frat boy has stumbled up the steps and passed out on the front porch.

I set the phone on the coffee table and stand, walking to the door. Pushing up on my toes, I peer out the peephole.

"Jesus!" I jump when a face appears distorted from the glass. I exhale and look again, getting an eyeful of a familiar sharp jawline.

Yanking open the door, I glare at the man on my porch, "What the hell are you doing here?"

Axel leans against the railing, dressed in a thick Wittmore U hockey jacket, black sweatpants, and scuffed sneakers. A brown wooden box is clutched to his chest. "Thank god," he says when he sees me, thrusting the box at me. "Take it."

I narrow my eyes at him. "What? What is it?"

"Take it," he says again, grabbing my hand and manipulating it to hold the box. "Please, before I do something I regret."

Reluctantly, I open the box and look inside. A baggie of weed, a pack of rolling papers and a lighter are stuffed into the small space. Understanding dawns on me. "You're trying not to smoke it."

He nods, pushing past me into the house.

"Hey!" I call, chasing in after him. "You can't just barge in here! Twyler could–"

"Twyler's at my house," he tosses out. "Probably getting her pussy eaten out by Cain right about now."

Well. Get it girl. "I still didn't invite you in."

"I almost caved, T." He sinks onto the couch, hands in his hair. "I tried to commit an epic fuck-up. I was this close, but I started walking, hoping the cold air would snap me out of it. I ended up here."

I sigh, snapping the box shut and shutting the door behind me. "Coming here wasn't a great idea. I've got to get up early for work." I don't add that I was one thumb swipe from committing my own epic fuck-up. Although, when I turn back, he's sitting on the edge of the couch staring down at my phone, it's clear he's on to me.

The screen is still open to Caleb, the hottie water polo player's profile page. His eyebrow raises and he sets those green eyes on me. "You were about to cave, too." I dive for the phone, but he gets it before I do, reading the profile out loud. "Caleb Bower. Wittmore sophomore. Likes dogs, working out, and–"

I snatch the phone from him and close the screen. "Axel! Oh my god! What if you swiped right?"

"Don't pretend like you weren't going to do that before I interrupted you."

"No, I wasn't." The lie comes out in a hiss. "I was watching TV and bored. That's all. No caving."

The look he gives me makes it clear he doesn't believe me, but it doesn't stop him from adding, "I just don't need to be alone right now. Can I hang for a bit?"

Being alone together proved to be a problem last time. It escalated quickly, from sitting on this very couch to a sex-a-thon in the bedroom. But he looks pretty pathetic and being alone sucks. I hate it too. "Fine. You can stay and watch TV with me, but you're sitting over there," I point to the armchair, "and I need you to promise you won't hit on me."

Because my willpower is only so strong.

"Sure," he says, rising and moving to the armchair. He shrugs out of his jacket, revealing a faded, tight gray T-shirt that clings to his chest. "So what are we watching?"

I grab the remote and a blanket and settle back on the couch, placing my phone on the flat arm. "Springfield."

"Like the town? Or the rock star?"

"It's the name of the town where they live. It's my favorite show from when I was in middle and high school." It's a teen soap opera about a bunch of high school kids as they learn about friendship and first love. Of course, there's a ton of heartbreak, scandal, and drama too. Axel still looks confused. "You never watched it?"

Everyone our age watched Springfield. It's a classic and launched the careers of half a dozen stars.

"Was it on cable?" he asks.

"Yeah. Every Sunday night."

He lifts his chin. "Well there you go. We didn't have cable growing up, and we were always busy on Sunday nights."

"Busy with what?" I ask.

"Obligations with my dad's job." He kicks his feet up on the coffee table and crosses them at the ankle. "So give me the gist of this TV show."

I start to explain it when my phone buzzes. We both look over. I won't lie, I'm hoping it's Caleb, but it's just a notification to take my vitamin before bed.

"You know, if you want to hook-up with a guy with a six pack," Axel lifts up his shirt, revealing the muscle cut into his abdomen, "you've got my number."

"Actually, I don't." I roll my eyes and force them back on the screen where Jen and Brock are flirting by their lockers. "Want to hook-up *or* have your number."

He grabs my phone, that hasn't locked since the notification came in, and goes to my contacts.

"There," he says, once he's added his in.

"I wasn't looking for a hook-up," I remind him. "And I'm definitely not calling you when I'm feeling horny."

He grins. "So you *were* horny?"

"I was *bored*."

And lonely. And yeah, a little horny. But mostly I was trying to keep myself from calling up Brent and making an even bigger mistake.

"Why not?"

I frown. "Why not what?"

"Why won't you call me?" He leans forward, elbows on his knees. "I'm hot. You're hot. We're clearly compatible sexually. We can scratch each other's itches."

"Because," I rub my temples. Is he always this infuriating to talk to? "I'm not chasing jerseys anymore."

"It's not chasing a jersey if I'm naked."

I give him a hard look. "I'm trying to be better. Just like you are. Hooking up with random athletes has done nothing for me, but give me a shitty reputation and essentially getting blacklisted across campus. If anything, you should stay clear of me, I'm like some kind of hook-up kryptonite."

"That's bullshit," he says. "We hooked up and I had a shutout. If anything, you're a lucky charm."

I laugh darkly and shake my head.

"What's so funny? You know we take our superstitions seriously."

I stare at his terrible mustache. Twyler told me he started growing it after they started winning this season and had vowed to keep it until they either lost or won the whole thing. "Oh, I know."

"Then what?" he asks, smoothing his 'stache down with his fingers.

"Do you know how long I've waited for one of the guys I've chased to say I'm their lucky charm?" He shakes his head and despite knowing better, I continue. "*Three years*. Three fucking years worth of hook-ups and late night booty calls. Being available whenever they wanted me. Showing up when I was exhausted or had other work to do. And the one time I'm not interested, when I absolutely can't be interested, you're showing up at my door flashing your abs and being all cute."

He grins. "So you do think I'm cute."

"Shut up."

On screen Jess and Brock stroll down the sidewalk of their quaint small town, eating ice cream and holding hands. It's sweet and so far from where I am with my life today.

"People want a girl like that," I say, pointing to the screen. "Someone innocent. Not someone with a body count like I have."

"Who gives a shit about body counts?" he asks.

"No one gives a shit when you're a man." Again, I look at the screen. "Spoiler alert: Brock goes on to have multiple girlfriends, including one he knocks up, and two he cheats on. No matter what, he's the hero. Jess? She's just the sad girl that can't get over him."

"Okay," Axel says suddenly. I look over at him. "I hear you, and I'm willing to be your safe space, if you're willing to be mine."

I eye him, those long legs stretched out and the tattoos on his bicep bulging from where he has it bent. "What does that mean?"

"I need to stay away from partying. You need to stay away from going back to your own bad habits. We keep each other accountable. No more epic fuck-ups." His tongue darts out and licks that hoop in his lip. "A safe space. Deal?"

If he hadn't come over here tonight I probably would have caved, and either hooked up with Caleb or felt like shit when he didn't match with me.

And even though there's nothing about Axel Rakestraw that seems safe, I find myself saying. "Deal."

I give him my hand to shake on it, and he slides his warm, rough fingers against mine. He doesn't shake it though, instead holding tight. "But, if you change your mind, and want some no-strings, no-pressure, killer orgasms? Just ask."

I pull away and ignore the crackle where our hands met, adding, "I won't."

∽

"So her father is the rich guy, right? Is that why her tits are out all the time?"

I roll my eyes. "I don't think those things are related."

"Sure it is. They're excellent tits." He leans forward, eyes narrowed. "Too excellent. They're fake. Only a rich daddy would give a high school chick implants."

"Those aren't fake," I argue. "Monica Morgan is gorgeous. She's got her own clothing line and models on the side. Those are her real boobs."

He shrugs. "If you say so."

Obviously he doesn't buy it, and I have no idea why we're even having this discussion. I'm not even sure why he's still here. I've done nothing to make him comfortable. I didn't offer him a drink or an extra pillow for the chair which is notoriously uncomfortable. I've made little small talk other than answering a few questions about the show, yet he's watched three episodes of Springfield, growing more interested with each episode.

I mean, it's hard not to. All the characters are gorgeous. The drama – delicious. I was surprised to hear he'd never heard of it. You would have had to live under a rock not to have an awareness of the show back then. It was super popular and the actors were everywhere at the time. All over magazine covers, social media, and commercials.

If I had to guess, I'd suspect his interest back then was on two things. Hockey and sex.

When the episode ends, I turn off the TV with the remote.

"That's all?" he says, watching as I yawn and then stretch my arms over my head.

"Yep. I have to work in the morning."

"Where do you work?" he asks, reaching for his jacket.

"The campus gym."

"That's cool." He stands and looks toward the door. "Can I go out the front door this time or are we still doing the window thing?"

I shake my head. "You can use the door, just don't make a show about it."

"Damn, my plan had been to walk out on the front porch and shout out that I'd been hanging out with you all night." He winks. "No one needs to know that all we did was watch soft porn."

I gasp. "That's not soft porn! It's about teenagers."

"T, two of the characters had sex in a shower. Sure, they didn't show anything, but that's like porn 101."

"Gross."

"Just calling it like I see it." He shrugs. "But I definitely know why my father didn't let us have cable."

"Was he strict?" I ask, walking him to the door.

"You could say that." He runs his hand through his hair. "Thanks for letting me come over and distracting me with tits and sex scenes."

"Even if they weren't my tits?" I joke.

"Oh, yours distracted me too, T." He gives me a lopsided grin that makes my stomach clench. "Bundle up all you want, I've seen them, remember?"

I fling open the door. "Go."

"I'm going," he laughs. "But really, thanks."

"You're welcome," I lean against the door as he steps out on the dark porch. "I refuse to admit that I was tempted to swipe on water-polo Caleb tonight, but I can acknowledge that I appreciated having company."

"No worries, T. I told you, I'm your safe space. Call me any time you get the urge."

He walks off with a smirk, and I take a deep breath. I did it. I made it through a night with a sexy, dangerous, varsity level athlete without taking off my clothes. Maybe he is my safe space after all.

∞

FOR SOMEONE ATTRACTED TO ATHLETES, organized sports isn't my thing. Sure, my parents put me in all the standard youth sports: soccer, volleyball, basketball, softball, but none clicked. I wasn't lacking athletic ability, I had good balance and hand-eye coordination, but the idea of chasing other girls around a field, court, or bases never held an appeal. Girls are mean, and competitive girls are worse. By middle school, it was clear that I wasn't going to find my tribe this way.

That didn't mean they let me off the hook–not exactly. My mother, in particular, saw the benefit of exercise with or without a team. Her view is that it's not just good for the body, but for the mind, and as much as I hate to give her credit for anything, she's right.

Working out definitely makes me feel better, primarily by reducing my anxiety. After a few more trials and errors, I realized that I didn't want to play games. I wanted to be strong.

I'd been coming to the campus gym since I got to Wittmore. I'd been happy to just use the facilities, coming in for spin classes or to use the free weights or cardio machines. But after everything went down with Brent and CJ, and I kept coming home to find Twyler and Reese snuggled up on the couch watching one of her disturbing documentaries, I bit the bullet and asked Abby, the gym manager, if they had any open positions.

Thank god she said yes.

"When Brian gets here, it'd be awesome if one of you can straighten out the mats in the studio," Abby tells me when I arrive for my shift that day. "The last class made a huge mess."

"I'll get them sorted." She opens her mouth and I quickly add, "And disinfected."

"Thank you," She grins, grabbing her jacket and shoving her arms into the sleeves. "Oh, also, the thermostat in the men's locker room has been acting up. Maintenance should be here in the next hour. If you'll show them where it is when they get here."

"No problem."

Loud shouts from the back corner echo off the high ceilings and she sighs. "Keep an eye on that back corner, will you?"

"The Wannabes are back?"

"Yep."

The Wannabes are a small group we dubbed the Wannabes due to the fact they want to be hard core weight lifters. They're fit, but they're too busy showing off and recording themselves for Chatty-Snap videos to maintain basic gym etiquette. The biggest offense, other than getting unconsented video of another gym member, is the fact they hog the free weight area and leave the whole area a mess. "I asked them to re-rack the weights this time but you know they never listen. Some are just too heavy for me to lift, so if you want to make a pass by them every so often to make sure they're keeping it straight, I'd appreciate it."

"My pleasure."

"Thanks, Nadia. I'll bring you a coffee on your next shift as thanks."

My boss heads out, leaving me alone at the desk for the first hour of my morning shift. It's past the early rush, and things are pretty quiet. I scan in members, who are primarily students with a few faculty members thrown in between. I also hand out equipment, like basketballs for the court, and towels for the pool. It's easy and pretty mindless, which is exactly what I need right now.

One of the perks of the campus gym is that it's free of varsity athletes. They have their own training facilities, which makes this my own little safe space.

Safe space.

I think of Axel showing up two nights ago, looking desperate and on the edge of making bad decisions and how he came to me for help. No one has ever looked at me as a reliable person to count on. It feels weird.

"Nadia?"

I look up. "Oh, Eric, hey."

I haven't seen my project partner since I overheard the awkward conversation between him and my former lovers after I left class.

"I didn't know you worked here." He holds out his phone and I scan his student ID.

"Yeah," I say, "I started a few weeks ago."

"Cool." He steps aside, and I scan in the guys with him. A few have the same Greek letters on their clothing–frat brothers. "I've been meaning to contact you about meeting up. We should get started on the project, don't you think?"

"Yeah, absolutely. We definitely should do that," I say, trying to quell the uneasiness in my gut. "This week?"

"We can, uh, meet at the Zeta Sigma house if you want? There's a study room or you know…"

If I didn't know, the smirky grin on his friend's face would fill me in.

"You know…" I say, mouth turning dry. Old me would have just said yes. I wouldn't want to rock the boat. I would have just done what was expected of me, and honestly, the urge to do that now is strong. It's the easy way to live, but I think about Axel on my doorstep, shoving that box of weed at me. Saying no to going to a frat house, alone, with a guy who was envisioning me giving him a blow job, seems possible. "Can we do the library? That would probably fit into my schedule better."

"Oh," he says, eyebrows furrowing, "Sure. No problem. I'll text you with a time."

I force a smile. "Great. Thanks, Eric, I appreciate it."

Behind me, Brian arrives, giving me the opportunity to cut the conversation short. After getting him settled, I say, "Abby asked me to straighten the mats in the studio. You okay here by yourself?"

"No problem," he says, already pulling out his laptop. We're allowed to do schoolwork when it's slow and Brian is an engineering major. He's always got some project due.

I'm on my way to the studio when I hear a shout from the back corner. "Great," I mutter, not in the mood to deal with a second group of guys this morning. I go past the cardio machines and the weight machines over to the free weight area. I hear their music blasting over the other noise in the gym–rolling my eyes at the fact they had to bring their own. Classic entitlement. Once I get past the ellipticals, I see a group of guys–the Wannabes–standing around a bench, the bar wracked with huge, heavy weights. Two of the guys are spotting, while another has his camera out recording the guy on the bench.

"Holy shit, he's doing it," someone says, voice carrying over the gym. "Did you get the weights?"

"Got it," the videographer says, a dumb grin on his face. "Personal record!"

As I get closer, I see the arms holding up the bar wobble, shaking–struggling–under the weight. Panic fills my throat, but before I can freak out, he, with the help of his spotters, get it back on the rack.

"Hell, yes!" a voice shouts in victory.

Oh, *hell no*.

I storm over to where Axel, the front of his T-shirt soaked with sweat, slowly climbs off the bench, shaking out his arms.

"What are you doing here?"

"T," he cries. "What's up?"

"Don't you what's up me. Why are you here?"

"Getting swole." He flexes, showing off his tattooed, bulging biceps. "Did you see that? Personal record."

My eyes dart to the unholy amount of weights on the bar. I grab him by the forearm and drag him away from the others. "I know you have your own training gym at the arena. What the hell are you doing in the campus gym with the normies?"

"Thought I'd check out the facilities. See what my tuition is paying for." He jerks his thumb at the Wannabes. "Those guys are great."

I glare at him.

"What?"

"You're on an athletic scholarship. You're not paying tuition."

"Oh, true." He rubs the back of his neck. "For the record, this isn't the first time I've been here. Sometimes I like to work out without the pressure of the team and just let loose. Test myself."

"By pressure, you mean Reese."

He shrugs. "Yeah. Everything's so intense with him, you know?"

Reese is definitely intense. It's a vibe that guys like him have–the team leaders. The ones headed for the pros. From everything I've seen and heard, Axel has the skills, but he may not have that same drive.

"Yo, Ax, come check this out before I post it," one of the guys calls, holding up the phone.

He doesn't move, hovering in that way that makes me acutely aware of everything about him. The tattoos, the muscles, the shiny piercings in his lip and eyebrow. The sweat.

He should smell terrible, but fuck me, all I'm getting is the strong scent of man.

I swallow and look around at the weights scattered all over the floor. "Make sure you put those back." I point to the sign over the rack holding the weight that asks people to return their weights to the rack after use. "We don't have a crew that comes along behind you to clean everything up like you do in the arena, and some of those are too heavy for the staff to pick up."

"Gotcha, T. We'll get it all cleaned up before we go."

I want to say more. To ask if he's here because he knew I was working, but that's foolish. He seems familiar with the gym and his reasoning makes sense. I get the need to have a little pressure taken off occasionally.

"Hey man, that was amazing." I turn and see Eric and his friends entering the area.

"Thanks," Axel says, wiping his face with the hem of his shirt.

Eric gives me a friendly smile and I hold my hand up in a small wave. They pass by, headed to a different section.

When I look back at Axel, his eyebrow is raised. "Know him?"

"My project partner in communications."

He nods, eyes following Eric across the gym. Behind him, I see Brian waving, trying to get my attention. The maintenance guy is here. "I need to get back to work."

"I guess I need to get back to getting jacked."

"God, you're the worst." I roll my eyes, but the smugness of his statement is cut by a wink and a quick grin.

The hardest part, I think, walking across the gym, is that Axel Rakestraw is definitely not the worst. And we both know it.

8

Axel

It's the giggling that gets me. Soft and flirty–a specific tone from a girl when she's into you. It echoes off the high ceilings of the Manor, taunting me from my roommates' bedrooms.

Fuck. I need to get laid.

I need to sink my teeth, and fingers, and dick into something soft, wet, and tight.

I could. There are two dozen girls in my phone that I could message right now and ask to come over, lead up to my room, and finally get some relief.

All of that seems weird now. I don't know if it's the sobriety or not wanting Reese's judgment, but in my heart (and maybe my cock) there's no doubt that getting to know Nadia better has made the thrill of having puck bunnies at my beck and call lose a little bit of it's thrill.

This. *This* is why men treat women as objects. Getting to know their thoughts and feelings about shit makes things complicated.

Because while I could be getting my nut off, I'm sitting on my bed, alone, staring at my laptop and the third hour of the drug education video I'm required to watch during my probation.

I'm almost done with the current segment: Marijuana and the Student Athlete when there's a knock at the door.

"What?" I ask, pausing the video.

The door opens a crack and Reid sticks his head in. "I'm out of condoms."

I raise an eyebrow.

"Got any?"

I jerk my head at the bedside table. "Top drawer."

"Thanks man."

He pushes the door open and I see his bare upper body and yep. He's buck naked.

"Dude seriously?" I say as he runs in, with his hand attempting to cover his junk. As if I haven't seen his hardware a million times in the locker rooms. "Jesus, put some fucking pants on."

"Sorry!" he fumbles with the box. "I was halfway in when Darla told me she was on antibiotics and we needed to double up."

He snatches a couple packs and exits the room, giving me a full view of his hairy ass.

Is it wrong that all I feel is jealousy?

I slam the laptop shut and reach for my phone, firing off a text.

GoalieGod: I hate this plan.

T: What plan?

GoalieGod: The no more epic fuck-ups plan. It's boring. And my balls hurt from lack of use.

T: I'm sure you'll survive.

GoalieGod: Don't tell me your pussy isn't lonely, T.

T: Jesus, you're pathetic. You know that?

GoalieGod: YES! That's what I'm saying. I'm thinking that maybe we should call off this deal. Or like give it a one night reprieve. I need some fun. And some pussy. And a fucking drink.

There's a pause.

GoalieGod: Sorry, I'm a terrible safe space.

T: LOL you really are, but if I'm being honest, you're right. My pussy *is* lonely and I'm all alone which makes it dangerous.

My cock tightens at the mention of her pussy and I groan into my fist, before typing.

GoalieGod: I wish I was alone. Everyone in this house is getting laid but me.

T: Even Reid?

GoalieGod: Specifically, Reid. He just came in here looking for condoms.

T: The girlfriend?

GoalieGod: Yeah. They're on and off but can't seem to shake each other.

T: Must be nice to have a consistent, reliable, safe person to fuck around with.

GoalieGod: Even if he's not headed to the NFL?

T: I'd settle for the NHL at this point.

GoalieGod: Are you trying to get me to enter the draft, T?

T: * winky face *

GoalieGod: It's not nice to taunt a desperate man.

T: You're right. It's not like I show up to your house, take off my shirt and flirt with you.

GoalieGod: Fair. Okay, you talked me off the ledge. I owe you one.

T: Night, Ax.

I've just put the phone down when there's another knock on my door. "Son of a bitch, Reid!" I grab the box of condoms. "Just take the whole goddamn box—"

I throw it at the door just as it swings open. The package hits Reese in the chest and it drops to the floor. "What the hell?"

"Sorry," I thrust a hand into my hair. "I thought you were Reid."

He gives me a hard look and then says, "Coach called." He bends picking up the box of condoms and shoving them in his pocket. "Your test results are in."

～

COACH BRYANT SITS behind his desk, the slip of paper in front of him. A gold pen clenched between his fingers, tapping on the desk. It's 8 AM. The rest of the guys are in the weight room–well, everyone but Reese.

He's standing next to Bryant's desk, shoulders back, arms crossed. He's not my friend in here, he's firmly in the role of captain. Eyes steely and he hasn't looked at me since I walked in.

I clear my throat, unable to take the silence anymore.

"I started the online drug education course you sent me. I'm about halfway–"

"This isn't about that, Rakestraw," Coach snaps, running a hand through his hair. "Your blood test results came back. I'm not even sure where to begin."

There shouldn't be anywhere to begin. I smoked–shared–one joint. That's it. The tense muscle in Reese's jaw tells me there's more. That I'd done it again. Fucked up.

"They found GHP in your system," Coach says, sliding the paperwork over.

"GHP?" I repeat, taking the paperwork but not looking at it. "That's–".

"Typically used for incapacitating people–most often women."

"Fuck." I sink into my seat. "That can't be right."

"There's a list of side-effects on the back of that paper. Did you experience any of those?"

I flip the sheet and read down the list, my spine tingling. Nausea, vomiting, memory loss, drowsiness and confusion. There are more– euphoria and impaired muscle coordination...

I think back to that morning–to the night before. How out of it I felt. Foggy headed and nauseous. I'd overslept, and according to Chantelle, had passed out on her. I thought I'd gotten blackout, which isn't like me, but maybe I wasn't just drunk. Maybe I'd been–

"This has to be wrong," I toss the paper on the desk. "I wouldn't ever take something like that. If I'm going to get high, I sure as fuck want to remember it."

Reese shoots me a look and shakes his head, but Coach ignores me. "After talking to the medical officials we think that it's entirely possible that you were drugged–even if accidental."

"You do?"

"Cain vouched for you. Said that the night of the party you were fine, but suddenly had slurred speech. He also assumed it was too much alcohol, but your behavior following that night tracks with the effects of GHP." Anger flickers in his eyes. "The NCAA showing up for unannounced drug testing at the same time as you getting drugged? Sounds like sabotage."

I look at Reese, who is looking at me. This time not just with anger, but something else. Sadness? Pity? I don't like it.

"Your probation stands, as well as your follow up drug test in two weeks. We'll push back on the NCAA's findings and request further investigation. I'll submit a report this morning."

My head spins trying to follow what's happening. "I've been impressed with how you've stepped it up over the last week, Axel, and I don't want this to cause any setbacks."

"Yes, sir."

"Don't disappoint me."

"I won't."

He gestures for us to leave, Reese following me out into the hall. I turn and say, "You vouched for me?"

He doesn't respond, just jerks his chin toward the exit. "We need to talk."

"What about?"

"Who the hell spiked that drink."

∼

EVERY MEETING between athletes is going to take place in one of two places: the playing field of their choice or over food.

Reese and I are sitting at a sticky table in the back of a truckstop diner, with massive plates of eggs, bacon, pancakes and more in front of us.

"Why did you vouch for me with Coach?" I ask, pouring syrup between each pancake.

"Because I know you didn't intentionally take that drug." He crushes up his bacon and mixes it in with his eggs. "Like you said, even when I think it's over the top, you like to be there for the fun." We both take a big bite of our meals, chewing in silence. Once he swallows he says, "Tell me what you remember."

"Not much," I admit. "Smoking with the rowing boys in the Jeep–just a couple of hits too. Then I had a couple of beers while we were playing quarters." I scowl. "We can blame your girlfriend for the amount I had to drink due to her winning streak."

"Yeah that's on her." He grins and slathers strawberry jam across his toast. "What else?"

I think back. "I remember you and TG leaving the game table and Reid taking your place. I did a lot better against him. Oh," I lift my fork pointing it at him, "I remember when the football team showed up. Reynolds looking all smug about his three fucking touchdowns."

"Right," Reese says, forehead furrowed. "We were outside by then. I only knew Reynolds and McMichael were there when you came out with Nadia."

"Yeah, she mentioned that we talked that night. I have no fucking memory of that at all."

"So you remember those guys coming in, and then nothing else?"

I search my memory, but it's nothing but an infuriating black hole. "Nothing. It's just gone. Which makes a lot more sense knowing someone fucking dosed me at some point." I take a sip of juice. "You really think it was sabotage? Who? Easton? St. Andrews? Thatcher? They're our biggest competition right now."

"Maybe," he says. "There's something I remember from the party."

"Yeah?" I take another bite of pancake. "What's that?"

"When you and Nadia came out you were slurring your words. I asked you then, how much you had to drink and you told me about the weed and the beers." His jaw tightens. "You also told us that you'd had Nadia's drink and that it tasted bad."

"I took her drink?"

"Yep." He sets down his fork. "You also told us you 'saved' Nadia from Reynolds–a conversation or something. She was hedgy about it."

"Son of a bitch," I swear, and my confusion turns into something hotter–anger. "He's not supposed to talk to her."

Or worse. Give her drug-laced drinks.

"You and I both know Reynolds or McMichael are above the rules."

I rest my fork on my plate, my appetite gone. "So what do we do? Kick his ass? Tell Coach? Call the cops?"

"As much as I want to do all of that, we have no proof, and accusing the captain of the football team seems a little risky without it." He sighs. "And maybe I'm off base. Maybe Coach is right. Someone took the opportunity at that party and drugged you, then called the NCAA. It's pretty coincidental."

Shit. He's right.

"So do we tell her?" I ask, not wanting to be there when she hears it. Nadia's taken a lot of hits and I don't want to be the one that gives her another.

"I don't think we tell her or Twy until we know something more. Let Coach submit the report for an investigation. Maybe we'll find out it was another team, after all." He picks up his toast. "Until then, we just keep an eye on her when we're out."

Although it does nothing to soothe the uneasiness in my gut, I nod in agreement. "Sure, no problem."

I promised Nadia that I would be a safe space, and now that means something different.

If I can do one thing, it'll be to ensure that no one is going to ever fucking hurt her again.

∽

OVER THE LAST THREE-AND-A-HALF YEARS, I've learned that one of the best times to be on campus is during the soft lull around the weekend with no football or hockey games. It's not quite dead, but people use it to take a quick trip home, or hunker down in the library to catch up on classwork. We still have practice, of course; Coach had us in the arena half the day on the ice running drills and then watching film. As a reward we hit the Badger Den to chill.

Other than the local regulars, it's mostly guys on the team, their girlfriends, and a few puck bunnies. Oh, and Nadia. I saw her come in with Twyler, her shiny dark hair that brushes her shoulders.

The last time I saw her, she was at the gym in a cute little uniform. Even though I'd told her the truth about coming there to get away from the intensity of the arena gym, I may have made an effort to go when I could see her.

She'd looked confident there, like the weight on her shoulders had been lifted for a moment. Well, other than maybe when her project partner walked by. Not sure what's up with that. But now she leans against a table top in a skirt that shows off her long, toned legs, and a soft looking, gray sweater with a neckline that reveals her sexy collarbones. Girls don't always get that just seeing the little parts makes us hot–less can be more–and Nadia probably thought she was wearing something that would discourage guys from hitting on her but she's wrong about that. While I wait at the bar, a steady stream of guys from the team approach her and give it a shot. It's clear she's not interested, letting them down with a soft, sympathetic smile, before going back to her phone.

It's fucking awkward. That's a word I definitely would have used to Twyler when she first started coming around. But Nadia? The description doesn't fit.

"Hey," I say to Mike behind the bar. "Give me two of those Reapers."

His eyebrow raises at my order, but dude has been in business long enough to know better than to ask questions. Plus, I think, as he slides the black and silver cans across the bar, he's probably just glad I've got my shirt on.

"Thanks," I say, passing over a folded up bill.

As I carry the drinks over to her table, some townie–ten years too old–is leaning against the table.

"Come on now," he says, "let me buy you a drink."

"I'm fine," she says, "but thanks."

"You sure? A pretty little thing like you shouldn't be sitting alone."

"She's not," I say, stepping up to the table. "She's with me."

The guy spares me a lazy glance. "Listen, buddy, if you've got a girl like this, why are you leaving her all alone?"

I tilt my head. "Because she's an independent woman and should be able to sit at a table in the bar and not have assholes not taking no for an answer."

He straightens, doing his best to push back his shoulders, but blinks when he finally takes me in. My size, the tatts, and eventually my face. "Shit. You're the goalie. Rakestraw, right?"

"Right." I set the can in front of Nadia and give her a wink. "Hey, darlin'."

I wait for her to balk, to throw the can back at me, but she smirks and replies, "Hey, baby."

The guy looks between us, eyes growing wide. "This is your girl?" His hands go up. "Sorry, dude, I didn't know."

"Well, you do now." I toss my arm over her shoulder and give her a squeeze. "So maybe give us a little room."

"Sure, sure." He steps back, shoving his hands in his pockets. "Keep up the good work out there. You keep playing the way you are, you guys are gonna take it this year."

I nod and give him a look so hard and pointed, he finally takes the hint and leaves.

"I could've handled that alone," she says, popping the top on her drink with her sharp, painted nails.

"I know." I open my own can. "But I owed you one. Remember?"

She grins and lifts the drink to study the side. "We studied Reaper and other canned water products in my marketing classes. They're specifically for non-drinkers to have something to hold in their hands and not look out of place. It's a six-hundred million dollar industry at this point." She takes a sip. "Predicted to hit seven in two years."

I taste my drink. Yep. Six dollar canned water tastes just like it does from the tap. "Maybe you should advise Cain to invest some of his rookie bonus in Reaper. Or a sponsorship. He'd be the perfect spokesperson."

She narrows her eyes at me. "I know you're joking, but it's probably a good idea. Reese's jawline alone could sell sand to people living in Death Valley."

"You're probably right." I laugh, and settle into the seat next to her. "Decided to stick around this weekend?"

"Yeah, it's too far for me to go home, not with Thanksgiving in a few weeks."

"Florida, right?"

Her eyebrow raises. "You stalking me, Rakestraw?"

"If I'm going to be your safe space I needed to do my research, which happened to lead me down the rabbit hole of your ChattySnap account to some sexy photos of you very tan on the beach."

A small smile plays on her lips. "I miss it."

"Being tan?"

"The beach. Well, and being tan." She holds out her arm and pulls up her sleeve. "I've never been so pale in my life."

"Yeah it was an adjustment for me too," I admit. "Plenty of sun in Texas."

She looks surprised. "Ah, Texas. That explains the accent and the liberal use of the word, darlin'."

I laugh. "Busted."

"So, how did a boy from Texas end up playing hockey instead of football?"

"Oh, I played for a while. Every red-blooded Texan boy has a helmet and pads before they hit kindergarten, but a friend introduced me to hockey when I was in middle school and I never looked back."

"And your family was okay with that?"

"Not in the slightest," I say, taking a big swallow of water. "But getting their approval has never been a priority for me."

"What does your father do?" she asks.

"He's a minister."

"Oh wow." Her eyes skim over my tattoos. "A Southern Texas minister whose son is a tattooed, pierced, hockey player. No wonder you moved halfway across the country to go to college."

"You have no idea, T." Thanksgiving week is going to suck. Thank god, I've got a pass to make it short and get back for the game. "I do miss the food though, like the kolaches, so that's something to look forward to."

"What's a kolache?"

"Only the most amazing pastry in the world." My mouth waters thinking about them. "Traditonally, they're filled with fruit or cheese or something, but in typical Texas fashion someone decided to load them up with meat, like sausage and add peppers, and fuck me, they're so good."

"Are you getting horny talking about pastry?" she laughs, giving me the first genuine smile of the night.

"I told you this no-fuck-ups plan is killing me. I'm horny for just about anything." I sigh dramatically and change the subject, because talking to her about it isn't helping. "Why did you pick a college so far away?"

She shrugs. "Just looking for an adventure, I guess."

I nod, feeling like she's leaving something out, but who am I to judge. I sure as hell am.

"You should come to the Friendsgiving we have before break." Her response telegraphs across her expression before she says it, but I add, "It's just the four of us that live in the Manor, and a few other guys on the team, plus a few girls. Twy will be there and Reid's girl. Jefferson may or may not bring anyone." She still looks hesitant. "Come. We can keep each other honest."

"Okay sure, it sounds fun." She finally relents. "I'll talk to Twy about what to b-bring."

Her last word falters and her body tenses, eyes glued over my shoulder. I turn and see why. Brent and CJ just walked in.

"What's he doing here?" she asks quietly, but I hear the small tremor in her voice. She's scared and that just pisses me the fuck off. "They have an off week. Shouldn't they be gone?"

"Hey," I say, forcing her to swap places with me, so she's no longer looking in his direction. "He can't get to you. Not here. Not with me around."

But even I know that's a lie. Someone did try to get to her already–or at least there's a strong possibility. I'm not buying the sabotage theory. Someone wanted to incapacitate her. Hurt her. Over her head, I see the moment he realizes Nadia is here. He lifts his chin and jabs CJ in the ribs.

She sets her can on the table. "I should go."

"Hell no, T, this is our bar. The Badger Den is a hockey bar and you're with us. He's the one that can get the fuck out."

Of course, there's no real rule he can't be here, but the way he's watching the two of us makes it pretty clear he came here for a reason.

"Do you trust me?" I ask, licking my bottom lip.

To my surprise she looks up at me with those big brown eyes and says, "Yes."

The way she looks, the way she says 'yes' makes my chest feel achy and weird, but there's no time to wonder if I'm having a heart attack. I slide my hand down her back and over her curvy but firm ass and squeeze.

"Axel!" she hisses, looking around–no, looking for Twyler. "What the fu–"

Pulling her to me, I tilt her chin, and kiss the dirty word right out of her mouth.

Her lips are warm, soft, and even though there's the slightest resistance, probably because I surprised the hell out of her, it's short lived. Her lips part for me and I ease my tongue in, tasting her the way I've wanted to for weeks now–maybe longer. I've thought about this for a while. What kissing Nadia again would be like. If those thick, puffy lips taste as good as I remember. Fuck yeah they do, and once this is over she'll probably knee me in the balls, so I graze my fingers over the skin just below her skirt and keep her held tight, wanting it to last. Sliding my hand from her chin to the back of her head, I go all in. Kissing her like this may be the only chance I'll get.

Her fingers wind into the front of my shirt, drawing me closer, and I grind unabashedly against her lower belly. Hell yes, all those days of pent up–

The thought, and my body, are yanked away from her soft heat.

I shift gears in a heartbeat, ready to take on whoever–I assume that fuck-face Reynolds–and my hands clench into tight fists. When my vision clears, it's not the football player, interrupting us, it's Captain America himself, Reese.

"I almost punched you, asshole," I shout, fighting against his grip.

"What the *fuck* are you doing?" he growls, both hands tight in my shirt.

I grin, cocky and assured, both at the girl standing across from me, touching her lips like she isn't sure what just happened, and at the target of my move, Reynolds, as he grabs his friend and exits the bar.

Reese hauls me away from Nadia and the main part of the bar, pushing me down the back hall with a hard shove. "I told you to stay away from her." He pinches the bridge of his nose. "Twyler is going to flip out."

I adjust my jeans, trying to relieve the pressure of my raging hard-on. "Jesus, chill out. I wasn't fucking around with her. I was helping her."

"With your tongue down her throat and your hand up her skirt?"

"Yeah, dumbass." I take a deep breath, still caught up in the sensation of her teeth dragging over my lip. "Because Reynolds and McMichael came into the bar and I could see the wheels spinning in their TBI rattled skulls. I did what I needed to. I protected her in the only way that matters to neanderthals like them."

I staked a claim.

Reese sighs, and leans against the brown paneled wall. "Are you sure that's all?"

"Dude, yes. You should have seen her when they came in. She was scared." I feel that anger rising again. "So until we find out who spiked that drink, we need to keep her safe–and that's exactly what I was doing. That was *all* I was doing."

"Okay," he nods, "I believe you."

Thank god he does, I think, as he holds out his hand and I take it, because the way that kiss left me reeling, I wouldn't trust a word coming out of my mouth.

9

Nadia

The cold night air feels good on my overheated skin and I take a deep, unsteady breath and try to get my bearings.

Mental bearings, not physical.

After Reese dragged Axel down the back hall, I took off, slipping out the door that leads to a small outdoor seating area and then ducked into the alley between the bar and the pizza place next door. The scent of burnt, greasy crust fills the air. There's a small table with a couple of chairs behind the pizza place, the table littered with empty beer bottles and a full ashtray. A place for workers to hang out during their shift. I drop into one of the seats and take a deep breath, trying to get the scent and taste of Axel Rakestraw out of my head.

Easier said than done.

My lips still burn from the way he claimed my mouth. It was spontaneous but controlled. Hard and soft, skilled in a way that made me cling to him, desperate for more. Axel has all the qualities that I find sexy. The athleticism. The commanding presence. The confidence and swagger that comes from being the best. No matter how hard I try to forget it, I know what it feels like to have him inside of me. To have his tongue bring me to orgasm, and that kiss brought it all rushing back.

I tug at the front of my sweater, fanning myself.

When he'd been abruptly pulled away, my first thought had been the absolute need to get his mouth back on mine. But then I thought maybe it was Brent, and that brought another flood of confusing emotions. Hope? Anger? Fear? When I saw it was actually Reese, eyes murderously set on Axel, the feelings were instantly replaced by something else: guilt.

Axel's nickname for me is scarily on target. I just can't stay out of trouble.

I'm supposed to stay away from epic fuck-ups and men on the hockey team, but everytime I get near that sexy, tattooed, goalie, I fall right back into bad habits.

My phone buzzes.

Twyler: You okay?

Nadia: Just outside getting some air.

A shadow blocks the neon pizza light.

"There you are."

Axel.

Just seeing him sets my skin aflame and my nipples tighten when he grabs one of the plastic chairs and drags it across the asphalt with a loud scrape. He sets it across from me, and I shiver when our knees touch.

"You're cold," he says, oblivious that my reaction is due to his proximity, not the heat. He shrugs out of his hockey jacket and leans over, wrapping it around my shoulders. I'm instantly engulfed back in the scent I'd been trying to escape from inside.

"Thanks," I say, reluctantly snuggling into the warmth.

"I explained everything," he says, leaning back. "I told him I was just giving Brent the signal to back off."

"Good." I nod and stare at my knees.

"Did I cross a line?" he asks. "Because if I did, I apologize–"

"No." I look at him. At his handsome, dangerous, face. "Brent needs to understand that I'm not getting back with him. In any way."

"Is that what he wants? To be with you?"

"Brent Reynolds wants his cake and to eat it too. I'm not stupid enough to think that he actually wants to be with me. He just wants to use me, that's all, and if he can't he'll be content to make me miserable."

I haven't forgotten his threat of blackballing me. If my communications class is any indication, the message is out.

"You're not stupid," he says, giving me a hard look. "He's a massive dick, T. Just an absolute piece of shit. You're better than him."

"Am I?" I ask, without thinking. "Because the no fuck-ups plan feels lonely. Confusing. Embarrassing that I want to be wanted, even if it comes with a bunch of strings." I tilt my head and look at him. "But that's not the worst part."

"What's the worst part?"

"That if he'd talked to me tonight, and asked me to go back home with him, I'm afraid I would have said, yes."

Axel shifts, turning to me. The neon sign behind his head filters through his hair, casting it in a pinkish glow. I fight the urge to squirm under the intensity of his gaze. He touches my chin and forces me to look at him. "I get it. I'm lonely too. I don't trust myself to take an inch or I'll go a mile, and screw it all up again. Kissing you in there got me harder than steel." His tongue darts out and those bottle green eyes drop to my mouth before popping up again. "It's the only time I've felt right all week."

We stare at one another, his thumb sweeping under my jaw, giving me time to make the decision on my own. My body reacts to the simple touch, a sign of how deprived I feel. This is when I should walk. Stick with the plan. Deny how he makes me feel, but instead my lips part for him; opening in invitation.

He reacts instantly, but this time when his mouth meets mine, it's slow and sweet, without the fuel of doing it for someone else. It's between us and I don't fight him when he lifts me up, dragging me onto his lap.

Straddling him, his hands smooth down my skirt to keep my ass covered, but holding me tight, making sure our bodies are flush. Fuck, he isn't kidding about being hard. It's painful, but the good kind, and I grind down against him wanting to feel him through the thin cotton of my panties.

He groans, breath hot against my mouth.

"This is a bad idea," I say, unconvincingly, resting my hand on his shoulder.

"Is it?" He pushes the hair off my neck, laying a wet kiss against my throat. "Because it feels pretty damn right to me."

We writhe against one another, fully clothed, our hot breath clouding in the cold air. Axel's hands push under my shirt, fingers searching, only stopping when they meet lace.

"Your tits are perfect, you know that?" He pulls the lace aside, the pad of his fingers circling my nipple.

"Yeah, well, so is your body." I lift his shirt, getting a peek of his abs. "It's ridiculous."

He grins, tweaking my nipple, and I cry out, the jolt from my nipples to my pussy electrifying.

The weeks of celibacy build into something frantic, the need to be felt, to be touched, bigger than anything else. Axel kisses me again, taking my breath from me as I start to pant. The friction between my legs, his hands on my tits, his tongue–

"Oh fuck," he growls, thrusting into me. The seam of his jeans rubs deliciously on my clit and when he presses down on my nipples, the world turns upside down and explodes.

"Holy shit," I breathe, collapsing into him. His hands are still clenched around my hips, dragging me against him, until he groans so deep it rattles in his chest.

"Jesus," he exhales. "I just came in my pants. I haven't done that since I was fourteen."

We breathe together for a long moment, my heart and pussy

throbbing like hummingbird wings. The sound of voices snap me back to reality and I pull back. "Oh God, I'm–"

"Don't you fucking dare apologize, you hear me?" His big hand slides behind my neck, pulling my forehead to his. "Don't feel guilty, or slutty or anything else. That was you and me in a safe space, got it?"

I nod, but I can't help thinking we may have just had our biggest fuck-up yet.

～

GOALIEGOD: *I think I got denim burn on my dick.*

My eyes roll everytime Axel's screen name pops up on my phone, but this time my skin also gets hot.

GoalieGod: How's your pussy? Need some aftercare?

My pussy is… fine, a little sore, but overall pleased with getting some much needed relief last night. Although the idea of Axel checking up on me, gives me tingles all over my–

"Order for Bertha!"

The barista shouts out Twyler's name–well her cat's name–some weird inside joke between her and Reese. I shove my phone into my pocket and ignore the texts. Two girls are in line behind my roommate–sorority girls according to the letters on their crewnecks. One flicks a stare at me for a long moment, before rolling her eyes and leaning into her friend to whisper.

I'd try not to be paranoid, but there's no doubt these girls have heard the news: Nadia Beckwith is blacklisted.

GoalieGod: But seriously, Reid has an industrial sized container of aloe vera if you need some…

I smile down at the phone, the sorority girls pretty much forgotten.

"So…" Twyler says, grabbing the ice coffee and a straw off the counter. "I hear you kissed Axel."

"What?" Startled, my hand squeezes my cup of coffee, popping the plastic lid off and sloshing the hot liquid down the side. "Shit."

"Nadia!" She frantically grabs a wad of napkins from the dispenser. "Did it burn?"

"No," I say, ignoring the throbbing in my finger. "It's fine."

"Let me look at it." She gestures. We're still in the campus cafe, and she nudges me toward a chair. We both drop our bags and sit. Before I get my coat off she grabs my wrist, checking my hand.

"I mostly just made a mess," I tell her.

"It's a little red but I'm not seeing any blistering." She frowns. "Give me a sec."

She hops up and runs over to the counter, returning a moment later with a spoon. Popping open the lid of her coffee, fishes out an ice cube with a spoon and wraps it in a napkin before handing it to me. "Use that."

"It's fine, Twy." I take the napkin and press it against my finger. "Thank you, though. You're good at your job."

"My internships with the hockey and basketball teams have taught me to be prepared for just about anything." Tucking her hair behind her ear, she shoves her straw into the lid of her ice coffee and then leans in. "So Axel."

Crap. Well, that distraction didn't pay off. What do I say? He laid a toe-curling, tongue sweeping, set my lady-parts on fire kiss on me in the middle of the bar? Oh, and then I crawled in his lap in a dark alley and rode him like a stallion?

"I promise it was no big deal," I tell her. "He just saw Brent come into the bar and wanted to give him the idea that I wasn't available."

"No better way to prove that than with another guy's tongue down your throat."

I eye her. "You're taking this very well for someone who made it very clear I'm not allowed to mess around with anyone from the hockey team."

She takes a sip of her drink and sighs happily at the caffeine hit. "Reese told me Axel was just looking out for you."

Was he? Was he looking out for me or just looking to get off. Not that I'm judging him. What Axel and I have going on doesn't have the lopsided situationships of the other athletes I've chased. First, I'm not chasing him. At all. Second, we're using one another. I mean, he asked before he kissed me.

No other guy has done that before.

I watch her closely. "And you're okay with that?"

"What I'm not okay with is Brent showing up and bothering you." Worry lines crease her forehead. "Have you thought any more about reporting Brent and CJ?"

The expression on her face is hopeful, leaving me no doubt to what Twyler wants me to do. "I still don't want to."

"I know. But what they did to you," her voice lowers even more, "secretly recording you while you were having sex and posting it online on a paid subscription site… it's not okay."

I know she means well, but every time she talks about it. Every time I remember it, it brings it all back and I hate it.

"They took the video down." I press the red area where the coffee hit my finger, trying to feel something other than shame. "That's all I wanted."

"They're also supposed to leave you alone." She stirs the straw. "And last night makes twice he's been at the same place as you."

"The first was a post-game party. He had more of a right to be there than I did. And there's no reason to think I'd be at the Badger Den." I wink, trying to lighten the mood. "Hockey players aren't my thing, you know that."

I'm not sure why I add that on. I guess I just don't want any more drama. Or maybe I want to pretend that Axel isn't getting under my skin. But most of all, I think that I know that even if Twyler is okay with me kissing Axel, she sure as hell wouldn't be okay with me dry humping him in the back alley.

"I do, which is why when Reese told me you two were kissing I was surprised. But then I figured you guys may have just been inspired by us."

I frown. "What do you mean?"

"Using a kiss to distract an ex? That's straight out of the Reese Cain playbook." She points across the room and gets a dreamy look on her face. "Happened right over there."

"Oh," I nod, playing along, "right. That's probably exactly what it was."

She checks her phone. "Shit, I need to get across campus."

"Same. I've got a project meet up."

We stand, gathering our bags and coffees.

"Listen," she says as we approach the door, "if you need to use Axel as a buffer between you and Brent right now, I think you should."

"Wait, what?" I look at my friend to see if she's joking. Nope. She looks completely sincere. "*You* think Axel and I should hang out together?"

"He's a good guy," she shrugs, "and he's dealing with a lot, being on probation and everything. You both probably need a friend right now."

A safe space.

"Maybe." I reach for my scarf and remember I never got it back after class. "Although, I'm not sure he'd be into you offering him up to be my protector like that."

"Oh, he's into it." She zips up the front of her jacket and smiles. "It was actually his idea."

~

Nadia: Just had an interesting conversation with Twyler?

GoalieGod: Was it about teaching you deep tissue massage? Because I volunteer if you want to practice.

Nadia: It was about you offering to 'protect' me from Brent.

GoalieGod: Safe space, darlin'.

Nadia: That was a one time thing.

GoalieGod: Not if I have anything to say about it.

The shiver that runs down my spine has nothing to do with the cold, November air, and it doesn't fade when I step into the business building.

Eric and I finally agreed to meet up to discuss our project at one of the study rooms provided in the communications department.

He'd been cool about meeting here, and I felt better about not going somewhere private. Boundaries. It's something I've been working on... well, apparently other than when it involves Axel Rakestraw.

When I get to the room, Eric's already there, sitting at the table with his laptop open. He looks up and smiles.

"Hey," I say, stepping into the room. "Sorry I'm late."

"You're not late." He pushes out the chair next to his. "I was early, so I figured I'd start some of the research."

"Well, that's different," I say, peeling off the layers and taking my own things out of my bag.

"What do you mean?"

"The last time I did a group project in this class it was with Austin and Rocky and neither of them even opened their laptops once."

"Oh yeah, I had to work with Darius, who don't get me wrong, is a great guy but..."

"Dumb as a bag of hammers?"

"Let's just say..." he taps his chin, "unmotivated for academic pursuits."

"Oh you're good." I laugh. "Let me guess. Planning a career in sports related PR?"

He winks. "Nailed it."

Whatever tension I felt eases a little with the easy banter between us. Eric's a nice guy and to be fair, I never actually heard Eric say anything demeaning about me with the other guys.

"So how do you want to go about this?" I ask, ready to get started.

"I've been looking over the instructions..."

Ultimately, we split up the work–he'll do most of the research and I'll write up the paper. Then we'll present it together.

"We can do most of this by email, don't you think?" I say.

"Yeah, that should work," he agrees. "Oh fuck."

I glance over and see the annoyed look on his face. "What's wrong? Did we forget something?"

"*I* forgot something," he says. "Your scarf. I've had it this whole time and I keep forgetting to bring it to you."

"Oh, that's okay. I can get it later."

"I'm the worst at that. Like, I set it right by the door to remind me to bring it with me and I still fucking forgot." He gives me a small grin. "I promise I won't be a flake on our project."

"I'm not worried about it," I say. "Who needs a warm neck anyway?"

He laughs. "You know, I could bring it by your place if you want. You live over in Shotgun, right?"

It's common to know who lives in the community right off campus. There are a ton of parties over there, specifically at the Manor. But my skin prickles anyway.

"It's okay. I'll get it from you in class."

"Or, if you're not busy, we can go back to my place and grab it now."

I force myself to look at him. Eric's expression is innocent enough, with his wavy blond hair and innocent hazel eyes. But are they innocent? Does he want something more? That's the problem, I can't tell, but my body reacts, pulse ticking erratically, and a wave of nausea sloshes in my gut.

I slam my laptop shut and stand. "I need to go."

"Wait, what's happening?" he asks, watching me fumble for my things. "Are you mad about something?"

"What's happening is that whatever those guys told you about me, isn't true." Not anymore. "So if you think you can get me alone and I'll give you a blow job or you can come all over my tits, you're wrong."

"I, uh," he stammers, ears turning red. "I didn't think that. *At all.*"

"God, whatever," I sling my backpack over my shoulder. My heartbeat bangs in my chest and ears. "I heard you talking to Austin and Rocky after class."

Guilt flickers across his boyish face. "Shit. That was them. I promise–"

"Let's just do this project, present it, and turn it in."

"Nadia–" He looks like he wants to melt into the ground. Yeah, join the club, Eric. Whatever he was going to say, he swallows and adds, "Whatever you're comfortable with, that's fine with me."

His expression is sincere, and suddenly I feel like an idiot, and I do what idiot's do–run like hell. My hands are full with my coat and backpack and I keep my face down, not wanting anyone to see my tears.

That's why I slam straight into a brick wall.

A brick wall with hands that grip me by the arms and hold me upright.

"Woah, slow down, darlin'."

Son-of-a–

"Seriously," I hiss. "Are you stalking me?"

"I'm a communications minor. I had class." He looks me over and I avert my gaze, not wanting him to see the tears. He lifts my chin and scowls. "Who the fuck made you cry?"

"No one."

He smears a tear across my cheek with his thumb. "Bullshit. You running from someone?"

I shake my head, and realize his touch made my heartrate shift from fear to something else. Something that makes my body warm and flush with the memory of the night before. "What are you doing right now?"

"Other than kicking someone's ass, nothing." His jaw tics. "Why?"

I take a deep breath and confess, "I need a safe space."

10

Nadia

Axel takes my hand as we climb the porch stairs. I can feel the energy rolling off of him.

"Ready?" he asks, looking down at me, a glimmer in his green eyes.

"Not even remotely."

When I asked Axel to take me somewhere 'safe' I didn't think it would be to the old house on the edge of the business district. The one with the neon sign in the window announcing the name of the shop: Permanent Record.

It's a tattoo and piercing parlor.

"This isn't what I was thinking, when I said I needed a safe space."

"Me either, T," he opens the door, and a bell chimes overhead, "but the other option included the two of us getting naked and I don't think that's what you had in mind."

He'd be wrong about that, I think, but don't say, as I walk in behind him. Getting naked with Axel is exactly what I'd had in mind. I'd wanted to go back to one of our houses, let him peel off all my clothes, and forget about stupid boys and epic fuck-ups. Of course, that decision would have added another to the list.

I hate it when he's right.

We step inside a small foyer, that doesn't look like it's changed since it was a home. A glass chandelier hangs overhead and a massive coat rack takes up one wall. There's a room to the right and left. To the right is a sitting room, filled with comfortable looking seating and gorgeous artwork on the walls.

"So this is your safe space?" I ask, peering at one of the drawings.

"It's relaxing," he says.

"Having a needle jabbing into your skin is relaxing?" I ask in disbelief.

"I know it sounds weird, but it's true. The pain isn't that bad and after a while it becomes kind of soothing. I go into this, like, meditative space."

I stare at him, trying to figure out if he's messing with me. The expression on his face, tells me he's not. "God, you're weird."

"Unique." He gives me a cheeky grin. "At least that's what my mother calls it."

He looks over my head and I turn, seeing someone walking across the foyer.

"Hey man." A guy with spiked hair and tattoos twisting up his neck. He grins, thrusting his hand out. Axel takes it, smiling back. "Didn't see you on the appointment books."

"Hoping for a walk-in. It's for something small." He grabs me by the wrist and pulls me next to him. "Tony, this is Nadia. Nadia, this is Tony, my tattooist." He grins. "We're kind of in a committed relationship."

"We're not–" I start, taking a beat too long to realize Axel is talking about Tony and not me. "Oh, right."

"Although," Axel adds with a sexy grin, "Nadia and I have a special thing going on too."

"Nice to meet you, Nadia." Tony looks me over and I feel oddly insecure, not like he's checking me out, but noticing how bare my skin is. "I have a little time if you want to get something after I'm finished with Ax."

"Oh." My eyes scan the room, at the framed images on the wall. The artwork is all amazing. So delicate and intricate. "I've never really thought about getting a tattoo before."

It's a lie. I'd thought about it, plenty, but it only centered around one idea: getting a tattoo of my boyfriend or future husband's jersey number, 04 specifically.

Brent's number.

There is no freaking way I'm admitting that.

"Well, in case you need some inspiration, you can check out the portfolios on the shelves over there."

I follow his gesture, noticing the stacks of books in the room with the couches. The idea of picking a tattoo out of a book seems impersonal. Twyler has tattoos. They're on her upper thighs, covering the scars from when she used to self-harm. The designs are important to her, symbols from her favorite band, The New Kings. I don't have anything in my life that has that kind of importance. I never let myself get that deep into something that wasn't fashion or boys.

Now that I think about it, it's kind of unsettling.

Stepping away from the bookshelves, I walk into the other room. It used to be a dining room, but it's been upgraded to a sleek, clean, tattoo room with three stations. Axel's in the process of pulling his shirt over his head, revealing his incredible body. His pants are slung low, revealing the cut V between his hips. I'm momentarily struck dumb.

"Damn," a voice says what I'm thinking. I turn and see a woman come from the back of the parlor. She's pretty, with heavy eye make up and long black hair with pink streaks underneath. Her body is covered in artwork, tattoos, and piercings. There's one above her lip, a diamond, glinting like a beauty mark, and another at the top of her cheek. Her eyes drag away from Axel's impressive physique. "Sorry, he's just a goddamn work of art."

"No need to apologize," I say, "but yeah, he really is, isn't he?"

Axel's busy showing Tony an area on his hip, but he must feel me watching him as he settles in the chair, because he looks up at me and winks.

"Ovaries exploded," the girl mutters as a warm heat spreads across my limbs. "Make sure you wear protection with that one."

"We're not together," I say quickly.

"Hey, Jasmine," Axel calls. "What's up?"

"Not much," she replies. "Getting a piercing today?"

"Nah, just the ink."

"What about you?" she asks.

"Me?" My ears were pierced at the mall when I was twelve, and I did a second on my own at Jennifer Mitchell's house during a slumber party. At eighteen I got my belly button pierced over spring break, but it quickly became infected, and I'd sworn them off. "I'm just here with him."

"You've got those killer cheekbones and gorgeous lips, I don't really think you need anything. Although," she touches the row of earrings in the shell of her ear. "A helix or two would probably look good with your hair since you tuck it behind your ear."

My cheeks burn at the compliment, and Jasmine walks to the adjacent room.

"Yeah," I hear Axel say, "I think that's a good spot."

Curious, I walk back over and take a look at him lying on the chair. He's on his side, with one arm propped behind his head, and his jeans are unbuttoned and pushed down. I keep my eyes away from the dark shadow of hair, and focus on the exposed tattoos. Under Tony's bright lights, I can see them more clearly than I have before. There's no pattern to them, a collage of symbols and imagery. Skulls and pistols combined with butterflies and hearts. Hockey sticks and pucks. There's a pin-up girl on his bicep and an arrow above his heart. Script fills some of the space. Some single words or others a longer sentence. Most in cursive, making it hard to read. There's religious iconography, which makes sense with a minister father. There's a line of tallies on his ribs, the badger logo above it. I reach out and touch his warm skin, running it over the marks.

"Goals saved," he says, watching my fingers. "I get them updated a few times a season."

"Is that what you're doing today?" I ask, looking up at Tony who is holding a small sheet of paper in one hand and a wet cloth in the other. "Adding to the tallies?"

"Nah." Tony stands over him and presses the sheet of paper on his hip, just inside the defined muscle. "I like to commemorate important things in my life. Events. Success and failures. People."

After pressing the wet cloth on the paper, Tony pulls it back, revealing the temporary purple ink of a 'T'. The font is bold, varsity letter style.

"You're kidding," I say, gaping at the letter.

"Things have been pretty shitty lately, with the probation and stuff. You're the only good thing that's left a mark."

"Axel..." I say, my words cut off by the harsh buzz of the tattoo gun.

"It's not a marriage proposal, T," he says, taking my hand and linking his fingers with mine. "It's just how I keep track of things. Some people have a diary. I have my body."

Needle meets flesh and his fingers tighten against mine.

I don't watch Tony, my eyes are glued to Axel's: brilliant, pure, true.

I have to ask, because no man, especially not a man I'm not sleeping with, has ever made a gesture like this. Proof that I'm here. That I exist.

"You're sure this isn't another fuck-up?"

"Yeah," he says, looking down at Tony filling in the ink, "I'm fucking positive."

∽

THE PUCKS CLATTER across the ice, slamming into the players' sticks and the boards. The scoreboard says 1-1. I spot Twyler is sitting in the stands. She's in a Wittmore jersey, the number 15 on the back and Cain stitched over it. Half the reason Twyler switched from training the hockey team to basketball was so that she could sit in the stands and support her boyfriend without their positions being a conflict.

"Get it together, Wittmore!" she shouts, making room for me to get to the seat she saved for me.

"Hey," I say, nodding to the score, "how did that happen?"

"Lucky shot." She frowns. "The Badgers had been dominating the whole first period, but their forward got a breakaway and Axel couldn't get his hands on it."

I look down at the net, Axel suited up in his pads and gloves. He's alert and watching the play down at the other end of the ice. It's impossible to see his face with the helmet on, but I know he's pissed. Not at the team, at himself for missing that goal.

The puck ricochets off the boards, and the players shift directions, gliding across the ice with complete ease. Watching them, I understand a little better how they're all so confident. The simple feat of being able to skate and handle the stick and puck is physically impressive.

The whistle blows, and the lines change, one group of guys going on the ice, while another goes off. I feel Twyler staring at me.

"You got your ear pierced," she says, touching the shell of my ear. "When did this happen?"

I pull back and give her a face. It's still tender. "Yesterday."

"Did you go to Jasmine at Permanent Record?"

I nod.

"She's great. Tony, too. You should have told me you were going, I need to get a touch up on one of my tatts."

"Sorry." I give her a small smile and a white lie. "It was a spontaneous decision."

The only reason I was at the tattoo and piercing parlor was because Axel took me there to help me get out of my head. After watching him get the 'T' on his hip, something courageous lit in my chest, and I decided to do something too. Albeit, something much less permanent.

Down on the ice, the referee drops the puck for the face-off and the guys fight for possession. Wittmore loses and someone nearby shouts, "Stop him!" as the forward makes it into shooting range. Jefferson makes a play for it, but the puck slides past him, right into the forward's path. He rears back, slapping the hard disc with the edge of his stick and it sails through the air.

I tense, every muscle in my body tight, as the puck slings through the air. My only thought is how does anyone stop that? Yet Axel is there, snatching the disc out of the air.

"He did it!" I shout, both shocked and not. I don't get a chance to breathe before he responds quickly, hurling the puck back on the ice. His aim is true, and the puck lands right at the tip of Reid's stick. He's in perfect position, passing the puck to Reese up near the goal. Twyler jumps to her feet. "Go get it, Cain. Take the shot!"

Reese moves with unbridled power, taking a hard slapshot that sails past the other team's goalie and into the back of the net. The light flips on and the buzzer sounds. "He did it!" I shout, jumping to give Twyler a hug. Down on the ice, Reese looks up at her and grins, and my heart clenches.

Somehow my friend is living my best life. I wait for the wave of jealousy, but it's impossible. She didn't chase it. Love found her. Well, I guess Reese found her in that coffee shop and fate did the rest. It just makes me wonder if I've been doing it all wrong.

The second the buzzer sounds for intermission, and the organizers start up some game on the ice for the fans. I watch the guys skate off the ice–no, I watch Axel.

"Oh, I got you something," Twyler says, reaching for her bag. She pulls a Wittmore hockey jersey out and holds it up with the back facing me. The name Rakestraw is stitched across the top with the number 01.

I stare at the jersey, then up at Twyler's smiling face, and ask, "What the heck is this for?"

"For you to wear. You know," she gives me a look, "since you're dating."

My heart stutters. "We're not dating."

She gives me a 'duh' look. "I know, but Brent and CJ don't. Shanna definitely got the message she and Reese were done when I started wearing his clothes."

"She got the message because he looks at you like you're a three-layer cake and he wants to eat the whole thing with his bare hands."

She rolls her eyes, but I see the pink flush in her cheeks. "I just think that after Brent saw you kissing Axel in the bar the other night, it makes sense to imply that this is more serious than a one-night thing."

If she only knew about our real one-night stand. I run my hands down my thighs, the guilt of lying to her a weight on my shoulders. "Don't you think Axel would have a problem with it? You and I both know walking around in a guy's jersey means something. Something we're not. It would be like wearing a sign that says 'cockblocker' to any other girl he's interested in."

She shrugs, shoving the shirt into my hands. "He's not interested in anyone else right now. Or at least it doesn't seem like it. You know I stay over there a lot, and the parade of puck bunnies going in and out of there like Grand Central Station has come to a complete stop."

It feels weird to hear confirmation that he's holding up to his end of the pact. I never thought he'd really give up sex entirely. Why should he? That's not his problem. It's mine.

But I can't deny that hearing her confirm it loosens something in my chest, and I'm not sure how to identify the relief that follows.

"He's trying to focus on the game right now," I tell her. "At least that's what he told me. He feels like he let the team down when he failed the drug test so he's partying less. I guess that includes women."

Twyler nods. "Reese is really proud of the work he's putting into it. Between us, he wasn't sure if he could–or really–*would*, do it."

I don't tell her how hard making these changes have been for him–on both of us–and that we've been leaning on one another for support because I'm pretty sure her approval would disappear. "I think he's really trying."

"Well, if you want me to steal a hoodie for you the next time I'm over, I'm on it." Her eyes widen. "Oh, or you could get one yourself at Friendsgiving on Sunday."

Shit. I'd forgotten about that. "They're not really my friends, Twy."

"Of course they are. Reese, Reid, Axel…"

"I don't want to intrude."

"They want you to come. And even more, I *need* you to come." Her gaze flicks behind me and I know she's looking at the group of puck bunnies that come to every game and party. They have their own little section and they have no problem wearing various jerseys with the players' names on them. Discreetly, I turn, and see that one girl with long blonde hair has on Axel's number.

My nails dig into my thighs.

I've been that girl before, desperate for a player's attention. Her clear blue eyes meet mine and something passes between us. A familiarity. Does she know who I am? Does she know I slept with Axel? Kissed him in the bar?

Does she know he got my initial tattooed on his body?

Hell, I don't know if she's done the same with him and honestly, it's none of my business.

"Reid and Darla broke up, which means I'll be the only girlfriend," Twyler continues. "Jefferson's been on a tear through sorority row, so I expect at least a couple girls I don't know to be there, and I'm sure Reid will be licking his wounds with at least one puck bunny."

"What about Axel? You just said he's flying solo these days."

"And he's totally cranky about it." She grips my arm. "Please come? You don't even have to cook. I'll bring enough for both of us. Just don't leave me alone with these people."

"Fine. I'll come."

"Thank God." She sighs in relief and looks at my long sleeved work shirt with the Wittmore Gym logo on the chest, then down to the jersey. "You gonna put that on?"

I've gone three years without wearing an athlete's jersey. My goal had been to actually date the player first. For him to claim me. It had never happened. But Axel isn't a guy I want to date. He isn't going pro.

Like Twyler said, he's a friend, and he'd offered to buffer me from other guys, which is important right now.

I slip the shirt over my head, pulling it over my head. There's a torn, frayed spot at the bottom and when I lift the fabric to my nose, it has a warm, musky, clean scent. "Where did you get this?"

"Out of the team manager's room. They swap out uniforms all the time–this one was in the bin for damaged jerseys."

The music blasts, announcing the end of the participant game. The winners carry off their prizes, T-shirts and a few Badger plushies. The buzzer sounds and all eyes are on the players as they skate out of the tunnel. Twyler's on her feet, cheering on her boyfriend and my eyes are glued to the goalie as he heads across the ice to the net. Right before the whistle blows, his head lifts and he searches the crowd. It's impossible to know with that mask on, but I sense it when he finds me, and something hot slams into my chest. I exhale loudly.

"You okay?" Twyler asks, frowning at me.

"I'm fine, just a long day, you know." The whistle blows and the boys lunge into action.

"Long semester," she agrees. "I can't wait to have a few days off for Thanksgiving."

I nod, not feeling the same desire, but it's better than talking about the feelings coursing through me. "So Reid and Darla, huh?"

"Oh yeah, total drama," she says, eyes lighting up. "We heard the whole thing."

I smile, grateful for the distraction. "Tell me everything."

～

"Sure you don't want to come?" Twyler asks, grabbing Reese's hoodie and pulling it over her head. She fluffs out her long hair, letting it spill over her shoulders. "It should be fun."

The guys are having a party over at the Manor to celebrate their narrow win. It may have been narrow, but they're still undefeated and the vibe coming off the team tonight was intense.

"I really need to work on this project," I say, pulling my computer into my lap, "and I have to work early."

"Okay, but if you want to come up, just come in. The guys will be happy to have you there."

I don't react to that other than with a tight smile and feel a sense of relief when she's out the door. After all those months of not wanting me around the hockey team, she's shifted gears. It could be because she's not working with the team anymore, but I suspect it's something else: She just feels bad for me.

Checking my email, I see a message from Eric, adding me to a shared document for his notes. My emotions are still conflicted about how we left things–or well, how I freaked out on him and ran from the room. Was he being a douche? That's the problem. I have no idea. He looked genuinely horrified at my accusations, but it wouldn't be the first time I've been gaslit into feeling guilty over something I'm unsure about. I'm not used to nice guys, non-athletes, who don't feed on ego and over-inflated confidence. Maybe Eric had been genuine, just wanting to give me back my scarf and the easiest way to do that was to stop by the frat house.

Or maybe he's just like the rest of them, looking for an opportunity to hurt me.

Why are men so fucking confusing?

I type out a response: *Thanks. I'll get on this ASAP,* and shut the laptop.

My phone buzzes and panic hits my gut. Is it him?

I pick up the phone and stare at the text:

GoalieGod: SOS.

11

Axel

Holy shit, I made a mistake.

All I wanted was a slice of pizza and a bottle of Gatorade. Fine, two slices of pizza. I'm fucking starving after that brutal game. Instead of food, I found a fluffle of puck bunnies in my kitchen, half dressed and clustered around the island. I almost turned around and went right back upstairs, but fuck no. This is my house. My kitchen.

My pizza.

For the past couple of weeks, the guys have held off on partying, doing their best to keep me from temptation, but tonight they deserved it. It was a tough win–one that requires celebration. Booze, chicks, loud music, and fun. All things that are on hold for me until my probation is over.

While they went to the liquor store and announced the party across social media, I showered, changed into sweats and a black tank, and figured I'd stick to the second floor.

Then I got hungry.

At first, I handled it. Smiling. Talking up the girls. Giving them enough attention to keep things cool between us, while giving each one an easy brush off. It's a skill I learned from my father of all people. Being a minister is half man of god, half politician. Being smooth comes with the job.

I move like Moses, parting the red sea, if that sea was made up of short skirts, tight jeans, and unrelenting cleavage. When I finally get to the refrigerator, I stick my head in, letting the cold air wash over me.

A small hand rests on my lower back.

There's only one girl I want touching me right now, and I say a quick prayer that maybe she showed up. I turn, stomach and balls tight, only to feel a surge of disappointment.

Chantelle.

She hasn't gone full stage 5 clinger, but I can tell from the curve of her upper lip, and the low cut of her shirt, that she's determined to finish where we left off. That's not what puts me on edge. It's the cup of brown liquid she's holding out to me.

"I brought you a drink. You like whiskey, right?"

That's when I shoot off the text.

SOS.

"Thanks," I say, sliding my phone back in my pocket, and taking the cup. I can't help but inhale the spicy liquor. God, it's the scent of a thousand bad decisions and best nights ever. I miss it. "But I'm not drinking tonight."

"Oh," she says, giving me a pout. There's defensiveness in there too. People get weird if you're not drinking at parties, like it's a statement about them and not just a choice you've made for yourself.

Murphy, one of the younger guys on the team, walks by and I hand him the cup. "Go crazy, brother."

He grins, eyes darting to Chantelle. "Thanks, man."

I have a glimmer of hope that maybe she'll decide to go off with him, but her gaze shifts back to me.

"I thought for a minute you guys may not pull it off, but then

Kirby scored," she says, letting me know she was at the game. "I jumped to my feet so fast."

"You should tell him. He'd love to hear it." I gesture to my teammate doing a keg stand on the back porch. Reid is cheering him on, wearing only his boxers. The urge to strip off my tank and join them in a night of debauchery is strong. Even though I'm still pissed about missing that breakaway, the old me would have wanted to celebrate the win. The new me knows I can't risk it. I'm so close to being off probation.

"I don't know how you do it," she continues, while I unscrew the cap of the sports drink bottle and take a long sip. "I'd be so scared to have those pucks coming at me so fast."

While she talks, my eyes search the room. Maybe she's not going to come. I check my phone and see a message. It's not from Nadia but my Dad.

Rev: How's the sermon? Make any progress?

Nope. Not dealing with that now. The closer we get to the break, the more often he's going to bug me about the talk he wants me to give over the holidays.

I check again, making sure Nadia's message didn't get bumped. Maybe she didn't get it? Or maybe she's tired of holding my hand, but this wasn't a cry wolf. This is a code red.

"Axel?"

I look down and see Chantelle gazing up at me. Fuck. "Sorry, babe, I'm sucking the fun out of the room tonight. I just came down for a snack." I give her a tight smile, one that has worked on letting down chicks in the past. "I'm not feeling up to a party tonight."

"We don't have to party," she says, fingers curling into my waistband. Her nails drag over the still healing tattoo–no pain really, but it's tender. "We could head up to your room, finish what we started last time."

Wrapping my hand around Chantelle's wrist, I'm prying her fingers off, when I hear, "What the fuck is going on?"

I smell her before I see her, that fresh, flowery scent that follows Nadia everywhere. I turn and see her standing just inside the kitchen, hands on her hips. She looks livid, those big brown eyes furious, and her mouth twisted in a scowl. None of that matters though. I'm stuck on the fact she's wearing my jersey. Not *a* jersey. *Mine*. I see the frayed hem from where I got in a fight three games ago. Her hot gaze flicks from me to Chantelle. "Are you hitting on my man?"

"Your *what?*" Chantelle snaps.

I reach a hand out and grab Nadia by the hip, pulling her against my side. "Darlin', thought you were never gonna show."

She places her hand on my stomach and rises up on her toes, kissing the underside of my jaw. That simple touch is enough to make my pulse quicken and my dick get hard. "Sorry," she says, holding up a canvas bag. "I had to get my things together."

"You're fucking kidding me," Chantelle mutters, glaring at the two of us.

Ignoring her, I cup the back of Nadia's neck and tilt her face upward. I see the flash of uncertainty in her eyes right before I kiss her, but that hesitation slips away when our tongues meet.

Jesus, she tastes so fucking good.

"Whatever," Chantelle says, and in my periphery I see her flounce off, her little tennis skirt bouncing as she goes.

Licking her lips, I ask, "Is she gone?"

Nadia looks around my shoulder. "Yes." She moves to pull away, but I hold tight.

"Don't even think about it," I say, running my hand down her back and nudging her out of the kitchen. I want to take her upstairs, lock the door of my bedroom, and strip every piece of clothing off of her, but Nadia answered my SOS, not a booty call.

I push her into the laundry room and kick the door shut behind us. I slide the lock, making sure no one can barge in. The room is dark other than the light coming in the window from the backyard. I stare down at her as I press her against the washer with my hips.

"Thank you for coming," I tell her, keeping my hands on her waist. "Those girls aren't bunnies. They're sharks."

"You looked like you had a handle on it," she says, looking up at me. Her lips are wet from my kiss and all I want to do is taste her again. It dawns on me. All I want is her.

"Look, T, I'm trying to tread carefully here, which is fucking hard for someone who likes to come in hot." Her forehead creases and I keep going. "Wearing a man's jersey isn't something that is taken lightly."

She groans. "God, I told Twyler it was too much. That this is something reserved for girlfriends. I'll take it off–"

"Like hell you will."

I slam my mouth against hers, and she gasps from the force. I don't give a fuck. I kiss her hard and demanding, the way I'd wanted to out in the kitchen. Not just for Chantelle. For the whole goddamn room. But most of all, for Nadia.

But first I have to make her mine.

Her fingers twist in the front of my tank, my lips skate up her jaw. "Seeing you up in the stands was one thing," I press into her, letting her feel how much she turns me on. "But the jersey... fuck, T. The only way I want you out of that is if you're getting all the way naked with me. Not here. Up in my room."

Her hand presses against my chest, pushing me back. She swallows, those brown eyes holding mine. "Is that what you want?"

I take a breath, trying to come to my senses. It's nearly impossible with my heart pounding like a drum and my dick attempting to drill its way out of my sweats. "Look," I finally say, trying to formulate the right words. Trying not to completely fuck this up. "I know this isn't what you signed up for when we made our pact. I'm not feeling very safe for you right now and if you want to go, you can go. We'll head out the backdoor and I'll walk you home."

We're on the edge of a sharp blade, one where we decide how this is going to move forward. Do we keep being one another's safe spaces or do we become more?

"I don't want to go home," she admits.

"Thank god," I mutter and drop another kiss on her mouth, licking my way past her lips to the warm heat inside.

"But," she pulls back, "I also don't know how far I'm ready to go."

All I want is for this girl to trust me, to know that I'm not here to hurt her.

"Tell me what you want, T," I say, kissing my way down her neck. I tug the collar to expose more skin and kiss along the ridge of her collarbone. She shivers and I run my hands up her shirt, feeling her pebbled nipples underneath. "What makes you feel good? Tell me and I'll make it happen."

She doesn't respond, her fingers clinging to my sides. She's anxious and I don't understand.

I lift her chin, but her eyes dart to the side. "Okay, what's going on?"

She shifts, then admits, "No one's ever asked me what I want before."

My eyebrows raise. "No one?"

She shakes her head, cheeks blooming red. "They pretty much called me over to, you know, meet their needs."

Fuckers.

"And those girls were hitting on you and it's obvious you're turned on," her eyes drop to where my boner is trying it's hardest to join the conversation. "I just… I don't want to be that girl you call just for sex."

Shit, now *I'm* the fucker.

"I didn't text you for sex. I texted you because you're the one I turn to when I need things to slow down. When I need to get my head on straight. Chantelle isn't the one that made me feel like this." I take her hand and place it over my erection. "That was all you, understood?"

Her response is quiet, but I hear her say, "Understood."

"And for the record, those other guys are worthless pieces of shit who probably don't know their way around a woman's body." I run my thumb over her bottom lip, puffy and swollen from our kisses. "Any man who doesn't want to hear the sound of you falling apart when you come is a damn fool. I can't get it out of my mind."

"Oh god." She drops her face into her hands. "That night never happened, remember?"

I wrap my arms around her and lift her, setting her on the washer, so I can see her face. "Sorry, but it's imprinted. I think about it before

I go to bed, and first thing when I wake up." And a dozen more times a day, but I'm trying to win her over, not scare the hell out of her. I rest my hands on her knees. "You trust me?"

She bites down on her bottom lip and nods. "I do."

"Then let me take care of you." I slide my hands up her legs, over her thighs, and hook my fingers into the waistband of her leggings. "Lean back and lift up a little." Resting a hand on my shoulder for balance, she obliges and I ease both her pants and panties down her thighs. "That'a girl."

I bend, kissing the soft skin inside her knees, making my way up her legs. Nadia isn't one of these stick thin, thigh gap, kind of women. She's fit from working out, but there's still meat on her bones, and it's hot as hell. The higher I move up, the more she starts to squirm, her thighs clamping closed.

"Settle down, T, " I apply a little pressure, keeping her spread, and lick my lips, "let me eat your pussy."

"Your mouth," she says, falling back on the washer, "it's filthy, you know that?"

"Yeah, well, welcome to sex with a preacher's boy." I swipe my fingers along her clit, already slippery wet. She hums at my touch, and I bend, getting a taste of her. She moans, her fingers raking through my hair as her hips rise to meet my mouth. "There we go."

I've been with a lot of women, but never one that I wanted to please as much as Nadia. She deserves to feel safe. To let loose. To feel a man take care of her, without wanting something in return. I know I've done my job when her thighs start to tremble and her nails dig into my scalp. Her breathing grows heavy, chest rising and falling, the moan of pleasure in the back of her throat. Sucking on her clit, she shudders around me, knees clamping around my ears.

"Axel, oh my god," she whispers.

The orgasm hits like a jolt, shuddering down her limbs. She holds onto me, clinging to my head, and damn, I can't get enough.

Unfortunately, women get sensitive down there and as much as I hate it, she squirms away, uttering, "Wow."

"Yeah?" I ask, giving her my hand and help her sit back up. Jesus, she looks even sexier now all flushed with an orgasm wearing my number. "Good?"

"Better than good. That was amazing." She reaches out and runs her fingers over my mustache. "And that? Yeah, keep that."

If it means I'll get another chance with her, then I'm never shaving again.

"So, do you want me to…"

"Nope." I take her hand and kiss her fingers. "That was all for you."

12

Nadia

With every bone in my body feeling like it's turned to liquid, we emerge from the laundry room, back into the party.

Can they tell Axel Rakestraw just gave me the best orgasm of my life? Does a woman look different after that?

I'd asked myself a similar question after my first time, when I lost my virginity to Will Holt. I was fifteen. He was twenty and one of my older brother's best friends. Our next door neighbor that I'd had a crush on for years. His attention felt so good, and I knew he was experienced. I'd seen the girls he had come over, and they seemed so cool and confident. Like they knew some secret I was dying to know.

Axel's fingers tighten around mine as he leads me through the kitchen, only stopping to grab a pizza box off the island. He slides me a heated look, either ignoring or unaware of the glares coming from Chantelle and the other puck bunnies. It's not my first public walk of shame. No, that had come after Will Holt sent me home with cum still sticky between my legs. It is the first time the guy went down on me without asking for anything in return. It's also the first time the man didn't ditch me. Not yet anyway.

"Come upstairs?" he asks, his mouth close to my ear.

I nod, but call out, "Wait," stopping to grab the canvas bag I'd left in the kitchen. I keep my eyes peeled for Reese and Twyler, but they're probably playing quarters on the back porch or left early. Good. I don't want to deal with either of them right now.

When we reach the stairs, he takes the bag from me. It's heavy.

"What the hell did you bring?" he asks, moving to open it.

"You sent an SOS." I attempt to snatch it back. "That's my bag of tricks."

The upstairs is quiet. I've never been up here before. Four doors line the walls, each closed. We pass one and I hear a muffled voice. "Christ, Sunshine, sure you can take it?" A groan follows, then, "Good girl."

My eyes widen and Axel and I exchange a look. "Good girl?" I mouth, shocked. Those two are quieter than a church mouse back at the Teal House. "You listen to this when she sleeps over?"

"Yes," he groans, opening the door to his room. He leads me inside, turning on the light on the bedside table. "Between their quiet, lovey-dovey sex, Reid and Darla fighting and then making up all the time, and Jefferson's wall-fucking, it's like drought conditions over here."

"Poor baby," I say, flashing him a sympathetic smile, then stop short at the state of his room. If Axel's body is a diary of his life, his walls take it to the next level. It's an explosion of personality.

There's the obvious posters of sexy girls, suggestively holding hockey sticks while wearing thigh high athletic socks and knotted jerseys. But there are other pictures of players I assume are his idols, messy ink drawings that look like tattoo ideas. Over the cluttered desk is a long shelf of empty beer and liquor bottles–tokens from the last three and a half years. I spot stacks of spiral bound notebooks and can't help but wonder what he's writing in them.

Clothes spill out of his closet and a rack of scuffed barbells sits in the corner.

"This is..." I start, but I'm at a loss for words.

"A lot, I know." He runs his hand through his hair, making his tattooed bicep bulge. On anyone else, I'd side-eye the gray sweats and black tank at a party, but on Axel, it's ridiculously hot. "I wasn't allowed to really decorate my room growing up, so when I finally had my own space, I went a little overboard."

"I like it." I've been in my share of athlete's rooms, dorms and apartments, and you can tell the guys don't do much in there other than sleep and fuck. "It's chaotic. Kind of like you."

I turn, taking in the three hockey jerseys pinned to the wall near the bathroom, but the main feature, hanging over the headboard is a massive Texas state flag and a cowboy hat hanging on the bedpost.

He jumps into action, tossing items of clothing off his bed and onto the pile by the closet. "The sheets are clean," he says, fanning a comforter over the top. "Jefferson's mom insisted we get a cleaning lady in here twice a month." His teeth drag over the ring in his lip. "And, you know, I haven't had any women over." His eyes meet mine. "Until now."

"Right," I say, unsure of where to go next. With other guys I would know. There was only one reason they brought me to their room. Is Axel any different? Finally, I exhale and admit, "I don't know what the expectations are here. You just gave me an earth-shattering orgasm and–"

"First, I don't believe in transactional sex," he says, jaw locking tight, his eyes on mine for a long moment. He nods down at the canvas bag. "Second, I really want you to show me what you brought in that bag."

"Oh." I smile and lift it up. "Yes. I call it my Axel Rakestraw No More Epic Fuck-Ups SOS Kit."

"That's quite a mouthful, T." He climbs onto the bed, legs crossed. He pats the empty space in front of him. "Let's see it."

When I got the SOS text, I packed the bag with whatever I could find in the house. I wasn't sure what to expect, but Axel being surrounded by hot puck bunnies wasn't a stretch. What did surprise me was my reaction. I've been jealous before. Shanna, the woman Brent traded up for, comes to mind, but this was different. I wasn't just jealous. I was territorial. Enough so, I didn't hesitate staking my claim.

"Okay," I say, settling across from him. I reach into the bag and start pulling out items. "First we have a 500-piece puzzle of the Wittmore campus." He picks up the puzzle and studies the front. "Twyler's mom bought that for us when she came to visit."

"Cool. The arena's on here," he points out.

"I also have two decks of cards, one is normal playing cards, the other UNO."

"Do not let Reid see those UNO cards." He shakes his head. "Dude is fucking rabid."

"Over UNO?"

"Yeah. Something about high stakes competition growing up. He's got a bunch of siblings." He smirks. "There's even a story about someone getting stabbed with a fork during one particularly dramatic game."

"Wow, okay." I take the UNO cards and drop them back in the bag. In its place, I pull out a long box. "There's also Scrabble, or…" I rummage around for my laptop, "I've downloaded the complete second season of Springfield."

"You're offering me the choice between a puzzle, some games, or soft core porn?" His eyebrow lifts. "Obviously, I'm choosing the puzzle."

"Bullshit," I challenge, grabbing the laptop. "You already sacrificed yourself once tonight. You deserve a little soft core porn as a reward."

"Thank god," he says, falling back on the pillows. "If I don't get to see at least some sideboob tonight, I may cry."

I set the laptop in the middle of the bed. He grunts, grabbing it and placing it on his lap while reaching for me with a strong arm. He pulls me against him and I'm engulfed in his scent. His skin is warm and he smells so good, spicy and clean. My body reacts to him even more than it did before–now I know for sure how good he can make me feel.

"You think Bryce and Tess are going to take another shower together?" he asks, breath hot on my ear.

"Brock and Jess," I remind him, but his smirk tells me that he's fucking with me. "And no, I don't think they'll take another shower, but I'm sure they'll up the ante somehow. Maybe the hot tub? Or a threesome?"

"Awesome." He leans over and turns off the light, shrouding us in the dark other than the screen. I lean back, marveling at how this all happened–this easy relationship with an orgasm giving, trashy-TV-watching, super star goalie.

For once in my life, I don't want to overthink it. Wrapped in his arms I settle against him and just enjoy the moment.

∼

THE NOISE JOLTS ME AWAKE.

Thump. Thump. Thump.

"Ugh, not again."

The voice is rough with sleep, and attached to a very hard, very warm body. I'd fallen asleep for the second time in Axel's arms. This time we're both fully clothed.

"What is that?" I whisper, cheek planted against his chest.

Another loud thud slams into the wall and a stack of notebooks slides off the shelf and onto the floor.

"Jefferson," he mutters, hand reaching between us to adjust himself, while never letting me out of his grip.

Oh. The wall fucking. That's what he was talking about.

Out in the hallway, I hear the sound of a door opening and then a louder, more insistent pounding.

"Uh oh, he pissed off Cap."

"Seriously, dude?" Reese's voice carries through the walls. "It's three-fucking-AM. You're waking up the whole house. We've got practice in the morning."

"Shut up, man," Jefferson retorts. "You think you and Twy are all quiet in there, but you're not. Oh, Reese!" His voice rises into a high falsetto. "Oh, Sunshine!"

"Oh my god," I snort, then bark out a too loud laugh. Axel brings my face to his chest, smothering my laughter.

"You're gonna give us away," he says, quietly. "They may be okay with us hanging out some, but I suspect this crosses the line."

He's right. Twyler would lose her shit if she knew I was still in here–although right now, she's probably just dying of embarrassment that Jefferson called them out.

"Just go to bed, asshole," Reese says. "And fuck your girl on the bed like everyone else."

The doors slam, one then the other, and the house falls silent. Axel's hand is on my back and there's no mistaking the hard erection between us. It was like that while we watched three episodes of the show, but he never made a move–not once.

"Is it like this every night?" I ask, lifting my face to his.

"Only when Jeff brings chicks home. He spends a lot of time over on sorority row."

"I've heard those are your stomping grounds too."

He shrugs. "Used to be."

"Do you miss it?"

His green eyes hold mine. "Not as much as I thought I would."

Our bodies are close, every inch pressed against one another, including the rock hard erection he's been sporting all night.

"Twyler is so private. She's going to be horrified showing her face in the morning."

"The first night she slept over, she bolted before daylight."

"Sounds right." I smile, before it falters. "I guess I always saw the walk of shame as this badge of honor. Like I wanted everyone to see me coming out of a football player's dorm or apartment." I think this comes from my first time with my neighbor, too. "Walking home in the morning was never what made me feel shitty with the football players, especially with Brent."

"What did?" he asks.

"They didn't want me to be seen with them, but they also wanted me to just hang around. Wait for them while they were playing or at practice. Sit and wait until they got back from a party. It was boring and never as exciting as I thought it would be."

I was an afterthought. A quick and convenient way to get off.

"I was never good enough to be seen with them–like as their girl. No one was looking for me in the stands." I sigh, feeling so dumb. "I thought eventually they'd realize that I was the girl they were waiting for. See how I could be more to them than a quick fuck."

"Hey," he says, arms circling tight, "that's bullshit, you know that right?"

"It's hard when you know the only value they see in you is how much money they can make from selling you."

"Jesus." He exhales. "You are worth so much more than you understand. Those assholes were lucky you even gave them the time of day."

"Yeah, okay."

"Seeing your face up in the stands makes the game so much better," he says with a harsh ferocity. "It makes the win so much sweeter."

"Yeah?"

"Fuck yeah." He runs his hand up and down my arm. "And the jersey? I'd give you one for every day of the week, if I thought you'd wear it."

"Stop." I frown. "Then everyone would think we're sleeping together."

"Darlin' we literally just woke up in the same bed." He takes my face between his hands. "We *are* sleeping together."

"You know what I mean."

"And you need to know that the only reason I haven't tried to fuck you again is because you're not ready." My heart stutters, unsure of how to respond. Apparently he's not finished. "I'll be here when you are, but until then this is enough."

"A safe space," I say, more to myself than to him.

He nods, kissing me again, before tucking me close against his side.

It's hard for me to accept the truth behind his words–he's an athlete after all–I'm not stupid. He's under pressure and I'm a steady spot in the whirlwind of chaos, but I can't deny that the feeling of being in his arms makes it worth it.

∼

THERE WAS no walk of shame.

Axel waited until the guys left the next morning, brought me downstairs, and loaded me in the front seat of his black truck and drove me to work.

"You sure you don't need anything from the house? We can swing by and get it."

His hand is on my thigh, warm and steady.

"I have a locker there with workout clothes and an extra shirt." He pulls the truck up to the front doors of the gym. "Thanks for the ride."

"Thanks for coming to my rescue last night," he says, bringing my hand to his mouth. He kisses my knuckles. "Next time you owe me a game of Scrabble."

The morning passes by quickly. After changing, I stick to the front desk, checking students and faculty as they come in, from the cold bleary eyed to the determined. There's always a steady stream when we unlock the doors. Most are regulars. There's a certain type of dedicated gym-goer that consistently comes every day. Instructors clock in and head back to the workout rooms to teach spin, pilates, body pump.

"That was an awfully big truck you got out of this morning," Abby says, leaning back against the counter with a steaming cup of tea in her hand.

I laugh. Big trucks are common back home, but up here less so. "Axel's from Texas. I guess that tracks."

"Axel?" Her eyes widen. "Axel Rakestraw?"

I shouldn't be surprised she knows him. All the guys on the hockey team are pretty popular and recognizable. Axel more so with a prominent position and his dark bad boy looks.

Abby's in her mid-twenties. She was a student at Wittmore, and a member of one of the bigger sororities, who was offered the manager role of the gym after graduation. Her next comment confirms how well she keeps up with the student gossip. "I thought you only dated football players?"

"We're not dating. He's a friend of a friend, who is just... well, a friend."

You know, if friends give you amazing orgasms and snuggle in bed with you watching cheesy teen dramas.

The look she gives me over her tea tells me she sees right through my 'just friends' comment. But it's true isn't it? Sure, we're hooking up, but he's not asking for anything from me–just a safe place to hang while he waits for his probation to end.

God. Just friends is confusing.

"I'd have a hard time staying just friends with a guy who looks like that," she admits. "But he's got a reputation over in the Kappa house for being a player. Nothing scandalous, just... he's always chasing fun. If that's what you're into, you probably won't find a better guy." She sets her drink down as a member with wet hair approaches the desk. "Can I help you?"

Apparently one of the showers in the women's room won't shut off, and water is backing up. "Watch the counter," Abby says, grabbing her cell phone to call maintenance. She runs back to the locker room. The interruption allows me to drop the Axel discussion. Thankfully. What she's describing is the reputation Axel has had for the entire time he's been at Wittmore, but I also know that lately he's had to shed that to keep his spot on the team.

There's a lot more to Axel Rakestraw than sexy party boy.

"Nadia?"

I look up and see Eric standing at the counter.

"Hey," I say, fussing with a few objects on the counter as a way to look busy. "Forget your ID?"

"No. Not here for a workout." I realize he's alone, not with his usual posse of frat boys and dressed in street clothes. I notice he has something in his hand. "I wanted to bring you this." He places my scarf on the counter. "It's cold out there and Thanksgiving is coming... thought you may need it."

"Thanks," I pull the handmade scarf off the counter. "I appreciate it."

A student lines up behind Eric and I gesture for him to move so I scan his ID. Eric steps aside, but doesn't leave.

"If this is about the project," I tell him once the student is gone, "I got your notes. Everything will be done on time."

"It's not about that," he says, leaning over the counter. "I want to apologize. What you heard that day–it was gross and inappropriate. Although I wasn't the one that said it, I didn't stop it. I let Austin and Rocky say that awful stuff and I should have stepped in and defended you."

My cheeks burn at the memory of what they said. How they talk about me like I'm nothing but a body for their purposes. The real humiliation comes in because I know there's truth to it. I allowed that to happen.

Eric's not finished. "I understand why you thought I was trying to get you alone. And to be honest, I did want to spend more time with you. You're nice and yeah, hot, but in the context of everything it was a boneheaded move."

"I may have been a little hypersensitive," I admit, "and maybe took out some of my frustration on you and not the people who deserve it. They're pretty intimidating."

"Fuck, right?" he laughs darkly, shoving his hand in his hair. "I let myself get caught up in the whole thing. They're basically celebrities, you know? I'm a huge sports fan and having a class with them has been unreal." His jaw tics and he looks down. "I guess I just wanted their approval and I did it in a super shitty way." His eyes flick up to meet mine. "If you want to just finish the project and never speak again, I understand, but I just wanted to let you know that I really am sorry."

"I accept," I tell him. "And if you want, we can maybe get together after the break to run through the presentation?"

He grins. "That would be awesome."

We agree to talk after Thanksgiving break and after he walks off I take a deep breath, a weight lifting off my shoulders. I've got too much fear and anger in my heart and it feels good to let a little of it go.

13

Nadia

I'M STANDING at the front door of the Manor, trying to figure out how to knock and also not drop the foil covered platter in my hands.

"I'll get it!" A cheery voice calls from behind me. It's followed by the sharp tap of heels on the wooden porch floor and a gust of perfume. I turn and see two girls, both blonde, that I've seen at games or at the Den. One carries a bottle of champagne. The other orange juice.

Puck Bunnies.

"Not sure what that is," she raps on the door with her knuckles, "but it smells divine, and I wouldn't want you to drop it."

"Thanks," I say. "I think I'd cry if I dropped them. They took forever."

"I'm Bridget," she says and nods to the other girl, "and that's Heather."

"I'm–"

"Nadia," Heather says, smoothing down her skirt. "We know."

I could ask how, if Brent's blacklisting has reached them, but I'd rather not. Thankfully, the door opens and Reid stands in front of us in a wild paisley print shirt and loose jeans. He grins down at us. "Ladies, welcome to Friendsgiving!"

"Hey, Reid," Heather says, "love your shirt."

"Thanks," he says, obviously proud. "It's vintage."

Heather pushes the OJ into his chest. "Jefferson here?"

"Out back," he says as she and Bridget both step in. "They're frying the turkey."

"Thanks," Bridget gives him a smile and the bottle of champagne.

"I guess they're Jefferson's guests?" I ask, watching them cut through the house to the backdoor.

"I suppose." He eyes the platter in my hands. "Twy's upstairs changing. She just got here."

"Already?" The basketball team had an away game over night and according to her text, the bus pulled in about thirty minutes ago. As part of the staff, her duties aren't over the minute she walks off the bus. She has to stick around and help get all the medical supplies back in the training room or attend to any injuries before leaving. "She must have rushed."

"Reese picked her up," he says, closing the door behind me. Although the Manor is an older home like ours, it's been upgraded over the years. The living room is set up with comfortable couches and a big TV and the kitchen is an open concept, with a well-equipped kitchen that has a large eat-in bar. At parties it becomes a real bar, loaded with bottles and cups, but today it's filled with food. A girl I recognize as Reid's on-again-off-again girlfriend, Darla, organizes the dishes.

Guess they're back on.

Reid grabs a beer and heads outside, but not before stopping by Darla and giving her a kiss on the neck. "I'll go make sure they're not over-cooking the bird."

Still clutching the platter in my hands, I ask Darla, "Where do you want me to put this?"

"What category does it fall in? Main, side, or dessert?"

"Um," I stall, shifting from one foot to the other. This was dumb. I should have just brought rolls from the store or a green bean casserole. "I'm not exactly sure."

Darla gives me a look like I'm an idiot, and takes the platter out of my hands.

As she rearranges the space for the tray, shifting a pan of mac n' cheese to make room, the spicy scent of meat and peppers fills the room. On the staircase, Twyler walks down in jeans and a cropped sweater. For Twy, that's dressing up.

"Holy shit," Darla says. "Did you make these?"

With Twyler out of the house, the gym closed for the impending holiday, and too much time on my hands, I'd spent the day looking up recipes, buying ingredients and started baking. I'd made six batches overall, scrapping the first three, salvaging the fourth, and was pretty pleased with the last two.

Twyler says, staring down at the pastries, "What the hell, Nadia, since when did you go all Rachel Ray?"

"I, uh, saw it on ChattySnap. Apparently they're popular in some regions for Thanksgiving and figured I'd give it a try."

It's a lie, of course. I'd made them for Axel. He'd looked so miserable talking about his family, only perking up when he spoke about the kolaches.

A loud shout echoes from the backyard and Darla and Twyler move over to look out the window. "Seriously? Would it kill him to wear a shirt?"

There's only one person Twyler could be talking about and my pulse kicks into gear at the thought of him. Sure enough, when I look out the window I see Axel; shirtless with all those muscles and tattoos on display. He's laughing at something Jefferson said while Kirby moves around in a dramatic reenactment of a hockey move.

The two puck bunnies, along with Kirby's girlfriend, Claire, and a few other girls, stand to the side, watching the guys goof around. Are their eyes fixed on the way Axel's jeans cling deliciously from his hips? On the trail of dark blond hair tapering under the waistband?

Or maybe that's just me.

"First of all, it's forty freaking degrees." Twyler shakes her head. "And second, that's hot oil! He could burn himself."

Never one to let a potential injury happen on her watch, Twyler huffs out of the room and out the back door. I can hear her start up before she hits the grass. "Axel Rakestraw, step away from the turkey fryer."

Darla and I stay glued to the window like we're watching an episode of Springfield.

"Hey, TG." His eyes sweep over her. "You're looking good."

"Shut the fuck up about my girl, man." Reese's fist slams into Axel's bicep, then he looks at Twyler. "He's right, Sunshine, you're gorgeous."

Twyler is unfazed by either man. "Do you know what emergency rooms look like on holidays like this? They're packed. Primary reasons: knife accidents and burns."

"I'm not going to get burned," he says, watching Jefferson check on the bird. "Jeff on the other hand…"

"Jefferson is wearing a shirt."

"Baby," he drawls, clearly working to get a rise out of his roommate and mine, "I'm from Texas, barbecue is our thing. I'm not getting near that contraption. It's sacrilege." He smirks. "Although I appreciate your concern. Shows you care."

"It's not concern for you, dumbass." She rolls her eyes. "It's concern for the rest of us who will have a ruined Friendsgiving and have to smell scorched skin for the rest of our lives."

He gives her a grin, enjoying getting under her skin. "Fine, I'll go put on a shirt, but only because it's cold as fuck and I think my nipples may freeze off."

I'm not sure why I make myself busy when he comes in. Maybe because of Darla. Or because Murphy and his date just showed up. I turn on the faucet, cleaning up the dishes left in the sink. Maybe because I made this man, a friend, my safe space, the giver of amazing kisses and orgasms, his favorite dish.

And that means something.

"Wait, do I smell peppers?" He moves around the island, checking out the food. "Are those kolaches?"

I shift, looking for his reaction.

"Nadia made them," Darla says, outing me. "Have you had them before?"

His eyes search me out. "Yeah, I have. Can't wait to try them."

There's a strained huskiness in his voice, and my body feels hot. I tell myself it's because the oven is on and there's food warming on the stove.

"I'll be back," he announces. "Apparently, there's a dress code at this event."

Out back, Jefferson announces that the turkey is finished, and Darla and the others head outside. I hold back, grabbing one of the kolaches and wrapping it in a napkin. Taking a deep breath I go upstairs and knock on his door.

After a beat it swings open and Axel stands before me, rolling up one of the sleeves of his black button-down, revealing a tattooed covered forearm.

"I brought you a–"

He grabs me, pulls me into his room, mouth on mine before I can finish my sentence.

"Wow," I say, pulling back. "Is that how you greet all your guests at Friendsgiving?"

"Not even close." He grins, looking down at the pastry in my hand. "That's for me?"

"Oh, yes." My brain is fuzzy from that kiss. I hand him the napkin covered pastry. "I wanted to make sure you got one before everyone else."

He lifts it to his nose and sniffs, then licks his bottom lip before taking a bite. It's not dainty. No, it's the bite of a hungry man.

"Good?" I ask, aware that I'm buzzing with anxiety. Wanting a man's validation isn't new to me. But wanting it for something like this? It's strangely nerve wracking.

His eyes close and he moans, *"Fuck me."* He shoves the final bit in and grins around a mouthful. "Better than an orgasm."

"Really?" I ask, feeling proud.

"Okay, maybe not better than, but as good. It's fucking delicious, T." He grabs my hip and pulls me close, leaning in for another kiss. He tastes like the kolache. Spicy and warm with a slight hint of sweetness from the bread. "Just like you."

The way he's looking at me feels like I've been lit on fire. Like the hole inside of me is filled, not with pain and regret, but something warm and nourishing.

A shriek comes from downstairs. "Don't you dare drop it!"

"Guess the turkey is done," he says, fingers still pressed into my hip.

"Yeah," I nod. "We should go back down before Twyler notices we're both missing."

His fingers reach out, tucking a strand of hair behind my ear. "Thank you for making those for me."

"Hey," I let out a shaky laugh, "that's what friends are for."

I turn before he can respond, slipping downstairs to join the fray. Pete arrived with a girl he introduces as his sister, along with a few other guys on the team that I don't know. I help Darla make room for the new food, and Jefferson makes a huge show of carving the turkey.

When Axel comes down the stairs, looking sexy and disheveled and not like he just kissed the crap out of me, I try not to bristle at Heather sidling up to him, loudly offering him a drink. He takes it, but I notice he doesn't drink.

"You should have one, too," Twyler says.

"Huh?" I ask, dragging my eyes away from the pair. "One what?"

"A drink. I know you've been holding off when we go out, but this is a safe space."

If I've learned one thing over the past few weeks is that Axel Rakestraw is very dangerous, sober or not.

"I'm okay. I've gotten kind of used to it."

"Used to what?" Reese asks, stepping next to Twyler and sliding his arm around her lower back. A pang strikes my heart, jealousy, there's no doubt about it. I want that. The public affection. The casual touches. Belonging to someone else. Even now, Heather has no problem putting her hands on Axel.

"Not drinking," I admit, holding up my sparkling water.

"Who would've thought Axel and Nadia would both be sober," Jefferson says, obviously listening. He pours a glass of wine for the other girls.

"And celibate," Reid adds cheerily. I cough and every eye lands on me. "I mean Axel," Reid clarifies. "I don't know, uh, anything about Nadia's sex life."

An awkward silence follows until Axel strokes his mustache and flashes the room a grin. "Hey, we're undefeated, no one should question my methods."

The result is drawing the heat away from me, which I have no doubt was his intention.

"I think all the food is ready," Darla says, somehow the unofficial hostess of this dinner. "Grab a plate and dig in."

"Wait," Heather says. Reid groans, already dishing up a spoonful of mashed potatoes. Darla punches him in the gut and he drops the spoon. "Shouldn't we say a blessing or something? List what we're grateful for?"

"What about Axel," Pete says. "Your dad's a minister, right? You can kick off this dinner."

"Oh right," Bridget says, eyes widening. "Your dad is that guy on TV. From that huge church out in Texas, right? What's it called?"

"Kingdom," Pete supplies, earning a glare from Axel. "What? My aunt watches it on TV."

"My mom watches sometimes," Reid confesses. "Your sister is hot. How come she never visits?"

The look Axel gives his roommate is a death glare, but his girlfriend beats him to any kind of retribution by smacking him with a serving spoon. "What did you say?"

"Nothing, babe."

Bridget, on the other hand, studies Axel closer. "You're like a celebrity."

"Not a celebrity." Axel's tone is clipped. "But we should totally do the whole thankful thing." He saunters over to the food, grabs a plate, and piles my pastries on the top. "I'm thankful for undefeated seasons, kicking the Thunderbolt's ass, and these delicious Texas delicacies that taste better than the ones my mother makes."

Out of the corner of my eye, I see Twyler's gaze slide from Axel to me. Refusing to give an inch, I nudge Reid, "Go eat."

The guys fall like dominoes, forgetting a blessing or being thankful, ready to dive in to the feast. I grab my own plate and fill up on a hodge-podge of Thanksgiving-ish dishes, many store bought. We spread out around the room. I look for a seat and there's one next to Axel on the couch, Heather on the other side, her thigh glued to his. I don't miss the pleading in his eyes–an SOS–wanting me to save him from the puck bunny, but Twyler calls out my name.

"Nad," she pats the empty seat next to hers at the small dining table, "here."

"Oh cool." I give Axel an apologetic face.

Twyler takes a bite of her kolache. "Damn. These are good. How did you know to make them?"

Picking up my fork, I shrug. "Axel mentioned them being his favorite a few weeks ago. I got curious and looked them up."

"I'm glad you did," Reese says, shoving one in his mouth, "they're fucking delicious."

"What's up with that about his dad?" Twyler asks.

"He's a big-wig minister in Texas," he says. "One of those mega churches. He doesn't like talking about it."

"Why?" She stabs green beans with her fork and teases, "Does it mess with his bad boy image?"

"I think his father's expectations are part of why he's not looking at the draft," Reese licks gravy off his fingers. "Coach keeps trying to get him to reconsider, but so far he's not interested. I get the feeling his dad has other plans for him lined up after graduation."

"As a minister?" Twyler blurts, eyes wide. "Holy shit, can you imagine?"

I can't. Not in the slightest, but some of what Reese says tracks with what Axel has said himself. I can't imagine him not wanting to pursue a career in the NHL. Not every player gets that opportunity. Not even every player in this *room*.

"I wasn't sure if he had what it takes to go pro," Reese admits, "but after the last few weeks, seeing him take his probation seriously, I'm pretty sure if he wanted it, he could."

There's a million questions I want to ask about Axel, or maybe I just want to have his name on my tongue. Our relationship–even a friendship–isn't something I feel like I can openly talk about without Twyler getting suspicious. *Or worse*, passing judgment. So I sit back as the conversation changes, trying not to dwell on the feeling in the pit of my stomach when, across the room, Heather feeds Axel a bite of her mashed potatoes.

"Freaking puck bunnies," Darla says. She and Reid took the last two seats at the table. "They're like vultures."

"Sharks," I blurt, regretting it as everyone looks at me. "That's what I've heard before."

Reid snorts. "Sounds about right. All teeth."

Darla shoots him a glare, while picking up a roll from his plate and buttering it for him. Twyler and I exchange a look, before Reese brings up the New Kings concert they went to a few weeks ago. I don't look at Axel again until we've finished eating. To his credit, he seems like he's trying to create distance between him and Heather, moving over at one point to watch the hockey game Kirby pulled up on the TV.

To her credit, she's undeterred and follows.

The rest of the guys all wander over, ready to settle in when Darla bangs her fist on the countertop and shouts, "No one leaves until this kitchen is spotless."

"Is this why they're always on the rocks?" I ask Twyler as we take over sink duty. "Because she's bossy as hell?"

"I can't figure them out. Reid's a good guy, but he just never seems fully invested in the relationship." She runs a handful of silverware under the faucet. "My mom always says it's important for the man to be more into the girl than the other way around. I think Darla likes Reid too much, and he knows it. It makes him lazy."

I glance over at my friend. Two months ago she would have been at home, curled up on the couch in her grungy old hoodie, watching true crime. Now she's got a boyfriend, a group of friends, and is a relationship Yoda.

"Look at you being all relationship savvy."

"Yeah, being in a functional one helps."

I'd have no insight on that. Heather is still glued to Axel's side when Heather hands me a to-go container of leftovers and Reese kisses Twyler goodnight. She's headed back to the Teal house with me since they're leaving for Tennessee in the morning. Yep. A month in and they're spending Thanksgiving together. I mean, sure, his dad will be traveling with his junior hockey team for a tournament, but this is still relationship big.

If Axel notices me leave, I miss it. The whole night has left me feeling raw and conflicted. He was appreciative of the food I made for him. But maybe it was a step too far for two people not in a relationship. Girls make food for their boyfriends, not for the guy that gives them an orgasm occasionally. The further away we get from the Manor, the more I realize I fucked up. Big time. Like every other man I've made myself available to, I read more into it than was there, and when it came time to acknowledge it, I was nothing but a dirty little secret.

What the fuck is wrong with me? Why am I broken like this?

Back home, I'm in the middle of packing when my phone buzzes.

Mom: Excited to see you tomorrow!

Nadia: Me too!

Mom: Your dad will pick you up at the airport. Bring a raincoat!

I shake my head at the raincoat comment, and send a heart emoji in response. My mother is obsessed with the weather.

I don't mind going home. Getting some warmer weather will be nice as will seeing my family; my parents, older brother, and his fiancée. I feel like I navigate two worlds. One here and one there. Back home, I'm still their sweet, little, innocent Nadia. They were oblivious to my life then as they are now. They've always seen what

I've curated for them. Completely PG. They have no idea about the situation with Brent or CJ. It's one reason I refused to report it. My parents would be crushed.

I'm trying to decide if I can fit my raincoat into my carry-on bag when I hear a tap. There's no one in the bedroom door, and there's a second tap, this one coming from the window. Axel's shadowy figure is visible behind the glass.

I shut and lock the door before opening the window.

"What are you doing?" I whisper.

"Coming to see you," he says, climbing in without an invitation. "I missed you all night."

"Did you?" I ask, not hiding the sarcasm. "You seemed pretty well entertained."

He frowns. "You mean Heather?"

I shrug, turning to my closet for the coat. It's petty, but I'm not feeling generous right now. I'm tired. Hurt. Confused.

"I left Heather in a threesome with Jefferson and Bridget." He catches my hip and spins me to face him. "It was fucking killing me not to be around you."

The urge to fall into him is intense. To be held by those strong arms and forget all my insecurities. But that's what keeps me in this same place, right? Cycling through the same emotions over and over again. For once I resist.

"Hey," he tries to catch my eye, "are you really upset about it? Because I was just trying to play things cool in front of everyone."

Fair. It's all fair. I'm not in the position to ask for more but maybe that's the problem? I never do.

"I'm just..." I search for the word. The best one I can come up with at the moment is, "tired. It's been a long semester."

"It's almost over. My probation. Football season. All this petty shit driving us mad." He sits on the edge of the bed, but not before grabbing me by the waist and pulling me on his lap. "I'm sorry things have been so hard. You're such a tough, incredible, chick." He kisses my neck. "With impressive as fuck baking skills."

I laugh. This guy.

He looks over at the bag I'm packing. "Leaving in the morning?"

"My flight's at nine."

"You need a ride to the airport? Mine doesn't leave until later, but I don't mind going early."

"I'm hitching one with Twyler and Reese, they leave around the same time." I push the hair on his forehead back. "Are you worried about going home? You didn't really seem happy about your dad being brought up today."

He tenses, almost imperceptibly. "I just don't like to have my identity tied up in his."

"I can see that. It seems like he's pretty well known." I run my nail down the denim on his knee. "Reese says you may not go into the draft because of him."

This time his irritation is less hidden. The muscle in his jaw throbs and his eyes narrow. "You tracking my career now, T?"

"What? No. It just came up at dinner."

"I thought this was a safe space." He shifts, sliding me off his lap and onto the bed, before standing. "I should go."

"This is a safe space," I say, making sure to keep my voice low. "Since when is asking you about your family or hockey off limits?"

"When it's shit I don't want to talk about." He strides over to the window. "Or there's an ulterior motive."

"Ulterior motive?" I set my hands on my hips. "What the hell does that mean?"

"I don't know darlin'," I don't miss the wary expression of distrust on his face, "but when a notorious jersey chaser starts asking me about my aspirations with the draft, I get a little suspicious."

I'm shocked, but not enough to not say, "That's rich coming from a guy who promised *me* a safe space, but is just like every other athlete I've ever known." Lifting my chin. "You're using me as much as Brent did. Sneaking around, late night calls, pretending you're different, while keeping me a secret."

His chiseled jaw drops, and eyes darken, heated emotions flickering in their depths. Something sharp is on his tongue, and I brace myself for it, but whatever it is, he thinks better of it and snaps his mouth shut.

"I'm done with this," he mutters, turning to open the window.

"Same."

He moves quickly, out the window faster than conceivable for a man his size. In a blink, he's gone vanishing into the night, leaving no evidence he was ever here other than my broken heart.

How could I allow myself to do this again?

∼

Theme parks or big cities like Miami are usually what comes to mind when people think of Florida. Flashy lights, loud music and lots of tourists. Not everywhere is like that, there are areas that are more like small towns. Tight knit communities with nice neighbors and beautiful beaches.

I grew up in one of these places, a community called Kenwood. The streets are lined with historic cottages and thick shady trees. My parents were drawn here due to their affinity for older homes and renovations. Before my brother, Jason, and I were born, they lived in and renovated three homes, making enough of a profit to finally purchase the one they wanted to stay in long term. Jason is five years older than me. He and his fiancée, Kendall, are high school sweethearts and are both mechanical engineers. They're disgustingly perfect.

My goal is to decompress and try to forget about Axel Rakestraw.

Easier said than done.

Mom's energy level is on a ten when I wake up the first morning home. I barely get in a cup of coffee before she has us going in an endless cycle of cleaning the house, prepping for Thursday's dinner, and whatever other task she can come up with.

At least I'm busy.

"Mashed potatoes or sweet potato pie?" my mom asks, looking over an ancient, crumbling cookbook. I'm standing over the kitchen counter, rubbing off the tarnish on the good silverware.

"Sweet potatoes."

"Good idea." She scribbles something on her grocery list. "Oh, I saw Lucy Johnson's mother the other day. She says Lucy already has a job lined up for after graduation."

"Good for Lucy." I use my nail to get the polishing cloth into the decorative grooves on a serving spoon.

"Your brother had a job lined up by this point," she adds in a light tone, "but, of course, he had an internship the summer before and that helped a lot."

My mother had pushed me into getting an internship before my senior year. I didn't want to go too far from Wittmore–too far from Brent–so I'd stayed up there and waited tables.

"But..." she continues, "if you can't find anything you can always move back home. We're happy to help you out until you find something solid and get on your feet."

That sounds like a nightmare.

"I've been to the job fairs on campus," I tell her, "and I've started my applications. Don't worry, I'll find something."

She flips through the cookbook. "I guess if you're dating someone, it's possible you'll want to find a job where they are."

I'd been waiting for it, the questions about if, and who, I'm dating.

"There's no boyfriend, Mom."

"I thought maybe Twyler would set you up with one of her handsome boyfriend's friends."

"*Mom.*"

"Okay, okay." She holds up her hands. "You never tell me what's going on. You can't blame me for asking."

She always says this, pretending like she wants to know, but does she really? There were a lot of things in my past that she ignored. All those nights sneaking in and out of the house. The condoms she found that I claimed belonged to a friend.

My mother has spent her entire life taking broken things, houses in particular, and doing her best to shine them up and make them perfect. Sometimes I feel like one of those old houses. Everything can seem perfect on the surface, but change a light fixture or touch the plumbing and you realize that underneath, everything is falling apart. A simple project reveals a shit-ton of issues.

I feel like one of those old houses. Start peeling away the wallpaper and you'll find a rotting wall.

"I'm not keeping anything from you, Mom. There's just nothing going on. No job prospects. No boyfriends. *Especially* one of Reese's hockey friends." I feel the creep of anxiety climbing up my spine. I drop the spoon with the other clean pieces and say, "I think I'm going to go work on the hedges while it's nice outside."

She nods, unaware of the turmoil bubbling under the surface. "I'm going to finish this list so I can get to the market before traffic gets too crazy."

I step outside and into the sun. Fall is the nicest time in Florida. Not too hot, but not cold enough to bundle up like I would at Wittmore. I wonder if it's warm in Texas.

Nope.

I'm done with him, remember? *We're* done with each other.

Grabbing the hedge clippers I walk over to the fence line and start hacking. The manual labor feels good on my arms. I've missed going to the gym–getting out that stress release. When I finish the sides, I head over to the pool deck and snag a chair. Placing it under the hedge, I climb up and push up on my tip toes. The chair wobbles on the uneven surface and I grab the fence for balance, but drop the clippers into the neighbor's yard. "Son of a bitch."

"Still have a dirty mouth, I see."

Will Holt sits by the pool deck in his parent's backyard, legs sprawled in front of him, smoking a cigarette.

"Will," I say, heart hammering from almost falling, but I know that's not all.

His eyebrows raise. "It's been a long time, Nadia."

Up on that chair, I'm struck by a flash of memories. How he'd been my brother's friend. The cute guy next door. Cocky and smug. A jock. He picked on me a lot–throwing me in the pool, dunking me under water. The classic trope about the guy pulling a girl's braids to get her attention.

Will had definitely had mine.

"You home visiting your parents?" I ask, speaking around the lump in my throat.

"Nah, moved back home a few months ago." He waves to the pool house in the back. I don't look, a dark feeling burning in my gut. "They let me have my old digs. How's college?"

"It's good," I manage, wiping sweaty my palms on my leggings. "Almost over."

He nods, taking a drag on his cigarette. Exhaling he says, "Maybe we can hang out while you're home."

Panic crashes over me like a wave, a cold, clammy sweat on my neck. "M-my mom needs me to help her with a few things."

Jumping off the chair, it tips over and clatters on the pool deck. Rushing inside, I head straight to the toilet off the main hall, barely making it before dropping to my knees and heaving inside.

My first instinct is to call Axel. To hear his voice and have him distract me.

But Axel isn't my safe space.

I'm starting to think that nowhere is.

14

Axel

THE BLACK SEDAN that picked me up at the airport is waved past the security gate and starts the too short drive into the exclusive neighborhood where Nolan Rakestraw and his family live. My plane landed two hours ago in Dallas. I talked the driver my father sent into stopping for a quick dinner, but I could only procrastinate for so long.

The house doesn't so much come into view as it rises. I jokingly call it The Real Kingdom, after the name of Father's church, because that's what it is; that fucker built himself a castle.

Nolan Rakestraw comes from a long line of southern preachers, back to the days when they rode circuits on horseback, stopping in a new town every Sunday to minister to the desperate souls of East Texas. The call to follow in his ancestors' footsteps was strong, and my father happily took up the mantle. He wasn't self-taught like his father and grandfather. He went to college. Nothing like a state university. No football or women. It was a small, religiously focused, all male school, where he made the connections to take his natural born skills to the next level. College didn't give him the gift of preaching–of connection to his flock. That was a hundred percent DNA. How do I know? Because I feel it in my blood. This way with people, this charisma, and I do every fucking thing I can to shut it down.

All of that is enough to explain why I feel like I've got a rock building in my gut. I'm not foolish enough to think that's the only reason. I feel like shit about how I left things with Nadia. That is not how I wanted to end that with her and it's exactly why I don't let women get close.

I grew up under intense scrutiny. More than any NHL hockey player could ever imagine. People had access to me, to my family. We were on display. We were God's chosen. And they, I learned quickly, were the key to our livelihood, which meant the people of the Kingdom owned me.

That's the real reason that, as soon as I hit eighteen, I tried to put distance between me and my family. It doesn't make a difference. No matter how many tattoos, piercings, or saved goals I have, no matter how much I try to establish my own identity, I'm still Nolan Rakestraw's son.

I'm the heir to the Kingdom.

It's been a challenge, but Wittmore is the only place I have that isn't infected by him, so when Bridget brought up my family at Friendsgiving it was like a bomb went off in my chest. Nadia got hit by the shrapnel, which is totally not fair. She made me the most amazing kolaches. Those pastries were like an orgasm in my mouth, but more than that, I know it took time and effort.

It was maybe the nicest thing a girl has ever done for me.

No, no maybe. It *was* the nicest thing a girl has ever done for me. And the reaction I felt was fierce. It made me want to stake a claim in her. Let everyone else at the party know she was mine. Celebrate with her. It was only her concern about Twyler finding out that held me back. And, well, I sure as hell don't want Reese's foot up my ass. So when Heather started clinging hard, I felt like it was a good diversion but… I knew when she left she was upset. I tried to fix it. I went to her house after to show her my thanks, to kiss her goodbye, to express to her how fucking special she is, but then she asked about my dad and hockey and... I snapped.

Even if I can't have her the way I want to, I don't want to lose her as a friend. I've got to fix it. I just don't know how. Unfortunately, that's not my biggest issue at the moment.

The car coasts down the stone lined driveway, up to the imposing arched front entrance of the house. I take a deep breath and prepare myself to enter The Kingdom.

~

"How many more have you gotten since I last saw you?"

Shelby stands by my dresser, watching me flip through the clothes in my closet for a shirt. There are dozens hanging neatly on the rod. Crisp button-downs in pale, unassuming colors, along with neatly pressed pants that match the pair I've already put on. My mother's doing.

"Has she never heard of black? Gray? Dark blue?" I mutter, finally settling on a basic white one and yank it off the hanger. Shrugging it over my shoulders I see my sister is still waiting for an answer.

"How many?" my sister repeats, eyes sweeping over my torso.

"I don't know. Ten? Fifteen?"

She shakes her head, but I see the way she looks at the tattoos. She's both curious and judgmental. Not of the tattoos, exactly, but of the life that allows such freedom.

"What's the most recent one?"

It's the 'T' on my hip. Every time I catch a glance at the dark ink, it feels like a punch to the gut. I hold out my forearm instead. "This sun. I got it after seeing this amazing sunrise down at the river. I didn't want to forget it."

"Other people take photos, Ax."

"Well," I start, securing the last button and shoving the hem of my shirt into my pants, "I'm not other people."

"Maybe out there you aren't, but here you're still part of the flock. Hurry up or Mom's going to send someone else up here to get you."

Someone else: my father.

I already spent an hour with him this morning going over my part of the holiday sermon that I'll be doing next month. It's a family affair, a tradition that started when we were barely old enough to read. The congregation loved it though, and Father knows how to deliver. This time it's different. There's more pressure on me taking a bit more of a leadership role.

He hadn't been overly impressed, not that he'd tell me if he was, but I think he was just glad I'd actually started. He assured me that we'd go over it again once the guests leave. Yay.

The doorbell rings again downstairs and Shelby huffs. "Ax, seriously. They're waiting and unless you're willing to shave off that ridiculous mustache, I'm not going to cover for you."

"The 'stashe stays," I tell her. Still undefeated.

My eyes dart to the bottom drawer of my dresser where I've kept a bottle of Jack hidden for the last five years. Every other holiday party we've had here for the last three years I've taken a shot before heading down. Not so much liquid courage, but liquid sanity.

I can taste the spicy heat right now. I could send Shelby ahead, grab the bottle, and take a fast swig. Cut the edge. I don't think it would even count as an epic fuck-up.

Shit. That just makes me think of Nadia for the millionth time since getting home. Not just when I see the tattoo, but the second before I fall asleep and the instant I wake up. Like habit, I grab my phone and check her social media one more time, seeing if she posted any other photos since her last update. It was a single image of blue skies and palm trees. I'm glad to see she made it home, but just want to see her face–determine if I can get an inkling of her state of mind. Does she hate me?

What am I asking? Of course she does.

"Oh, who's that?" Shelby leans close. I shut off the phone and shove it in my pocket.

"No one."

"Are you stalking someone?"

"No," I snap, a little too quickly, and direct her out of my room. From the hallway, I can hear the loud voices echoing from the foyer. I reconsider the whiskey one more time.

"Oh gosh, you like someone." Her eyes are wide, gleeful as she races after me to keep up. "Is it serious? What's her name? Can I see her picture?"

"There's no girl, Shel." There's not, right? "You know I don't date."

She gives me a disappointed look. No one is happy about the fact that I've never brought a serious girlfriend home. At the top of the stairs, I ask, "What about you? Anyone special?"

The hint of a smile plays on her mouth. "I've been talking to David Jones."

"The music minister's son?" I snort. "That skinny kid that's been trying to grow a mustache since he was fourteen?"

"Yes." Her chin lifts defiantly. "And he can grow a full beard now."

"I bet." I roll my eyes and add, "I'm assuming Dad set this up?"

What better way to keep Shelby under his thumb than to have her marry another minister's kid.

"No," she says fussing with the bracelet on her arm. "We've known one another for ages and we've been working with the youth group. He's with the boys and I'm with the girls. It just... kind of happened."

Yeah right. "I'm sure the Rev approves."

"He does."

Midway down the staircase I grab her arm and pull her to a stop. "You don't have to do this, you know? You can go to college. Move out. Get a job."

She pulls away from my grasp. "Please don't."

"Don't what? Tell you that you have options?" I sigh. "You should come visit me. See what it's like on campus. Reese's girlfriend is amazing. You could stay with her and Nadia–"

"*Don't* start this today," she repeats. "I like David. He's cute, smart, and respectful. He *is* in college, studying business management, and he comes home every weekend to volunteer and to see me. Just because you're desperate to rebel against the future, doesn't mean that I am."

"You haven't even kissed him, have you?" I ask, narrowing my eyes, trying to see it.

"Of course not." She gives me a final, hard look, and continues down the stairs, the smile plastered on her face before she greets her first guest.

Fuck. I really need that drink.

~

THANKSGIVING ISN'T A FAMILY AFFAIR. Nothing about the Rakestraws is ever just 'us.' His argument is that the church built this home, and we should open it to members of the congregation and community to celebrate. Of course, none of these people are needy in any way. They're the same people that follow my father everywhere, kissing his ass, tell him he's amazing, agreeing to his every word, not to mention, funding his ideas and causes. Most of all: lining his pockets.

At some point Thanksgiving got so big that my mother started hiring help. I don't blame her. It's too much for one woman to do and my father sure as hell isn't helping. There's a valet outside, a man at the door receiving guests and taking coats, and waitstaff rushing around in all black, weaving through the guests offering appetizers and drinks. Over all this buzz, I can hear my mother commanding the army of servers in the kitchen as the scent of turkey wafts through the house.

"Sweetie, you look like you could use a drink." This comes from a woman I assume is from my mother's bible study.

"That would be awesome." I've been hovering–fine *hiding*–in the alcove near the library for the last hour, hoping I didn't overwork my wrist from the repeated handshaking I was forced into when the guests arrived.

She snatches a glass of brown liquid off one of the passing trays and presses it into my hand.

"Oh," I give her a tight smile when I realize it's iced tea. This house is an alcohol-free zone, even on holidays. "Thanks. It's crowded in here."

I don't know if it's unnaturally warm or not, but my skin is itchy and hot.

"Your parents are so gracious to open their home to everyone." She grins. "It's wonderful, but definitely a little chaotic."

I nod and repeat. "So wonderful."

"Slow down, Preston!" she calls when a few kids run past us, out the back door to the wide, green lawn. I watch them wistfully, wishing I could follow them. When I was their age, I loved these events. But now... I swallow a sip of the sickly sweet tea and hope it washes away the dread. "Put them in clean clothes and they turn into wild things."

"Get some turkey in them and they'll be ready for a long nap."

"Maybe I can slip them a little bit before dinner starts." She laughs and then looks at my hand, her gaze lingering on the tattoos and rings on my fingers. "I don't think we've formally met, I'm Donna. We joined the Kingdom last year."

"Axel."

"The Reverend's son. I've heard of you."

"Cautionary tale?" I ask. "Or in reference to the prodigal son?"

"Oh no, your parents have nothing but praise for you. They're so proud."

I fight a snort at that, but yeah, outwardly, I'm sure they put up a good front. Inwardly, the disappointment is thick.

Donna rests her hand on my arm. "You go head in the den with the other men. We'll call you when dinner is ready."

It may be my imagination, but I'm pretty freaking sure she feels up my bicep and I take the offer to escape. The den is in the back of the house–my father's other sanctuary. Dark wood paneling lines the walls and comfortable leather seating fills the space. Football is on the massive TV. The Cowboys' game will be on later today–dinner scheduled around the event. Trays of appetizers have been set out on a buffet in the back and I head straight for it instead of joining the other men. I don't miss that my father is talking to David–Shelby's new beau.

I've got a stuffed mushroom in my mouth when I'm approached by one of the men.

"Axel, right?" he asks, stacking crackers and cheese on his paper plate.

"Yes, sir," I say after swallowing.

"Jim Brown." He offers his hand and I shake it. "You're having one heck of a season up there at Wittmore."

"Oh, you're a hockey fan?" I nod to the others hovering around the screen. "Don't let them hear you, or they'll try you for treason."

"I grew up in Michigan. We love football and hockey." He gives me an appraising look, seeming to look past the tattoos and piercings. "You carried the team in that game against the Hounds."

"That's giving me a little more credit than I deserve. Our offense still got the puck in the net, but their offense was just relentless." The defense was struggling that day and I'd been worn the fuck out by the end of it. "Even though we won, I wouldn't be sad to see them knocked out of the playoffs."

"I heard about your probation. Hopefully that hasn't been too disruptive."

"It was a stupid mistake," I admit. "But everything should be cleared up by early next week."

"Good, you wouldn't want something like that to hinder you from the draft."

I grab two more mushrooms, because Jesus, these things are like crack. "I'm not entering the draft."

"You're not?" He frowns. "I've seen the reports. You're high on the list."

"There are bigger things than hockey." A heavy hand lands on my shoulder. My father is the man behind that sentiment. "Axel has plans to join the Kingdom after graduation."

Jim nods, but I sense his disappointment. Mostly because I feel it myself. "I understand. A greater calling. Can't ignore that."

"No, you can't," Dad says. "Now, I just got the nod that it's time for dinner. Let's head to the dining room before it gets cold."

On the way to the dining room, I pause and indicate for my father to do the same. "About the probation. I was going to tell you–"

"No need," he holds up his hand. "I already know all about it."

"You do?" I frown. "Did Coach Bryant call you?"

His jaw sets, but he doesn't answer my question about Coach. "Just because you're across the country doesn't mean I don't keep up with your activities."

And like that, all the pieces fall into place. I'd wondered why the probation status hadn't made the news, not even locally. My father somehow managed to control it. "The toxicology report implies some kind of dosing?"

Shit. How far is his reach? I shift uneasily. "It seems like it."

"You know what they say: bad company corrupts good behavior."

Leave it to my father to throw shade on my friends with a bible verse.

"Well, it'll be done by Monday. I'll retake the test and I can put it behind me."

"I should hope so, Son," his voice lowers. "I've allowed you a lot of freedom during these years. As much as I dislike it, I'm aware that edgy, tattooed, experienced young leaders are a draw to the modern church, but embarrassing the family publicly is where I draw the line. Our reputation is all we have."

"Along with our faith, obviously," I add, not hiding the sarcasm.

I can tell by his expression that he thinks I should wear this weight for eternity, but my mother waves him to the head of the long table. The feast is too big and everything is placed on sideboards for a buffet, but the massive turkey sits in front of his seat, the carving knife and fork next to the gold rimmed plate, ready for the king of the castle.

"Reverend," a squeaky voice interrupts my father's preparations. Everyone looks over and sees David Jones step forward, pale and swallowing nervously. "If I may…"

"David, what's on your mind?" my dad asks and I sense a set up.

My gaze darts to Shelby who is standing by my mother, eyes wide, watching her boyfriend approach our father.

He fumbles in his pocket and the church ladies barely contain their whispers as he reveals a black velvet box. "I'd like to ask for Shelby to be promised to me."

Promised. Jesus Christ. I don't know what's worse. The commitment of an engagement ring or the shackles of a promise. Shelby gasps and the dread in my gut unfurls. I feel her slipping further away–further into their grasp. At least I had a chance to run free for a minute, but Shelby, she's never had a chance.

"We'd be honored, Son," he says, speaking for my sister. To her credit she looks thrilled, hands covering her mouth, bouncing on her toes. David turns, his grin wide and bright as the sun. The whole room vibrates with excitement, watching him push the gold ring on her left hand.

Although she's the one making the commitment, I can't help but feel the noose tightening around my neck.

∽

Thank god for football.

With the game starting mid-afternoon everyone inhales their dinner, and while everyone heads to the den, I step outside.

For the first time, I realize that I miss the cold of the northeast. The Texas air is too warm, and I crave the cold slap on my face to wake me up and the sharp needles in my lungs to prove I'm alive. Or maybe I won't breathe easily again until I make things right with Nadia.

I have to apologize.

Pulling out my phone, I see a slew of notifications from the team, all wishing Happy Thanksgiving. My roommates group chat is filled with photos: Reese and Twyler bundled up around a firepit. Jefferson on the beach with his family on some tropical island. Reid's is nothing but him gnawing on a turkey leg. I send out my own best wishes, including a selfie.

I scroll down and another notification pops up and my thumb swipes across the screen, opening it to Nadia's ChattySnap profile. My heart races when I see her in a bikini, standing in waist deep, clear blue, pool water. Her hair is wet and slicked back, the afternoon sun casting a glow over the curves of her sexy body.

I'm so entranced with her, that it takes me a minute to realize she's not alone. I zoom into the figures in the background. There's a couple–a guy and a girl–behind her. I recognize him as her brother from other photos she's posted. But the other guy? Who the hell is that?

I skim the caption. *"Thanksgiving is for real friends and family. Hope you get to spend the day with yours."* She tags a few accounts, but I already know it's @will_holt1.

A lesser man would be crushed.

But I've spent my entire life fighting against odds. It may be my generation's old Texan spirit–the need to rebel and fight for what's mine.

I shoot off a text: *Happy Thanksgiving, T. Hope you made it through the day fuck-up free. I know I barely did. My biggest fuck-up yet was leaving things the way I did the other day. I'm sorry. There's no excuse. I only hope you'll forgive me.*

It's not enough, but it's a start. Nadia Beckwith may not know it yet, but that's what she is–*mine*.

15

Nadia

Everything is fine.

That's what I tell myself as I sit across from Will Holt at the dinner table on Thanksgiving afternoon. After avoiding him and the backyard, until my mother sprang the invitation on the family two hours ago.

"Beth, this is so lovely," Mrs. Holt says, gingerly setting a roll on her plate, "we can't tell you how appreciative we are."

Mr. Holt agrees, piling turkey on his plate. Apparently their trip to Gainesville was canceled last minute when his sister tested positive for the flu.

"Any time," my father says. "We're always happy to have extra. Beth and Nadia made enough for the whole neighborhood."

At my name, the visitors shift their focus to me. "Your football team is doing well this year," Mr. Holt says, as he wrinkles his nose at the green bean casserole and passes it on without taking any. "That quarterback, what's his name?" He thinks for a moment. "Reynolds. He's the real deal."

"The hockey team is undefeated, too," I blurt in the world's worst attempt to change the subject. Next to me, Jason's eyebrow rises and I toss in, "And basketball team is in contention to go to the final four. Wittmore is, uh, competitive athletically."

"Well, I still wish Will had continued playing football." Mrs. Holt gives her son a sad smile. "You were so good."

Will Holt has been good at two things in his life; smoking too much weed and drawing naive girls into his pool house. If he'd ever really been good at anything else, like football, the other two took priority. He'd quit the team by senior year.

Thankfully, conversation shifts to Jason and Kendall's upcoming wedding, and I pretend to focus on my food. Pretend, because I have no appetite. I barely have since seeing Will. I lie awake at night, replaying our relationship, delving into all those feelings I'd thought I'd left behind when I moved to Wittmore.

I also have to stop myself from texting Axel.

He's just another man I've been using as a crutch. Another man that likes me better as a secret.

Clammy heat rises on my skin and I shift uncomfortably in my seat. The second dinner is over and it's appropriate to leave the table, I hop up, grabbing a stack of plates.

"Are you okay?" Kendall asks, following me into the kitchen. "You look pale."

"Just feeling a little hot. I guess my body hasn't adjusted to the heat."

"Nah, it's not just you, it's roasting in here," she agrees. "Jason and I were talking about taking a swim? Got a suit?"

The pool sounds good.

Even better is when the parents decide to head over to the beach with a bottle of wine to watch the sunset. Will, thankfully, goes home, and I quickly change into a green two-piece stuffed in the back of my drawer.

"I'll get in the pool," I tell my brother and Kendall as I toss my towel and phone on the edge of a chair, "but no PDA from you two, got it?"

Kendall laughs, but my brother raises his hands from under the water, proving he's not feeling her up below the surface. Dipping my toes in the water, I'm happy to see the heat is turned on. My mother swims laps every morning, and although it isn't quite warm, it doesn't have the chill of late fall. Taking a deep breath, I submerge myself, pushing off the wall with my toes and swim underwater.

The quiet is familiar. Comforting. We'd spent our childhood in the water, hours every day, and I feel more comfortable here than anywhere else. I stay under for as long as I can, until my chest tightens with the need for air, and I break through the surface.

I've barely inhaled when my breath is knocked from me again. Will sits on the edge of the pool by the stairs, legs dangling in the water. Smoke unfurls from the tip of his cigarette. "I think the first time I saw you, you were pretending to be a mermaid."

"Yeah, well I was eight and I was pretty sure if I stayed in the water long enough, I'd grow a tail." I adjust my top, making sure I'm covered, but it only draws his eyes to the movement.

"Nad," Kendall calls. "Can you grab your phone? I told my mom I'd take some pictures today and totally forgot."

"Sure."

I lean over the pool deck and grab my phone that I'd left on my towel. Instinctively, I check for messages and see that Twyler texted a picture of her and Reese, along with her sister Ruby and her mom. A few others come by, but the one I'm hoping to see isn't there.

Well, it's not just a message I'm looking for. It's an apology. Clearly, that's not going to happen.

"Hoping to hear from your boyfriend?" Will asks.

"No," I say absently, shooting off a reply to Twyler. "I don't have a boyfriend."

"Good to know."

I shoot him a look.

"What's that for?" he asks. "You've been a little cold to me all week. What's got those tiny bikini bottoms in a twist?"

"Nothing," I reply, wading back into the water. "Ken, you ready?"

"Yep."

She and I set up a few selfies, adding in a few with my brother. I make no real effort to include Will, ignoring him as he sits in the background, smoking cigarette after cigarette. Jason never had a clue what went on between us. He would have lost his shit back then, knowing I was sneaking across the property line to go hook up with his much older friend.

I snap one last picture where the light looks amazing on my hair and post it to my own account, with a wistful statement about family. Being home has been okay, but over the last few months, since Twyler and Reese started dating, it kind of feels like we've built a whole other family up in Wittmore. I miss them more than I expected.

A splash behind me sends a wave of water up the side of the pool, but it's the low voice right behind me that sends a chill along my spine. "I thought you had big tits before, Nad, but damn."

I spin and see Will in the water, walking over to me. He's stripped off his shirt and his upper body has lost the tone it had from years of regular workouts. The bloat of a beer gut hovers at the surface of the water. "Don't be gross."

"By speaking the truth?" He shrugs. "Come on, you and I always had a good thing and now we don't have to sneak around." His eyes dart over toward Jason. "Unless you want to."

"Not interested." I start to move, but his hands meet the edge of the pool, one on each side, caging me in. I search over his shoulder for Jason and Kendall but they've gone back on their promise of no PDA and are making out on the other end. "Please move."

"Why? Are you too good for me now? Because you weren't back then, when you came sniffing around non-stop, begging for my dick."

"I was fifteen, Will, I wasn't begging for anything other than a little attention."

"Cut the good girl act. You were a whore then just like you are now." He smirks. "Yeah, I've seen the videos. How much do you make from those? I should probably get a cut for teaching you all of that in the first place. A finder's fee for breaking you in."

I don't know if it's the way he's talking to me, so dismissive and rude, or the mention of the video that makes me snap, but the anger rising inside of me unleashes.

"You're a fucking pig," I seethe. "I wasn't a whore. I was a naive little kid that you took advantage of. You didn't break me in–you fucking *raped* me." Hot tears blur my vision. "Not just once, but every fucking time you lured me into your shitty, filthy, little bedroom, and in every fucking way you wanted."

"Rape? Jesus Christ. You showed up to my house day after day with those little bikinis on, or one of those short little skirts, and you think that wasn't an invitation?" He snorts. "You're fucking crazy. No wonder you're selling yourself online. What else are you worth?"

The slap shocks me as much as it does him. Almost as much as me saying the word rape after all this time.

"You fucking bitch!" He lunges for me, but I swim out of the way.

"What the hell is going on?" Jason is already halfway across the pool, Kendall behind him, her expression a mixture of fear and worry. "Did he touch you?"

"Nothing." Will is already on his way out of the water, the skin on his face already turning red. "I thought maybe she wanted to hang out. Apparently not."

Jason and Will start to argue, and I use the opportunity to get out of the water, leaving my phone and towel behind. Dripping water and leaving a trail of wet footprints, I enter the kitchen, stopping at the counter, when I break down.

"Hey." Kendall follows me in, drapes a towel over my shoulders, and wraps her arms around my shivering body. "What the hell happened?"

"He..." I start, but that old fear forces me to swallow it back down.

"Whatever you say he did, I'll believe you." She pushes the wet bangs out of my eyes.

"You will?"

"Absolutely. And if you want to tell me about it, I'm here to listen."

With the bandage finally ripped off this year's old wound, I do what I should have a long time ago, let it all out.

∽

KENDALL STAYED FOR HOURS, waiting while I showered and got my emotions under control. Once I was in my pajamas and under the covers, I told her what happened. Not just tonight, but all those years ago, that first time. It was scary as hell to admit it all, to brace myself for her judgment, but it also felt good. Like the heaviest weight, one built out of fear and shame, had finally been released.

"You know it's not your fault," she tells me, once it's all out.

"My brain does, but my heart doesn't," I admit. "Taking that blame was the only way I could survive at the time. Pretending like it was a choice seemed easier."

"That's what fuckers like Will Holt do to the people they hurt. They commit the crime, and then put the blame on the victim."

The story of my fucking life. Or it has been. I don't want it to be any more.

There's a tap on the door, then Jason's voice, "Ken, Nad, you guys okay?"

Kendall looks at me and I nod.

"Yeah," she says, rising to open the door. When he sees me, I see the line of concern across his forehead and a split in his lip.

"He hit you?" I ask, sitting up.

"Not as hard as I hit him." He hands me my phone and I see his scuffed knuckles. "You left this downstairs."

I take the phone from him and pull the blankets back up to my chest.

"Thank you, for the phone and having my back." I look to Kendall. "Both of you."

"Always, Nadia," she says. "Don't forget it."

I've given her permission to tell my brother everything. I don't mind him knowing, I'm just not sure I can face him. I did ask her not to tell my parents. Maybe one day, but not yet.

I exhale when they shut the door behind them. I turn off the light and reach for my phone. There's a few messages, but one makes my heart skip a beat.

GoalieGod: *Happy Thanksgiving, T. Hope you made it through the day fuck-up free. I know I barely did. My biggest fuck-up yet was leaving things the way I did the other day. I'm sorry. There's no excuse. I only hope you'll forgive me.*

Nadia: Can we talk when we get back?

Not even a heartbeat goes by before he responds.

GoalieGod: *Absolutely.*

I make the decision then to head back to Wittmore sooner than later. I know he has a game tomorrow night. What I have to say can't wait.

∼

AFTER THE STRESS of telling my parents I was leaving early and then navigating the crowded airports at the holiday, I arrive at the Teal House, worn out and exhausted. It was a long day, after an even longer Thanksgiving, but I'm ecstatic to be back at our tiny, cozy house hundreds of miles away from Florida.

Shotgun and the Teal house are quiet. When I get inside, I see Twyler's open suitcase on the bed. She's on the road with the basketball team and won't be back until tomorrow afternoon. The men's hockey team just finished playing Amsterdam U over at the arena. I checked the score in the Uber, and we were up by two.

I dump my bag in my room and head to the kitchen, filling up a pot with water and turning on the stove to make some ramen. I'm not upset everyone is busy. I think I need a minute to get myself together, especially with Twyler. She has a way of seeing right through me, and right now I feel fucking transparent.

When I told my parents I'd changed my flight they hadn't been happy. I told them I had a project due–which isn't completely false. Eric and I need to get our presentation finalized. Mom's spidey-senses could tell something was wrong, but Jason must have smoothed it over. I owe him one. Him and Kendall, both.

I drop the brick of noodles into the pot and add in the packet of spices. Once it's cooked, I fill my bowl and head back to my room. I've just set the bowl on the bedside table when I hear a tap at the window.

Axel.

Just seeing him creates a reaction in my body. I rush over and unlock the window.

"Hi." His eyes sweep over me.

"How did you know I was home early?"

"Reese may have mentioned you were getting back while Twyler is gone."

I frown. "If you know she's gone then why are you coming to the window?"

He shrugs and gives me a lopsided grin. "This just kind of seems like our thing, but if you want me to go around–or leave–I will."

"No," I say, stepping back to give him room. "Stay."

He steps through the window and shuts it behind him. Standing in the middle of the room, I take him in. He's dressed in his post game suit, which means he didn't even stop off at the Manor to change. The tie is already loosened, and he looks sexy as hell–smells it too–all clean and soapy after his shower. His damp, blond hair a shade darker than usual.

"I need to–"

"I'm sorry," he says, cutting me off. "That shit I said last time? That was me just dumping my baggage on you and it wasn't fair."

"It's okay, I know a lot about baggage."

He shifts and I realize he's nervous. I get it, I'm nervous too.

"I was way out of bounds. You'd just done something amazing for me–so sweet and kind–and instead of thanking you like I wanted to I got stupid paranoid and shit all over it like an absolute dumbass. I won't even bother with excuses, because there are none." He swallows. "I just hope you can forgive me."

"I forgive you," I say, with zero hesitation. "I shouldn't have accused you of using me. We made an agreement and you were just doing what I asked."

"So are we good?" His eyebrow arches. "You're important to me, Nadia, and I'm not willing to leave until we get this straight, not until you're willing to talk about where this can go."

"We're good," I tell him, my pulse beating stronger, "and I want that too, but…"

"But what?"

"Something happened on Thanksgiving. Something I want to share with you and may change the way you think about me." I know I've changed in the last twenty-four hours. Knowing I need to get comfortable for this, I climb onto the bed and I pat the spot next to me. He may need to get comfortable too. "If you have the time to listen."

"I've got all the time you need, darlin'."

He kicks off his shoes and takes off his coat. My ramen sits uneaten on the bedside table–my appetite lost in a jumble of nerves.

"What's this about?" he asks, taking my hand. I trace the 'Y' on his knuckle.

"Me."

"You?"

I nod. "This week I ran into someone from my past. Someone that hurt me, although it took me until just now to realize how bad." I tell him about running into Will–and how things escalated in the pool.

"That fucker called you a whore?" He looks ready to crawl out of his skin.

"It wasn't the first time," I admit.

"Well, damn, T, that just makes it worse."

"I know. And I allowed it," I confess, "in a way I kind of encouraged it. I thought that's how older kids talked to one another. I thought that was what I had to do to get his attention. I let him say and do a lot of things to me that I didn't want or like."

Our eyes meet and he knows. I know he understands. "Fuck."

"I was so in over my head. He was this cool older guy. My brother's friend. I trusted him. I wanted his attention. His *validation*. So when he," I swallow, "when he made me do things to him, I didn't fight back. I didn't really know how to or if I could."

Axel's arms wrap around me, the stiff collar of his shirt grazing my cheek. He holds me tight and I sink into it, breathing him in. Safe space.

"He–"

"You don't have to tell me." He turns to face me. "Not unless you want to."

"I want to."

I tell him about all of it. The way he flirted with me around other friends, getting me to drop my guard, then inviting me over to the pool house by myself. "He was my first kiss," I tell him. "The first penis I saw and touched. The first one to go inside of me." I give him a pointed look. "Nothing was off limits, because I didn't know how to say no."

"Jesus, T. He was older and more experienced, preying on his friend's kid sister. A fucking predator."

"I knew it was off. All of it. There was the pain I felt, physically and emotionally. The shame I experienced during the act and when I snuck back home, crossing our yards, pretending to be the same girl I was when I went over. I just didn't know what to do. How to get out of it. Who to tell. So I just took it, until he got distracted by other girls and I grew up and ran as far away as I could." I swallow past the lump in my throat. "Unfortunately, I didn't leave it behind me. I brought all of that toxic behavior with me."

"You're not toxic." He brushes the back of his fingers down my cheek. "You're kind and beautiful and smart."

"Maybe not," I give him an appreciative grin, "but there's something in me that seeks this kind of validation–even if it's from terrible people." I inhale. "I'm ready for it to stop."

"You already have. You stood up to that asshole neighbor and to Mr. America, Brent Reynolds. You're not the same person you were when I first met you." He tightens his grip on me. "I mean, you were hot as fuck then and hot as fuck now, but you're different. More self-aware. More confident."

"I don't feel confident."

"It takes time." He shifts so that he can see me better. "When I started playing goalie I was fucking terrified. Of the puck. Of the stick. Of the aggressive guys holding and hitting both. And just when I'd get comfortable, I'd move up a level and it would start again, this time with a bigger, faster, better player." He chuckles. "The first time Reese took a shot on me I almost wet myself."

"You were scared of him?"

"Not of him, but looking like a fool going up against one of the top power forwards in the league. I was afraid he'd prove to Coach Bryant I didn't deserve my spot and I'd get sent back to Texas."

"What happened?"

He rolls his eyes. "We both made fools of ourselves. He was nervous too and whiffed the shot but I was so jacked up I went for it and tripped over the ice, busting my chin." He points to the thin white scar. "Blood got everywhere."

I laugh, imagining the two of them embarrassed and pissed. "I get it, but I don't think it's the same."

"What's the same is that confidence isn't something that's given to you, T. It's earned. Practiced. And the past few weeks you've been practicing how to be a woman that doesn't need to chase jerseys and looking for validation from the wrong kind of people."

Huh. There may be some truth to that.

"And even when you tried to screw up," he says, a slow grin quirking his lip, "I was there to keep you from any epic fuck-ups."

"You helped me?" I bark a laugh. "Please. I'm the one that had to keep helping you! You're weak, Rakestraw. Weak!"

"I'll show you weak," he mutters, and in a move I never saw coming, attacks me with his fingers, tickling my sides. I yelp and squirm, trying to roll off the bed and escape, but he catches me with those strong, quick hands. Dragging me to the middle of the bed, he flips me on my back. Hovering over me, he's all muscle and strength, and sexy masculinity. "Do I look weak, T?"

Chest heaving, I shake my head, unable to lie. "No."

His jaw tightens and his pupils darken. "Fuck."

"What?"

"I want to kiss you right now."

"Why aren't you?"

"Because you and I just had a pretty serious, unsexy talk and I don't want to trivialize it by getting a boner right after you allowed yourself to be vulnerable with me."

"You *always* have a boner." I feel it between us right now and my skin grows hot with want. "Kiss me."

"Are you sure? Because I don't want to be another man that hurts you."

I reach out and cup his face, running my thumb down the scar he just showed me. I know my truth in this moment more than I ever have before. "You're the only man that's ever given me a choice, Axel. That's provided a place of safety, while making me feel wanted." I push up and kiss the hard line of his jaw. "This is what I want. You're what I want."

"I'm not fucking this up," he tells me. I want to ask what he means, but there's no need. He shows me in the first kiss–gentle, his fingers barely lifting my chin so he can slowly lick my lips.

"You taste like salt."

"It's the ramen."

"Well, it's fucking delicious," he says, with absolute sincerity. His thumb strokes down my jaw, an ask for me to open. I part for him and the next kiss is deeper, unrelenting with intent, our tongues meeting in a desperate rush. "Jesus," he breathes, "you always taste so good."

My response is a hum, then I suck his piercing between my teeth, a distraction as my fingers move between us, unfastening the buttons of his dress shirt. His body always shocks me; lean, hard, muscle, decorated with ink. He shrugs off the shirt, tossing it on the floor. In a surge, I rise up and lick his nipple.

Sucking in a breath, his hands thrust under my shirt, muttering as he cups my breasts, "Fucking hell, these tits."

His nipple peaks, a hard pebble against my tongue. Mine do the same when he yanks down my bra, flattening his palms over the top.

We both shift to our knees, the rest of our clothing coming off in a rush, until we're just in cotton and lace.

I gape at him.

"What?" he says, hand gripping his cotton covered shaft and giving it a long stroke. The movement tugs down the waistband, revealing the 'T' tattoo. My heart flips.

"You look like an underwear model, that's what."

A grin tugs at his lips. "Yeah?"

I roll my eyes, but it's just a diversion. I can't decide where to focus. On the hard cut abs? Or the tattoo of my initial? Or gah, the outline of his cock threatening to escape his boxers? I've seen a lot of men's dicks, but none make my stomach twist with excitement the way Axel's does.

"Admit it," he says, looping his arm around my waist and pulling me close, making me feel every hard inch of his body. "You like me, which is good, because I'm crazy about you."

His words are light, but his gaze is intense. It's weird. Good. Strange. I start to turn my face overwhelmed by it all, *by him*. He holds me in place, asking, "What's going on in that pretty little head?" His green eyes hold mine. "Too fast? Too much? Too naked? Talk to me, T."

"No man has ever been like this to me before."

His eyebrow rises, wanting more.

"You're sweet. Silly. You say dirty things but it's not..."

"Demeaning?" he asks, the smile gone. "Because if you ever feel that with me–"

"I don't," I say quickly. "Ever."

"Good," he says, running his hands over my hips, "because all I want is to make you feel good. Safe. But I'm not gonna lie, I've wanted to get back inside of you for weeks now, wanted to feel you clench around me." He licks under my ear, sending a ripple of goosebumps across my skin. "I want to see your sexy body over me, or under me, or maybe both if we're not too tired."

I laugh. "We both work out, we should be good."

"Trust me?" he asks, fingers toying with the bottom edge of my panties until they dip underneath, brushing along the seam between my cheeks. A rush of heat pools between my legs.

I nod.

"Then say it, darlin', tell me what you want."

What do I want? One thing. "Fuck me, Ax. Hard. Like you mean it."

A switch flips: gone is the man tip-toeing around my feelings, around my fears. The following kiss is rough and his body commanding as he nudges me to my back. Splayed before him, he stares at me for a long moment, before he works his way down my body. His mouth is blistering–*taunting*–as he works those quick hands to remove the last scraps of my clothing.

He's worshipful. Reverent. Kissing my belly and between my thighs. Roughly, he spreads my legs and his tongue swipes over my clit, that mustache tickling. I cry out, pulling him back up. "No?" he asks, lips shiny.

"Not now." I want him near me, on me, in me. I like the weight of his body over mine; strong, safe, protective. Using my feet, I push his boxers down his hips, removing the last barrier between us. His erection is thick, and I reach for it, running my hand down the length. "I want you in me when I come."

He shudders, growling at my touch.

"It's been a while," he tells me, thrusting into my hand. "If we're doing this, it's gotta be soon."

"I'm ready," I say, kissing him again.

"Please tell me you have condoms." His jaw tightens. "Because your roommate's boyfriend took mine."

I wrinkle my nose, not wanting to know, and reach for the drawer of the bedside table. The soup sloshes, cold now, coating my hand. Axel's hand closes over mine, bringing it to his mouth to lick off the juice before tearing into the package.

He never stops kissing or touching me, even as he preps himself. The other guys I've been with only focused on themselves. There was never any tenderness. I was just an object to use. A plaything to get them off. With Axel, it's the opposite. This moment is about the two of us, every touch a give and take.

"You ready?" he asks, running his fingers over the wet heat between my legs. He presses one into me, then another, pumping in slowly, stretching me out. My hips rise to meet him. It's not enough. I want more. "Yeah, fuck, your pussy is soaked."

With his arms on either side of me, he looks down at me, holding my eyes. He presses against my entrance, but hesitates.

"What's wrong?" I ask, my body feeling so brittle, like it's going to break if he doesn't get inside me and hold me together.

He pushes the hair off my forehead. "You're beautiful, Nadia."

The first time we were together it was just another fuck-up. A way to get lost, to run from my problems by creating bigger ones. This time, when he enters me, sheathing himself deep, I feel it in my bones. My blood. My heart.

"Good?" he asks, the muscles in his throat tense as he holds himself back.

"Perfect." I lift my hips, urging him to move, wanting him as deep as he can go. He gives me what I want, thrusting hard, letting loose. I cry out and his forehead drops to mine, sweaty and warm. The tight band inside of me coils tighter and tighter, our bodies in sync, until I snap first, the orgasm unfurling inside, spreading a pulsating warmth across my nerves.

My body tightens around him and he groans, fingers digging into the meat of my hip as he stutters to a halt, spilling inside. I take him, the hard thrust of his hips, the way he buries his cock between my legs and his face in my neck. I feel him—every slick inch of skin, every heavy breath as he empties himself into me.

My nails dig into his back. I can't get him close enough.

Intertwined, our chests rise and fall, as our bodies float back to earth. His fingers link with mine, the YOLO face up.

For the first time in my life, I know one thing for certain: doing this with Axel, letting him in, allowing him to love me? It definitely wasn't a fuck-up.

16

Axel

Just because I'm caught in that blissed-out state between orgasm and sleep doesn't mean I can't feel Nadia trying to ease out of my grip and off the bed.

"Nuh-uh," I mumble, face pressed into her neck, "where do you think you're going?"

"Bathroom?"

"I already cleaned you up," I remind her. I'd found a clean cloth in the bathroom and wiped her down before getting back in the bed to hold her close. "You're trying to escape."

"This is my house, how can I escape?" But there's an edge to her voice and she relents, admitting, "I was just giving you some space."

"What gives you the impression that I want space?" My arm is tight around her waist, keeping her against my body. My cock twitches, the want building again, but it's not sex, it's just her. "I mean, the full-sized bed is a little tight, but it just makes it easier to cuddle."

She turns. It's not graceful. The bed really is too small for my body alone, much less hers. I keep my hand on her hip, holding onto her until she faces me. "You're saying you want to stay and cuddle."

I'd fucking move in if she'd let me.

"You think I'm not a cuddler?"

She rolls her eyes. "I think you're too lazy to move."

"You want me to leave?" The concept dawns on me. God, how much brain fog do I have? "You're kicking me out?"

She frowns, eyes searching mine, then sighs. "I don't know what you want from me."

"What are you talking about, T?"

"Every man I've ever had sex with has made it perfectly clear that I'm not invited to hang out."

"Even when it's at your house?"

"No one ever comes to my house. I'm always the one that goes to theirs," she says.

I know that this goes all the way back to that first time with that bastard Will Holt, who I plan on eviscerating in the near future.

She continues, "That's why I'm not exactly sure what to do here."

"I'm not leaving." I reach out and trace the line of her jaw. "And you're not either. We're going to fucking cuddle. And do that other thing couples do."

Her eyebrows rise. "What thing?"

"Pillow talk, or whatever."

"You want to cuddle and talk?"

"I mean, I wouldn't say no to round two when my cock comes back from the dead, but yeah. I missed you over the break. I thought about you every day. I hated the way we left things and I wasn't able to talk to you." I thrust my hand in my hair. "No matter how big of a house my father builds, it still feels too small."

"Do you want to talk about it?" she asks tentatively. "Because if you don't that's okay." I'm not sure why she's so hesitant, until it hits me. The last time she asked about my family I told her it was none of her business. Jesus, I'm an asshole.

"It's hard for me to talk about them," I admit. "And accusing you of ulterior motives was a dick move. I'm sorry."

"I know. We were both a little defensive that day."

Fuck, this girl. She's too good for me.

"Do you know who my father is?" I ask.

"I didn't," she admits, "not until we argued. I had some time to kill in the airport on the way home and went on a deep dive."

"So you know he's the head pastor of the megachurch, Kingdom."

"I watched a few of his sermons. He seems…" she searches for the right word, "…charismatic. I know you don't want to hear it, but I see the resemblance. In looks and presence."

I grimace. "Yeah, I'm aware."

"Sorry," she says, with the smallest smirk. "He's good at his job. I'm not even religious and I got a little caught up in his talk. I can see why he's popular. So what's the issue? Does he disapprove of your lifestyle?" Her fingers trace over a tattoo on my chest. "All the ink and tattoos? The women?"

"Yes and no." This is where it gets complicated, and where it's hard to explain who my father really is. "I had a lot of energy as a kid. Sitting still was like asking the Devil to sing in the choir, and he knew I needed an outlet. Mom signed me up for everything: football, baseball, basketball, but one day I went with a friend to a hockey game and I was hooked. Then it became pretty clear I was *good*. I made it to the juniors and the recruiters started showing up. He was always going to let me go to college–he just figured it would be a religious foundation and closer to home."

"But he let you go."

"One condition for me playing hockey at such a highly competitive and time consuming level, was that I still had to attend church–at least the youth portions. I could live with it, especially once all the girls started showing up."

"I know this is hard to believe, but I was already cocky at seventeen. I had my first tattoo," I shift, pointing to a lightning bolt, the name of my team, "and got my eyebrow pierced. I kind of developed this bad-boy persona that attracted a lot of girls and I wasn't afraid to pursue them."

"I bet," she snorts. "You're like the male version of catnip."

"Well, my father saw it a little differently, but yeah. I was popular. While I was trying my hardest to be rebellious, to tell my father he couldn't control me, but in the end, all I did was fall right into his trap. I became a mini-version of him, building his flock, and he noticed."

Fuck did he notice.

"He allowed me to come to Wittmore because it benefitted the Kingdom. The more popular I become, the more name recognition I have, the more it'll help when I go back."

She frowns. "What do you mean, 'go back?'"

"It's a family business, darlin'. Started with my great-great grandfather going all the way down the line." I meet her eye. "I'm next."

"That's why you're not entering the draft." Her eyes widen. "And why you've been living like a sailor on leave for the last three years."

"Pretty much." I roll on my back and tuck my arm behind my head. "I may not have the calling in the traditional sense, but there's no doubt about my destiny and it isn't tending goal in the NHL."

Nadia lifts up on her elbow, pulling the sheet with her to cover her chest. "You're an adult, Axel. He can't actually make you come back, can he?"

I shrug. "It's complicated. When he let me come up here, and agreed to pay for my education, I told him I'd come back." My word means something, and so does my family. "He's been preparing the congregation for my return this whole time. The prodigal son returns. I may live up here, but they're following me down there. There's a plan. A role I'm supposed to step into." I laugh darkly. "I even have an assignment for when I come home over winter break."

"People change their minds all the time, can they not see that?"

"Breaking that promise to him would be a scandal, and there's nothing like a megachurch scandal. It would hurt my mom and sister, who have sacrificed *everything* for that man and church." I shake my head. "I can't do that to them."

"What you're saying is that after graduation, you're heading back to Texas."

I nod, picking up her hand and running my thumb over her knuckles. "Unless God sends another flood, which I mean, is entirely possible. I've done some pretty sinful things."

"Epic fuck-ups."

"That's right." I rise up, and push her on her back, taking off the sheet in the process. Her body is perfect. She's perfect and that's why I confess, "And if there's only six more months of sinning and fuck-ups left, I want you to be the one I do it with."

~

"You didn't have to cook for me." I watch her move around in the tiny kitchen. She looks sexy as hell wearing my dress shirt that hangs down and grazes her thighs.

"I'm not sure this counts as cooking." She opens a cabinet and pushes up on her toes, reaching for a bowl, giving me a peek of lace and asscheek. "And your stomach was growling and you kept looking wistfully at my cold ramen."

I hop up and cross the room, crowding behind her to grab the bowls. Her ass brushes against my cock and fuck, well, this may not have been the best idea. Not if I want to eat something other than her pussy.

"I came over right after my game. I didn't get my standard post-win meal. And," I lift the hair off her neck and lean in, kissing her neck, "I'm pretty sure we burned a shit ton of calories tonight."

She turns, looking up at me with those big brown eyes. Her hair is a mess, bunched up from my hands. Under the shirt, I know she's not wearing a bra and the urge to feel her up, to make sure this is real, is strong–almost a compulsion. I want her. I'm pretty sure I'm never going to stop wanting her, but this is about showing Nadia that she's more to me than just a warm place. I can get that on sorority row. Here? I get a big bowl of carbs and an awesome chick to eat them with.

Grabbing the spoon, I ladle out the ramen, and pick up both bowls, then head to the living room. Steam rises off the top and the ceramic bottoms are hot. I set both on the coffee table and join her on the couch.

I twirl my fork in the noodles and take a huge bite. "Jesus, that's good."

"I'm glad my dollar package of ramen satiates you." She pulls a blanket over her lap, hiding those gorgeous legs. "I've got some pudding cups for dessert."

"You joke, but I'm a college athlete. We'll eat just about anything."

We eat in silence, the only sound is slurping–okay *my* slurping, she eats like a princess. Or she tries. A drop of soup dribbles down her chin and I grin.

"What?"

"I like you like this."

"Like what?" she shifts, anxious under my scrutiny. I don't let up. She needs to get used to it.

"Eating a cheap soup." I hook a finger in the neck of her shirt, pulling her close enough to get a peek down the front. "Wearing my shirt." I lick the drop off her chin. "Looking like you just had the best orgasm*s*."

Her lips part and I kiss her, tasting all that salty goodness. I release her though before it goes too far. Sitting back and taking another spoonful, I ask. "Want to watch Springfield?"

"Okay." She sets her bowl on the table. "What is this?"

"What is what?"

"This? Do you do this with all your hookups? Sit around, acting all cute, offering to watch shitty TV."

"First, do not degrade Springfield like that. It's a masterpiece of teen soap opera that occasionally has a ghost." She stares at me. "And second, no, I don't. Ever." I unscrew the cap of my water bottle and take a swig. My heart is pounding. I don't know why. I guess I've just never had to do this before. Never wanted to do it. But with Nadia, I want to make it perfectly clear. "And third, this," I point between us, "this isn't a hook-up. Not to me at least."

"Then you meant what you said in there? That you want to spend the next six months with me?"

There is no fucking way I can dump my emotions on this girl, especially after telling her about my future. I want Nadia. For the long term, although I suspect that living in Texas, moving to the Kingdom, isn't one of her goals. She wants a man in a uniform. A man getting knocked around and sweaty. Not one standing on a stage, preaching stuff he doesn't really believe to an unsuspecting flock.

But playing it safe has never been my style. YOLO. I've lived every day at Wittmore like it was my last. I'm not stopping now. If I can only have her until graduation, I'll take it. We'll figure out the rest then.

"What we did in there," I take her hands and kiss her knuckles, "and what we're going to do after we binge watch some Springfield, makes you mine. I don't mean just in the bedroom. Or when it's convenient. Or when one of us wants to get off. I mean all the time."

"You mean, public."

"As much as you want." I run my hand through my hair, suddenly aware that she may not want the same thing. "As much as you'll give me."

"Axel Rakestraw–committed boyfriend?" She tries it out, then shakes her head. "Are you sure?"

"You think I can't commit?" I ask, raising an eyebrow.

"In theory, yes, but isn't this wild, unpredictable goalie your whole thing?"

"That's the thing about goalies, darlin', we're the most committed player on the ice. When you've got a two-hundred pound power forward barreling toward you, hurling a puck seventy miles an hour, you have no choice but to commit or get seriously hurt." I pull her onto my lap. "Commitment isn't a problem for me, T. I've just never found the girl I've wanted to slow down for."

She exhales, eyes wide. "God, this is scary."

"Being in a relationship with me scares you?" Fuck, I'm doing this all wrong.

"No." She shakes her head. "Being in a relationship with you excites me. What scares me is the other thing we have to do; tell Twyler."

～

"You're clean."

It takes a moment for his words to process, at least until Reese slams his elbow into my side.

"Son of a–" I mutter, rubbing the spot. Coach's eyebrow rises. "Sorry, Coach. I guess I was just scared something would happen and the test would show up positive again."

"Check it yourself." He hands me the card with the test results. And sure enough, the blood test is clean.

"Thank god." I exhale, unaware of how I'd been bracing myself for bad news. "Because I'm clean as a damn whistle. I haven't touched anything for weeks. Not even a drop of alcohol."

Bryant nods. "You've shown a lot of maturity during this, Rakestraw. I'm impressed. Your focus has been on the ice, and the results are there."

My focus hasn't *strictly* been on the ice. There's a hot little piece of trouble I can't stay away from. Her body is more addictive than any drug I've ever taken.

"I did want to let you know that due to the presence of rohypnol in your prior test the NCAA reported it to local and campus authorities."

"They did?" I ask, sharing a look with Reese. "What does that mean?"

"It means they know someone on campus is dosing drinks with an illegal and controlled substance. Everyone is in agreement you were probably not the intended victim. Unfortunately, unless it happens again, or a witness comes forward, I doubt much will come of it."

It's a harsh reminder of why it's important to keep Nadia close and to stay alert. Whoever tried to fuck with her is still out there.

"Anything else?" he asks.

"No, sir." We both answer.

"Good." He jerks his chin. "Then get out of here."

Reese heads out the door, but I indicate to him that I need a minute. I hold back until Bryant notices. "I did have one more thing."

"Make it fast."

"I, uh," Shit. How do I start this? "I found out over the break that my father may have interfered with this situation. I was aware that it hadn't hit the press and just figured it was the athletic department PR team or something."

Coach leans back in his seat. "I'm aware that he made some calls."

"It was never my intention for him to do that. I made a mistake–two–the weed and then being unaware of my surroundings to the point that I was drugged. I accept responsibility for those."

"Son, I've seen your improvement over the past few weeks. Like I said, I'm impressed. You went above and beyond. Showing up early, adding in extra weight sessions, and from what I hear, your efforts exhibited with the team have filtered into your personal life."

Partying. Puck Bunnies. Burning out at both ends.

"I wanted to prove that I was serious."

"You have. Be proud of your efforts. I know that I am and so is the team." This time when he waves me off, I don't hesitate to leave. Reese is waiting in the hallway.

"Everything okay?"

"Everything's great," I admit. Which feels weird, but I'm not going to question it.

"I told the guys. They want to go celebrate. Badger Den?"

"Yeah," I'm already reaching for my phone. "But I'm not drinking."

"Still?"

"Yeah, I'm feeling good. Fit. I don't wake up with a hangover or wondering what I did the night before. I feel sharper in the goal and if this is my last season, I want to leave it all on the ice, you know?"

"Yeah, I know." If anyone would, it would be Reese. There's no one more dedicated to this sport and team. While he texts the team, I shoot off a message to Nadia.

GoalieGod: Passed my test.
T: Yay!
GoalieGod: Come celebrate with me.
T: Is this your way of getting me to come over?
GoalieGod: Nah. At the Den with the team.

For a second there's no reply. No little dots indicating a message is being written. Shit. Maybe it's too fast. Too soon.

"You ready?" Reese asks, tucking his phone into his pocket and grabbing his bag off the floor. "Everyone is headed over now."

My phone vibrates.

T: So we're doing this?

A surge of emotion runs through me. Adrenaline. Dopamine. Whatever it is that elevates life. That's what Nadia makes me feel. I shoot off a reply.

GoalieGod: Fuck yeah, we're doing this.

∼

"Your girl's here," Kirby says, his voice raised over the noisy bar.

Reese and I both look over at the front door. Twyler walks in first, hair up in a ponytail, wearing Reese's sweatshirt. My gaze skips over her. Nadia comes in behind her, cheeks pink from the cold December air. I haven't seen her since Sunday morning, when I reluctantly left her bed for practice. She'd had to work that afternoon and then Twyler got back and they spent the evening grocery shopping and running errands.

It took everything in me not to sneak back in her bedroom window, but that wasn't how she wanted Twyler to find out about us. Now, I lean back on the bar, waiting to see how she wants to play this. Because what I want to do is walk over there and shove my tongue down her throat, but that may be a little much.

"I thought her friend was into chasing football players. Guess she realized hockey players are better."

I turn and see that it's Murphy running his mouth.

"Shut up, Murph," Reese says, coming to her defense first. "She's had a hard few months. The last thing she needs is one of you sniffing around."

"Chill, Cap," he says, draining the last of the beer out of his glass, "I'm just wondering if anyone's given her an introduction to their stick."

"Fuck, Murphy," I say in a low drawl, "I don't want to have to kick your ass. I just got off probation."

"What? Suddenly you care about Puck Bunnies? You've got more notches on your bedpost than anyone on the team." He thinks for a second. "Well, maybe other than Jefferson."

He's not wrong, which is probably why I feel even more defensive. I've been a dick to a lot of women. Slipping in late at night, and leaving early in the morning. Thinking with my cock and nothing else. And I could kick Murphy's ass right now. Teach him a lesson in respect. I *should* kick his ass. Instead, I do the one thing that will keep me out of trouble and shut him the hell up.

Twyler and Nadia have just reached the bar, and I push off and go straight for her.

"Hey Darlin'."

"Hey." A sweet smile plays on her lips.

"I'm gonna kiss you, okay?" Those brown eyes widen, then glance around at the packed bar. I rest my hand on her hip and repeat, "Okay?"

Her gaze snaps back to mine. "Okay."

It's all the approval I need, and I slide my hand under her hair, cupping the back of her neck. With her close and in my grasp, I tilt her face just the way I want it.

Twyler's voice cuts over the crowd. "What the—"

But my mouth is on Nadia's, drawing her in. She's nervous, I feel it in the kiss, but I take my time, like we're the only two in the world, coaxing her lips apart, until her tongue meets mine. *Fuck* she tastes good, minty. Sweet. Mine.

I take my time releasing her because I know every damn eye in the bar is on the two of us.

Good.

"Jesus Christ, Axel!" Two hands shove me from the side and I stumble back. "What the hell?"

"Damn, TG." I rub my arm dramatically. "You're strong."

"Shut up," she barks, before her anger shifts to her boyfriend. "Did you know about this?"

"What?" he asks, eyes narrowing at me. "No. I swear."

"B-but when? How?"

"We became non-drinking buddies." I throw my arm around Nadia's shoulders and press a kiss on her temple. "And then we became more."

She opens her mouth again, but thinks better of it, saying, "Nad, can we talk?" She gives me a dark glare. "In private."

"Of course."

She starts to extricate herself from me, but I'm not quite ready to hand her over to the she-wolf pacing a few feet away. I drop my mouth to hers, kissing her again, wanting everyone to know this is real. When I'm satisfied my point has been made, I pull back, and run my thumb over the shell of her ear, over her piercing. "I'll grab you something to drink."

"Thanks."

Twyler steps forward and grabs my girlfriend's hand and drags her across the bar to an open booth. When I drag my eyes away from how amazing her ass looks in that skirt, I see that every guy on the team is staring at me, shocked.

Especially Murphy, who I give a hard look. He and the rest of the guys make the wise decision to go play pool, leaving just me, Reese, Reid, and Jefferson at the bar.

"What?" I say, using their dumbfoundedness as an opportunity to hit the bar. "Hey, Mike, two cans of Reaper?"

"Sure thing."

"Dude, I told you to stay the fuck away from her," Reese says, rubbing the back of his neck. "She's vulnerable, you know what she's been through."

"I do. Way more than you do." I take one of the cans Mike sets on the bar and pop the top. "This isn't something we rushed into. We're friends. We know each other." I take a swallow of water and then admit. "I like her."

"God dammit, man. Seriously?"

I grin. "So fucking much."

Reid, lifts his beer and points across the room, where the girls seem to be in a deep, animated, discussion. "What do you think they're saying?"

"Probably that Nadia is going to be just another in a long stream of broken-hearted girls leaving the Manor," Jeff says. "That you only think with your cock and are in no way boyfriend material."

"Sounds about right," Reid says. "She thinks you're a ho."

"Oh, Twy is definitely telling her that I'm a useless fuckboy," I say, under no delusions.

"I mean..." Reid says, "she's not wrong. You have a reputation for being a slut."

"So does Nadia," Jefferson says. "You can't deny it. Chick's been chasing jerseys since she got on campus."

"That's over. For both of us." I'm not letting these dumbasses get under my skin. "We're well aware of our mutual reputations and don't give a fuck."

"Well, good. Congratulations." Reid lifts his glass. "Here's to not giving a fuck."

I knock my can against his glass, and Jefferson does the same, before heading over to watch the game on the big screen, leaving me and Reese alone to finish the conversation they'd interrupted.

"Give it to me."

"Give you what?"

"The lecture. An ass kicking. Whatever you need to do to make this right between me and you and me and Twyler."

"All in all, I don't hate it," he says, surprising me. "She needs someone that understands what she's been through and I think you do. But what happens at the end of the year?"

I know Reese and that question is about more than me and Nadia.

"We've been honest with each other. She knows about my family and the obligations I have to them–where I'm headed after graduation." I swallow back the lump building in my throat. "And I know about her goals–the kind of life she wants to live."

A life I can't give her.

"So this isn't a long term thing?"

"It is what it is, for as long as we want it." I shrug. "Anything more than that is between us."

"Fair," he admits. "If you make each other happy, and you keep killing it on the ice, it's really none of my fucking business."

I tilt my head toward the booth, where the emotions seem to have settled down. Nadia glances over at me and my heart skips a goddamn beat. Whatever they're discussing needs to wrap up soon. I'm ready to be out and proud with my girl.

"By the way," I say to Reese, as I start across the bar, "you owe me a box of condoms. I'm gonna need them."

17

Nadia

"Sorry I'm late." I shove my bag under the front counter. "I stopped to grab a coffee and the line took forever."

"It's fine," Abby says. She's sitting in front of the main computer, entering data. "It took me twenty minutes to find a parking spot this morning. They keep closing lots for all the construction."

I remove my coat and stuff it next to the bag. "I swear this campus gets more crowded every year."

"That's what happens when you have multiple championship teams. It happens every time we have an impressive season, like the football and hockey team have had over the last few years."

"Are you saying people pick a college based on sports and not academics?"

She laughs. "I'm definitely saying that. Why do you think the school spends more on the athletic programs than anything else?"

She nods toward the back of the gym. "It also doesn't hurt to have guys like that walking around campus."

I follow her gesture and see a couple of guys lifting weights in the back corner. I don't know what or who I expected, but the flip flop of my gut is instantaneous when I realize it's Axel. He's in one of those T-shirts the guys at the gym wear with the arms and neck cut out for more room. His arm muscles flex as he goes through a set of bicep curls.

I haven't seen him since the night before, when we "went official" at the bar to Twyler and everyone else. After her initial freak-out, she'd handled it pretty well, but I thought it may be best for Axel and I to stay at our own places that night. Give everyone a minute to acclimate to us as a couple.

Give *myself* a minute to acclimate to having Axel Rakestraw as a boyfriend.

"You know him right?" Abby asks.

"Yeah, I do. We're uh..." I don't have to look to know he's staring at me. I feel it and my skin gets warm and hot, "friends."

Okay, I guess maybe I haven't fully acclimated.

"I need more friends like that," she says, then catches herself, "you know, if they were four years older." Her eyebrow raises. "Does he have an older brother?"

I grab the bottle of antibacterial spray and a clean rag. "Just a sister–younger." A sister he seems to care a lot about. I'm curious about Axel's family–the dynamic seems intense. My family isn't religious, no more than hitting the big holidays at our local methodist church. Although he and his father seem miles apart, it's also not completely impossible to reconcile Axel with the charismatic man I've seen clips of online.

Twyler had asked me where this relationship was going–was it long term. I told her that we were dating for now. Axel was honest with me about his future plans–how he'll go home to Texas to minister with his father. But I can tell it weighs on him, a conflict he's carrying if he doesn't want to fully admit it. I know athletes, and Axel is good. He has what it takes to go pro, but only if he wants it. That's what I can't discern about him. Does he want it? Because what I've learned about him is that he's a man that goes after what he wants.

He pursued the hell out of me.

I struggle to reconcile that with the man covered in tattoos–including the letters YOLO on his fingers. He doesn't seem like the type to compromise.

"I'm going to go wipe down the machines."

"Thanks but first, can you do me a favor?"

"He really doesn't have a brother, Abs, I promise."

She rolls her eyes. "I know, that's not the favor."

"What's up?"

"There's a prospective student tour coming through in about fifteen minutes. They'd be thrilled to see a star Badger in action," she explains. "Will you ask if he'll stick around? Maybe even talk to the group? If I can get a picture I can submit it to the social media page."

The campus tours make a stop at the gym every day–it's a big selling feature for the university. "Yeah, sure, I can ask him."

With my bottle of cleaner and rag, I cross the gym over to where he's moved away from the other guys and is sitting under the leg press machine–mid press. His shorts slide down, revealing his thighs and god, they're thick and muscular from all that hockey.

"Hey," he says, grunting as he lowers the weight. Sweat beads on his forehead and he lifts the hem of his shirt, wiping his forehead, showing his slick abs. "I was hoping you'd come by."

I drag my eyes away from his muscles. "Huh?"

"T, you can see me shirtless anytime you want–no need to drool over me while I'm working out."

I swat him with the cleaning rag. "I'm not drooling."

He lifts a shoulder. "You want me, it's okay to admit it"

I do want him, but like hell I'm going to feed his ego.

"Stop being so vain." I roll my eyes, trying to pretend like just seeing him like this isn't making me crazy. "My manager asked me for a favor."

"What's that?" He climbs off the machine and grabs his water bottle, taking a big swallow.

"Will you stick around for the next student tour? She wants to wow the admissions department with a couple photos of a star athlete working out."

"Star athlete, huh?"

"Her words, not mine."

He smirks, but then says, "You know I'm not really approved to workout without Coach's approval."

"Oh shit, right."

"I mostly just come in here to see you." His tongue darts out, licking the ring in his lip. "I missed waking up with you."

"I missed it too," I admit. "I just felt like it was better to take it slow. For the sake of everyone."

He nods, leaning a sweaty arm on the machine. "How about this? I stick around, take a few pictures for the gym and you come to my game tonight."

"You won't get in trouble?"

"I'll smooth it over," he says, running his fingers over his mustache. "It looks good for the team too when we do a little extra PR."

"I was already coming to the game, but if that's the deal you want to strike, sure."

Across the gym, the tour guide enters the front door, followed by a small group of high school students and their parents. Abby walks over to greet them and I say, "I better go put this stuff up and see if she needs any help."

I duck into the back hall and have my hand on the supply closet door knob when I hear, "T, wait up."

I turn and Axel is behind me, crowding me in against the door.

"I wasn't finished with my demands."

I tilt my head. "Okay, what else?"

"You wear my jersey to the game."

Again, not a hardship. "Done."

His eyebrow arches. "With nothing on underneath."

Heat spreads through my belly. "I can do that."

"And after the game, you come home with me–spend the night in my bed."

The way he's looking at me–oh boy–yeah this is a man that knows what he wants.

"Fine, but..." I start, already knowing I'm going to agree no matter what. I'm just trying to have some dignity here. "You have to wear a Wittmore gym T-shirt."

"Deal," he says, holds out his hand.

I clasp it with my own, feeling the jolt of electricity running between our fingertips. Each touch is a commitment to something bigger than myself. Something I'm not sure I can control. Something I'm ready to run head first into. "Deal."

Apparently a handshake isn't enough for Axel Rakestraw. With our hands linked he pulls me against his chest and bends, his mouth covering mine, in a strong, sexy, kiss. When he pulls back he grins and says, "So where's that T-shirt?"

～

Wittmore is down by one as the timer ticks down to the second intermission and I'm in my seat ignoring how hard my nipples feel in the cold arena without the added layer of a padded bra.

"It'll be okay," Twyler says, although I think she's talking more to herself than to me. "They'll pull it together."

They guys are playing awful. Even with my limited understanding of the game, it's pretty obvious something's off. "I'm sure Coach Bryant will light a fire under their asses during the break."

"You see that?" she says, pointing down to Reese on the ice. He's skating around the goal, just having missed another shot.

I narrow my eyes at the number fifteen jersey. "See what?"

"His shoulder. See how he's rolling it back?"

All I see is a blur of black and gold badger uniforms smacking a puck around the ice.

"I think Reese's shoulder is bothering him. He keeps stopping short when he takes a shot." She worries her bottom lip. "I should go down there and check."

"Twy, you're not his trainer any more. I'm sure Coach Green can handle it."

"I may not be his official trainer, but I know his body better than anyone."

I snort. "I don't think having an intimate knowledge of his penis counts."

"That's not what I mean." She glares at me. "Reese is stubborn. He probably won't even say anything and just suffer through it– which will only make it worse." She swears quietly. "God, he's an idiot. I never should have switched internships."

Down on the ice Axel and the forward from the opposing team start shouting. A stick clatters against the ice and Axel lunges out of the crease.

"Oh fuck," I mutter, watching with wide eyes. Whistles screech, and a referee darts between the two players, pushing them apart.

Thank god the buzzer sounds, ending the period.

"Axel seems pretty agitated," I say, as Reid corrals him, urging him off the ice. He yanks off his helmet, revealing sweat soaked hair. "I know he's pissed he let in that goal."

"Well, Rodgers needs to stop buzzing around the crease." Rodgers, the power forward for Eastern, seems to be particularly focused on messing with him. "It's not illegal, but it's obnoxious as hell, and he's obviously trying to get Ax to do something stupid."

I don't know what Axel is like after a loss. Being undefeated is an amazing accomplishment, but it also adds another layer of pressure for these guys and everyone around them. Although I've never had this level of investment before–publicly dating a player– I do know what it's like to be around an athlete after a bad game. That's part of the role of a jersey chaser. You're there for the wins and losses. Some guys are angry. Others depressed. Most get wasted, drowning their sorrows, or getting high. Others like Brent and CJ put on a brave face for the crowds and then come back home and release their tensions in private. I learned quick how to navigate their emotions–how best to support them–which in hindsight, was just me putting myself in another risky situation.

I have no idea how Axel will act after losing and I'm a little scared to find out.

"I'm going down there." Twyler stands abruptly, grabbing her bag.

"What?" I ask, standing with her. "You can't do that."

"You think they won't let me in?" she's already working her way down the aisle. I follow, trying not to step on anyone's feet. "To fix their star player? They're not that stupid."

I'm not sure why I keep following her, probably because I assume this is going to end up a disaster. While she walks she unzips her bag, digging out a lanyard and slinging the ID badge over her neck. She starts toward the stairs that lead down to the locker rooms and I grab her arm. "Wait."

"I've only got a few minutes before intermission is over, Nad."

"What if it's me," I blurt.

She frowns.

"What if I'm the reason they're losing? I'm the new thing. The variation. My presence, my relationship with Axel could be what's fucking up everyone's mojo." I swallow. "What if he regrets asking me to come."

My best friend stares at me with her big blue eyes. "Don't be ridiculous."

"You know how they are about superstitions. Look at Axel's stupid mustache!" I struggle to take a deep breath. "What if he blames me?"

Twyler takes my hand and leads me down the stairs. "I'm still not sure what's going on with you two, how serious this is, or what's going to happen long term, but I know that Axel is more together now than he's been since I've met him. He's steady. Sober. Focused. Reese never thought he'd see him get his shit together." She stops in front of a door with a security box. "Don't think we aren't aware that this change in him happened around the time he stopped chasing puck bunnies and you two started hanging out."

"He was on probation."

"And reeling." She waves the badge in front of the sensor and the door unlocks. "Something got his head on straight, and we both think it was you."

We enter the locker room. My senses are assaulted by the worst smell I've encountered in my life. "Oh my god," I gag, holding my shirt over my nose.

"Holy shit," she coughs, "they stink, right? I swear I got desensitized."

"It's terrible."

"Wait here," she says and gestures for me to the equipment room off the hallway. She strides off before I can argue, and I hear her shout, "Cain!"

"Twyler?" Reese's voice rises over the other guys. "What the fuck–"

"Get in the training room. Let's check your shoulder."

"It's fine, Sunshine," he grumbles. I don't miss the laughter and cat-calls that follow from his teammates.

"Yeah, we'll see about that."

Satisfied she's not being tossed out immediately, I step into the equipment room. The room is painted yellow and black, a badger logo on the wall. There are cubbies filled with skates and helmets hanging on hooks attached to the wall. Bins are piled high with pads and slotted racks holding dozens of beat-up sticks.

A rustle sounds behind me and I turn. Axel stands in the doorway, wearing full goalie pads. "Well, isn't this a surprise?"

"Hi." I swallow, taking him in. He looks massive suited up. "I know I shouldn't be in here. I'm just waiting on Twyler."

"She told me to come down here and get a new strap for my helmet." He snorts. "Like that's going to help the shit show going on out there."

Irrational panic, mixed with a heavy dose of insecurity, rises in the back of my throat. "I should go." I push past him. "You need to stay focused."

He grabs my arm, keeping me in place. "You don't distract me."

I don't miss how his eyes dart down to my chest. I roll my eyes and say, "There's only one difference tonight, Ax. Me. I'm throwing things off balance. You guys have all your superstitions and rituals. I can't just come in here and not screw that up."

"Bullshit."

"What?"

"I'm calling bullshit. Rodgers being a dick is throwing me off balance. Getting in the goalie's head is his speciality. You, on the other hand, have been coming to the games for a while." He tugs at the hem of the jersey. "Wearing my name and number. The only difference is we're fucking now."

God, his mouth. "That's a big difference."

"Not to me."

I roll my eyes. "Us... doing *that*... is huge. It takes things to a new level."

"Sorry, darlin' you and I took things to the next level the day you wore that jersey the first time. That was the day I claimed you." He pushes the hair off my neck. "And we won. Ritual locked in."

He means what he's saying, and if there's one thing I know about the role of being an athlete's girl, is that it's my job to make him think he can get the job done. Axel doesn't need confidence. He has that in spades. My man needs a challenge. "If that's what you believe, then you need to go out there and prove it."

"Yeah?" His grin is cocky. Infectious. "How so?"

"If you want me to keep coming to your games, wearing nothing underneath this jersey," I lean forward, tilting my face to his, "then you better go out there and win this thing."

～

WITTMORE WINS.

After the game, Axel strolls out in one of those sexy suits wearing the confident grin of a winner. Fans clamor around him, the crowd bigger and bigger every week, and he and the other guys stop to sign autographs. I feel the heat of his eyes keeping track of me while I wait by the edge of the parking lot.

He deserves the attention. He managed a rebound in the second half, shutting out Eastern's offense. Bonus points for not throttling Rodgers in the process. In fact, the forward took a swing at Kirby and ended up in the box for the final minutes of the game.

"Hey," he says making a beeline toward me. This is the stuff I'm not used to. Being the girl waiting out in the parking lot, not deep in a cell phone or waiting at home. He grabs me before I can overthink it and lifts me up, kissing me hard on the mouth. "Believe me now that you're not bad luck?"

I smirk. "I believe you were sufficiently motivated to win that game."

"Darlin' it's time you understand that you're not shaking me. You're my girl, and if we lose we lose, that's got nothing to do with you and me."

"What about all your superstitions? You're telling me you believe in them?"

"To an extent," he says, grinning and running his fingers over his mustache. "But that kind of thing can fuck with your head as much as anything else." He tosses his bag in the bed of his truck and grabs me, pinning me against the side of the cab. "I want to see if you really were a good girl and followed directions, or if you were just fucking with me."

He doesn't wait for an answer, shoving his hands under my shirt to fondle my breasts. "Fuck," he groans, thumbs rolling over my nipples and sending a shiver down my spine. "Forget everything I just said. Now you're going to have to show up to every game like this."

My limbs turn to jelly, loosened by his greedy touch. I'm thankful that he opens the door for me, helping me inside the cab, even though his hand lingers on my ass a minute longer than necessary, making it worse.

"You're too far away," he says when he gets in the truck. Leaning over, he grabs me by the waist and pulls me down the bench. He smells clean, fresh, a far cry from the stink of the locker room. He plants a kiss against my neck. "That's better."

Tucked against his side, he makes the short drive to Shotgun. His fingers inch under the jersey, knuckles grazing the underside of my breast. It's good. Teasing. The air crackles between us. It's not all one-sided, I can't stop touching him either, running my hand down his thigh, feeling the hard length of his erection grow thicker with every pass.

By the time we reach the Manor, we're both squirming in our seats. The windows at the house are bright with light and people spill off the front porch. All the parking spots in front of the house are taken, so he drives around the back alley behind the house. It's dark back here. Discrete, although the music blaring from the house as the post-game party gets started is loud enough to rattle the windows.

I shift, preparing to slide out the passenger side door, when he holds onto me. "Listen," he says, peppering my throat with kisses. "We can go inside, talk to everyone, play a few games, listen to Reid's shitty DJ'ing, and then go upstairs and fuck, *or,* and hear me out," his fingers are back on my tits, toying with the nipple, "we fuck right now."

There's really no choice.

"Now," I tell him, my body completely on the edge. "Fuck me now."

He adjusts the seat and reaches over, dragging me onto his lap. His hands are hard and strong, greedy, and everything about this feels so fucking right. This whole day has been tinged with emotions. The highs and lows of the game. The weight of dating Axel and not just being some puck bunny waiting in the wings. I'm flush with energy, nerves, and *adrenaline.* All of it has combined into something combustible that needs a release.

I kiss him under the hard line of his jaw and loosen his tie and button down, while his strong hands push down my leggings.

"Christ," he grunts, realizing I'm not wearing panties. "Okay, maybe it's a good thing I didn't know you were up there like this or I would've let in more goals."

"You're the one that said bare," I remind him, rising up. It spurs him into action, unfastening his pants and pushing them down. He brings us together, two bodies aligned and I feel him swell between my legs. "We made a deal, I'm just holding up my end of it."

"Such a good girl." He pinches my ass and I rock into him, letting our sticky heat build. The car is dark, but there's enough light coming off the back porch that I can see him watching me. I still have the jersey on, and something tells me he wants me to keep it that way. Even so, I feel wildly exposed, but I also can't seem to care. Axel's body is a masterpiece, the hard cut muscle and all the tattoos. There's a post-game, frenetic energy running through him. It's addictive. *He's* addictive and I can't seem to get enough.

Kissing me, his arm shoots out behind him, grappling to open the glove compartment door. Yanking out a string of condoms, he tears one off while I stroke his length. He hums, when I rub my thumb over the slippery tip. "Darlin' slow down unless you want me to blow before I get inside."

I pull back, watching him roll the rubber down and he lifts me up, slotting us together. "Ready?" he asks, his green eyes holding mine. I nod, bracing myself for the feel of him. His cock is an invasion, thick and hard. I exhale, letting myself adjust to his size. "You good?" he asks, kissing my mouth, my neck. "Talk to me, T."

"I'm good," I tell him. So good. Better than ever before. The car is hot, sweaty, our breath taking up all the air. He fills me up, meeting me thrust for thrust, letting our bodies provide the friction needed to set me loose. His head dips, and he pushes the shirt up, taking my nipple into his mouth. He sucks hard, tongue lathing over the tip, and my head falls back as the jolt of ecstasy slams into me.

I ride him hard, spiraling out, until his movements grow erratic, his breath shifting to a groan. Axel's arms wrap around my body, holding me tight, and he whispers, "I've never felt so close to someone before," seconds before every muscle in his body constricts, and he comes in hard, unrelenting thrusts. My pussy milks him, clenching against his length, wanting every last drop.

His face drops into the curve of my neck, chest to chest, our hearts pound hard against one another. The way he holds me, the way he doesn't rush to move, to pull out and leave, makes me understand what it's like to be in his line of vision. The thing Axel Rakestraw wants.

This feeling? I'll take it as long as he's willing to give it to me.

18

Axel

"Nervous?"

"Yes." I swallow past the lump in my throat. "I've never done this before."

"You can do it, darlin'. Just take a deep breath. Everything's going to be okay."

I sound confident, but I don't admit that I'm nervous in my own right.

What we're about to do is a first for me, too.

I've never had a girl sleep over that I wanted to come back again.

A girl who makes my heart feel like it's about to explode out of my chest.

A girl that, every time I touch her, fuck her, laugh with her, I only want more.

So yeah, this is new to me too.

"Time to rip off the Band-Aid." I take her hand and push open my bedroom door, leading her to the hall. The scent of eggs and bacon waft up the stairs, followed by my roommates' voices. "I promise you, the guys will be so focused on food they'll hardly notice you're there."

"It's not the guys I'm worried about," she mutters, fingers tightening around mine.

Sure enough, when we get downstairs, it's not just my roommates in the kitchen. Twyler is there too.

"They emerge!" Jefferson says, lifting his cup of coffee. His black hair is a complete mess and there's a huge hickey on his neck. "You two sure vanished fast last night."

I pull Nadia into my side and loop my arm over her shoulders. "It's not as fun as you think to hang around a bunch of drunk assholes when you're sober."

"So, still staying clean, huh?" Reid asks.

I look down at Nadia and smile. "I've found something better than getting high."

She blushes and I kiss her forehead. Yeah, I'm going all in. When have I not?

"Thought maybe you'd pull a Twyler, Nadia," Jefferson cocks a grin at Reese. "You know, abscond before daylight."

"*That* was different," Reese says, pushing scrambled eggs around the pan with a hot pink spatula. "We weren't official yet."

Reid flips a pancake onto the plate. "Don't worry, I figured the smell of bacon would lure you two downstairs. We made enough for everyone."

"Thanks, Reid," Nadia says, and I'm briefly reminded that these two went on a date. She doesn't linger over him though, and eyes the huge platter of eggs and bacon Reese sets on the table, followed by the pancakes. "This is impressive."

"After a win like that, we celebrate."

"What do you contribute?" she asks.

"Ha!" Reese shouts. "Busted."

"I've got one job, darlin' and that's keeping the goals out of the net."

"I see your no shirt policy is still in effect despite having a guest,"

Twyler says, shaking her head at my bare torso. Nadia and Twyler share a smile, and I feel my girl's muscles loosen just a bit.

Good. This is good.

"Is my body too much for you, TG?" I ask, grabbing two forks and handing one to Nadia. "A reminder that Cain needs to hit the gym a little more often?"

"This isn't about muscles," Reese says, taking a stack of plates out of the pantry. "It's about common decency and hygiene."

"No one wants your armpit hairs in the food, dumbass," Jefferson says, although he's in a shirt with the sleeves cut out, which seems like just as much of a hazard. "Yo, Reid, where's Darla?"

"I know this will come as a shock but..." he starts making the three of us guys groan, "we broke up."

"Big surprise," Jefferson says.

"Again?" Twyler asks. "What did you do this time?"

"Nothing." He shrugs, then admits. "She's really critical of my post game fits."

"You mean those outfits that look like you're color blind and only shop at rummage sales."

"They're unique," he argues. "Classic. And I'm building a brand, something she–and obviously you–can't appreciate."

"Well, I like her," Nadia says. "She seemed really organized at Friendsgiving."

"Oh yeah," Reid says, "she's kind of..."

"She's uptight, man. Call it what it is," Jeff says, gesturing to the girls. "Go ahead and get some food first. Otherwise there will be nothing left."

I release Nadia so she can go fill her plate and watch as she and Twyler fall into conversation. They each grab a glass of juice and head to the living room.

"Breakfast with the roommates," Reese says, piling eggs on his plate and then handing me the spoon. "You guys are making it official."

"If that's the standard, then yeah, I guess so."

"I can't believe you're not going to hit up sorority row with me anymore," Jefferson complains. "Bridget and Heather were pushing for that foursome."

"Sorry, dude." I grin, not the least bit sorry at all. "I see your hairy balls enough in the locker room."

He scowls. "You know I do better with a wingman."

"I can be your wingman," Reid offers. "Now that I'm single."

"Please. I'm not falling for that again. You and Darla will be back together before the weekend."

"Not this time." Reid grabs a stack of pancakes with his fingers. "We're done. I can feel it."

With full plates, Reese and I walk away from the guys who have started to make plans for the following weekend. The girls sit opposite of one another, saving us seats. "I wasn't sure how this would go over," he says, nodding at Twyler, "but I can tell she's happy to have her friend around. Twy can handle being around guys more than most women, but occasionally it's a little too much of a sausage fest around here."

"I think Nadia's glad to have her around too."

"This just means if you fuck it up," he picks up a piece of bacon and pops it in his mouth, "you're going to have to deal with her."

～

WINTER BREAK STARTS in ten days.

I've got exams, multiple games, and a sermon to finish for my father.

The only thing I really want is to be with Nadia. That girl has a grip on both my heart and my balls. I can't get enough.

I legit want to follow her around like one of those pussywhipped guys desperate for another minute in her presence. I've spent every night with her this week, under the guise of getting some of this work done and all I've managed is to give *and have* multiple orgasms.

I'm a mess, behind on all my obligations, and that's why I've isolated myself in the athletic tutoring room on campus. It's quiet. No interruptions.

I stare down at the unfinished sermon and the bullshit topic my father picked out. It's not the first time I've spoken in front of the church. Shelby and I were raised to be part of the show, but even with making my visits fewer and farther in between, he's escalating my involvement. Before I left for college, we'd just read a few passages, light some candles, join in the ceremony of it all. Shelby's role hasn't changed much–women in my father's church are there to serve and support. But a son like me? The Heir to the Kingdom... my role is more complex. More of a leader. Not *the* leader mind you. That position is filled.

My phone buzzes and I reach for the distraction in relief.

Nadia: How's it going?

GoalieGod: Finished my paper for Communications and took notes for public speaking.

Nadia: And the rest?

She knows I'm struggling with this assignment from my father.

GoalieGod: Can staring at a blank screen for too long cause blindness?

Nadia: I'm grabbing some food before work. Need anything?

GoalieGod: Just ten minutes with you.

Nadia: I can probably accommodate that.

GoalieGod: And maybe a taco from the food truck?

I follow up with a text about being in the student center, room 110 and about fifteen minutes later I hear a tap on the door. It's locked from the outside, only accessible with a code, and when I open it, she's standing outside with a bag full of tacos and a smile.

"You found me," I say, taking the bag in one hand and pulling her in with the other.

"This is the athletic study room?" She looks around at the set up. It's nice. I won't deny it. New computers, comfortable desks. A couch and big screen. "I always knew you guys were spoiled, but this kind of takes the cake."

"Spoiled seems like overkill."

"Babe, the rest of us have to sign up to use the new technology, have to fight for comfortable seating, and if we're lucky the guy next to us isn't coughing and sneezing the whole time. Spoiled is the perfect word to describe this set up."

"Fine," I say, dropping the greasy bag on the table next to my notes, "we're spoiled."

Leaning on the edge of the table, I grab her hips and pull her into the hollow between my legs. "I missed you."

"It's been four hours."

"Yeah, tell my cock that," I say, pushing my hips into her playfully. "He's been thinking about you all day."

"You're ridiculous." Her hand runs up my chest and curls around my neck, where her fingers prod into my skin. "And super tense."

I tilt my neck, letting her fingers explore. "It's this stupid sermon. It's always a nightmare, but this year it seems worse."

"I thought you already had some written?"

"I did, but then I ditched everything I showed my dad at Thanksgiving. It just didn't feel right."

"What do you mean?"

My instinct is to shrug off her question, but Nadia's looking at me with genuine interest and concern and for once I want to tell someone–*tell her*. "It's hard to explain," I start, taking her hand and threading her fingers in mine. "Even to myself, really. I've always played by my father's rules: living my life up here at Wittmore, while fulfilling any obligations he has for me back home. But something's different now. Maybe it's the fact I'm graduating soon and I know I'll be sucked into that life forever. Or maybe it's the promise ring Shelby accepted at Thanksgiving, locking her into something when she's too young to make the decision." I shake my head, hating that her life is mapped out even more than mine. "Everything used to feel so far away, but now... it seems too close."

"Have you talked to him about it?"

I laugh. "There's no talking to the Reverend about anything. This isn't just a plan, T, in his mind this is destiny. My whole life, even him allowing hockey and tattoos, fuck," I run my hand through my hair, "probably even the women, is all about me coming ultimately home standing next to him."

Nadia looks away. "That's a lot of pressure."

Sliding my fingers under her chin, I force her gaze back at me. "It's even worse now because we're just getting started and I sure as fuck don't want to let you go."

I kiss her, wanting to feel the warm heat of her lips on mine, loving the way she opens up for me. Her hands dip under my shirt, fingers cool against my hot skin. "Your hands are so soft," I tell her, licking my way into her mouth. She responds, by spreading her fingers across my abdomen, toying with the trail of hair, leading under my waistband. I hum at her touch, stomach caving, while my cock tries to drill it's way through the denim of my jeans. I pull back, sucking in a gasp of air and press my forehead against hers. "I asked you here for tacos, not a makeout-shesh."

"Making out is good for releasing stress," she says, thumb releasing the button on my jeans. I feel her hand push under the waistband, beneath the cotton of my boxers, and she wraps her hand around my erection. "And don't tell me you're not horny."

"I'm always horny for you." She jacks me up and down, making a shudder run down my spine. I fall back in my seat and look up at her. "Jesus, girl, trying to kill me?"

She grins. "I just want to make you feel good."

"You always make me feel good." I'm brain addled, horny as fuck, and reach for her to drag her into my lap. Instead, she drops to her knees. Yeah, that snaps me back. "Nad, come on, get back up."

"No."

My jaw sets and a war strikes out between my brain and body. I haven't pushed her for anything like this. No blowjobs, no titty-fucks, nothing that could even be slightly perceived as taking advantage. She's had enough of that for a lifetime.

But hell, I want to see, *and feel,* her pretty lips take me in.

"Ax, this is what we do for one another. We take care of each other and right now I want to take care of you."

I swallow and touch her chin, running my thumb over her plump bottom lip. I cock an eyebrow. "Safe space, huh?"

"For both of us."

That's when it hits me that there's a difference here. This is on Nadia's terms and I need to acknowledge that. Settling back in my chair, I skim my fingers over her cheek, as she reaches for me, running her hands over my abdomen, feeling my muscles before she goes lower, grazing my engorged shaft. She moves closer, inching between my legs. She grips me by the base and bends, tongue darting out and licking the tip, teasing me before pulling back.

"Fuck," I whisper, trying to control the rise of my hips. "I knew you were trouble."

She looks up at me with those big brown eyes and says, "I love your cock," before making a sweet circle with those pretty lips and taking me in.

I groan at the feel of her covering me in wet, slick, warmth. Look, all blow-jobs feel pretty fantastic, but this one is enhanced by the stirring in my gut, the pulsing of my heart. The girl kneeling before me. *Everything* Nadia does is better.

Best.

It quickly becomes clear that my girl isn't a novice, that shit's for sure. A lot of guys would get weird about it, but I like her experience. There's no hesitation when she takes me in deep, tongue running over the ridge while she hums. She's got me panting, desperate to thrust. I push my hands into her hair, trying to control myself.

"Darlin'," I say, fisting her hair, "you take my cock so good."

"Mmmm," she hums.

"You gonna let me fuck your face?"

She looks up at me, chest heaving, her nipples hard and pressed into the fabric of her sweater. Her mouth is shiny, red, when she utters, "Please."

Pushing off the chair, I stand before her, accentuating the ache. Cupping the back of her head, I hold her in place, hips rocking in an erratic rhythm. "You're the fucking best," I encourage her, but then she cups my balls and white flashes in front of my eyes. Just when I think she can't take me deeper, I hit the back of her throat with a punch. "Fucking hell."

The surge roars, pounding in my ears, my heart, my balls. "I'm close," I warn, pushing her off with one hand, while scrambling for my hoodie tossed on the back of the other chair with another. "Back up."

"No." She grabs for me, sucking me back between her lips. She clamps down and runs her fingers over my balls and that sends me into orbit. I cum hard, and *a lot*, my balls seizing up and emptying. I keep an eye on her to make sure it's not too much. She doesn't just take it, she wants it, looking up at me with those sweet eyes while she sucks me off until there's nothing left.

Emptied and loose-limbed, I help her off the ground and wrap my arms around her, holding her close.

"That was fucking epic." I kiss the top of her head. "Way better than an epic-fuck up. And I hate to tell you, but now that I know you can do that, I'm going to badger the hell out of you to suck me off constantly."

"Good," she says, cheek against my chest. "I'm relieved. That's the first time I, you know..."

I frown, confused. "You what?"

"Swallowed. I was afraid I'd panic at the last minute."

I tilt her face upward. "You've never swallowed before?"

She shakes her head. "I was under so much pressure, I always gagged. The..." she inhales, "the other guys didn't seem to care as long as they got off."

My heart skitters–partly from wanting to chase down those assholes and pick them off, one by one, for ever making this woman doubt herself. The other part? It feels so fucking good that she trusts me like this. That she wants more from me.

"Thank you for giving me that." I brush my lips over hers. "I know being vulnerable isn't easy for you."

It was more than that, but I have no fucking idea how to articulate it. She curls into me and her hand flattens against my chest, and I know for sure she can feel how hard it's beating–I just wonder if she knows how hard it beats for her.

19

Nadia

THE CREDITS RUN on the latest episode of Springfield and I sigh in annoyance. "You know, Jane really is a dumbass for trusting Rich like that."

"Mmhmm," I tilt my head to look at Axel, and see that his eyes have fluttered shut. "Total dumbass."

"Axe," I say, shutting the laptop and setting it on the floor.

"Yeah, darlin'?" He rolls into me and shoves his hand in between my thighs, his preferred sleeping position.

"I think you need to sleep." I kiss his chin. "And I didn't plan on spending the night and don't have any of my stuff with me, so I'm going to head back to the Teal House."

His eyelids pop open. "Fuck no, you're not walking back by yourself this late."

I hadn't come over until nine, after my shift at the gym. He also had a late night at the arena, first on the ice, then watching film with the team. This weekend is their final game before the winter break–against their rival, Milton. Who, from what I understand, is the team they lost to in the championship last season.

"It's just a couple of blocks."

"I know how far it is, and I'm not comfortable with my girl walking back by herself." He covers a yawn with his fist. "I can either get up and walk you back or you can stay over. You pick."

He's naked in nothing but a pair of boxer briefs, his warm skin flush against my body. The idea of leaving is hard, but clean pajamas are the least of my concerns. My period started that morning and I've got one of those unrelenting heavy flows for the first twenty-four hours. I need supplies. Looking down at him, his eyes are already shut, sleep taking over. I brush this hair off his forehead. "I'll be back."

His grip tightens. "Where are you going?"

"Girl stuff," I say. "Let me see if Twy can help."

"Okay." He reluctantly releases me. "But don't leave without me, got it?"

Cocky fuckboy Axel is super hot, but protective boyfriend Axel? I'm about to melt from the inside out.

"I won't," I reply, easing off the bed. I grab his hockey hoodie and pull it over my head, before opening the bedroom door. When I glance back, he's already fast asleep.

I cross the narrow hall and pause outside of Reese's door, listening to see if they're quiet, maybe already asleep. If they're awake… I'm listening for a sign I shouldn't interrupt.

Twyler and I are still navigating this new arrangement, one she has originally been vehemently against. I understood her concerns. Even before the situation with Brent and CJ, I'd been getting into increasingly risky situations. I'd get on the dating apps and agree to meet up with guys on the football team in the middle of the night. I took no precautions. It was dangerous and dumb, trying to work my way in as a jersey chaser. All it did was get me in trouble and she didn't want that trouble messing with the hockey team.

But my relationship isn't about late night hook-ups or trying to elevate my status. It's about being with this amazing guy who has taken the time to get to know me.

Reese's room sounds quiet other than the soft murmur of a video playing. Knowing Twyler they're watching murder shows and there's nothing unsexier than that. I knock, rapping my knuckles on the door. A moment later it opens a crack and a shirtless Reese Cain fills the gap. "What–oh." His eyes widen, and his hand drops down below the waist. Is he naked? "Hey."

I look at the wall next to his face. "Can I talk to Twy for a second?"

"Yeah, sure." He clears his throat and glances back. "It's for you."

I hear the rustle of bedsheets and realize this was a terrible idea. Twyler and I are best friends and I've always been pretty open about my sex life, but she's much more private. I've probably just crossed a million lines and any progress we'd made about this situation is most likely ruined.

Reese vanishes and a moment later Twyler takes his place. Her forehead is furrowed. "Are you okay? What's wrong?"

Her immediate concern is both unnecessary and a little jarring. Just because I'm knocking on her boyfriend's door doesn't mean something's wrong.

"Nothing's wrong," I say. "I just... do you have any tampons?"

"Oh, uh, sure." She turns away and I hear her tell Reese she'll be back in a minute. She steps into the hallway and shuts the door behind her. "I left my backpack downstairs."

"Great." I give her the once over, noting the black hoodie identical to the one I'm wearing. The only difference is the number stitched on the chest and her legs are bare while I'm wearing leggings. "Looks like we match."

"It's so weird," she mutters, heading down the stairs. "You know that, right?"

"That we're both sleeping with hockey players who happen to be best friends?"

She looks at me over her shoulder. "There's that, but I mean, it makes a lot more sense that you're here than I am."

"Is it?" I ask. "You're surrounded by athletes twenty-four-seven. It makes way more sense than me being here. I didn't even care about hockey."

"Yeah, but you're the kind of girl they like. You make sense here." She nods at the hoodie. "That shirt looks like it was made for you." She tugs at the hem of Reese's oversized shirt that swamps her small frame. "I'm pretty sure most of them still think of me as a brother."

"Does it matter as long as Reese doesn't?" I follow her over to the couch where her backpack sits on the floor. "Because you're definitely the kind of girl he likes. *A lot.*"

"True." Her cheeks turn pink at the compliment and even though I know Twyler carries her own insecurities, Reese has made it perfectly clear how much he loves her. There's no reason for her to question herself. "Sometimes I still feel like I'm in a bizarro world."

She unzips the pocket on the side, pulling out a couple of tampons and handing them over. "Thanks, you're a lifesaver. I came straight from work and didn't plan on spending the night. We started watching a show and it got late. Axel didn't want me walking back alone."

She makes a face.

"What?" I ask.

"That was very gentlemanly of him."

"He's a preacher's kid from Texas, I think it's programmed into his DNA."

"But, and tell me if I'm understanding this correctly," her eyebrow cocks, "you're spending the night here and *not* having sex."

"You're understanding it correctly."

"Wow." She sinks into the couch.

I narrow my eyes at her. "What are you going on about?"

"I just didn't know he did that. Had girls sleep over without hooking up." She makes an apologetic face. "Not to be a bitch, but I've spent a lot of nights here, and for most of them, he wasn't here. And for the few that he was, and he wasn't alone, it was pretty obvious that no one was sleeping."

I sit next to her. "Well, if that blows your mind, then you'll be even more surprised to find out that we've been hanging out for weeks, spending the night with one another here and there, and only just started having sex."

Her expression seems genuinely shocked. "You're kidding."

"Nope. I didn't even give him a blow job until yesterday." I've thought about it all day, how sweet he was when I got on my knees, how he let me take control. I loved the way he gazed down at me when I kissed him for the first time, tasting the salty pre-cum on the tip. But the best part was when he came, completely lost. I felt powerful. "Although he did eat me out in the laundry room before Thanksgiving."

Her eyes dart to the laundry room. "Okay that sounds more on brand, for both of you."

"We've taken this slower than you'd think. Like, actually getting to know one another." I glance over at my friend. "I like him, Twy, a lot."

"And you're okay not knowing where this is going? Because Reese says he's been pretty adamant about not going pro."

"I'm well aware of his family obligations." I pull the cuffs of the hoodie over my hands. "I've never had a long term boyfriend before and I don't think he's ever dated anyone seriously. We've agreed to take it day by day and we'll see where we are at around graduation."

I can tell she wants to ask a million more questions, but this is where Twyler and I are different. She's had her life planned out for ages and the biggest struggle for her and Reese was coming up with a compromise on those goals. Now that they are, they're happier, and more focused, than ever.

For the first time in my life, I'm happy *now*. I'm not going to ruin it by worrying about tomorrow.

"Come on." I stand and hold up the tampons. "I need to go take care of this and get some sleep."

We're halfway up the stairs when she suddenly stops and faces me. "Other than the laundry room, are there any other public places I need to disinfect?"

I laugh, there's no hiding that Twyler thinks I'm messy. "No. We've been hooking up in our rooms, well," I think on it, "and his truck."

"Okay," she starts climbing, "good."

"Well, there was yesterday, but that's not anywhere you need to worry about."

"Where's that?" She makes a face. "Or do I not want to know."

"On campus. The tutoring room."

Her eyebrows shoot up. "Room 110?"

I snort. "Yep."

"That son of a—" She lunges forward, taking the remaining stairs two at a time. "That's where I gave him a blow job for the first time, too!"

I hold back a laugh, and race after her, but she's already flung open the door to Reese's bedroom. Inside, he sits up on the bed, still shirtless but wearing shorts. His expression turns wary when he sees his girlfriend's face.

"Is this a thing you guys do?" she blurts, before he can speak. "Some kind of bet?"

"Woah, Sunshine," he looks over her head at me and I shrug. "What the hell are you talking about?"

"Room 110!"

Reese grimaces, walks over, and as he shuts the door in my face I hear him say, "Twy, calm down."

Axel's bedroom door opens and he walks over, rubbing his head. His hair sticks up all over and he wraps his arms around me. "What's she losing her mind about?"

"Room 110. Apparently, we're not the only ones that hooked up in there." I lean into his warm body. "Did you know that?"

"Honestly, no." He scratches my back. "You're the first girl I've met up with there, and I can promise you that you'll definitely be the last."

"Why's that?"

"I want that memory seared in my mind forever." He pushes the hood aside on his sweatshirt and licks a spot on my shoulder. "Completely untainted by anything or anyone else."

This man.

Voices rise behind Reese's door. "Should we go tell them?" I ask. "Let them know it seems like an unfortunate coincidence?"

"Eh, a fight is good for those two." He nudges me back into his room. "The make up sex will be worth it."

∼

IF THERE'S a measure to test if my Blacklisting still stands, it's my communications class. The same cloak of silence exists between me and the varsity athletes Brent told to ice me out. A few weeks ago their approval had seemed so important. Their rejection had felt so painful. Now, I'm embarrassed I ever wanted validation from these guys.

It feels like a clear indicator that I've left that toxic part of my life behind.

Brent can have me ostracized all he wants. But what I've come to realize is that I don't need these guys or acceptance by any exclusive group on campus. I've got an amazing best friend, and the sexiest, most supportive boyfriend.

I'm good. Really good.

"In conclusion," Austin says from the front of the class. Rocky, his partner, stands next to him. "That's why we think student athletes should receive a salary from the University, like any other employee."

Rocky nods, throwing up a fist in support.

"Thank you," our professor says. "That was a very persuasive presentation."

I blink, wondering how this educator manages to live with supporting such bullshit. The past five minutes were painful to witness. Rocky ad-libbed his part, and Austin didn't even make the effort to remove his headphones. By the smug grins on their face, it's clear that they think they hit this one out of the ballpark, and I'm sure they'll be getting another 'A' to add to their transcript.

Austin has to pass me on the way back to his seat, and his massive thigh slams into the side of my desk. The action is jarring–my laptop jolting.

"My bad," he says with a smirk.

I open my mouth to say something back but shut it. He's not worth it.

Although, that doesn't keep the person next to me from muttering, "Asshole," under his breath.

I'm certain I'm the only one that can hear Eric's insult, and I give him a grateful smile as he adjusts my laptop back to the middle of my desk.

Our professor, oblivious to anything going on, approaches the lectern. "Those were very compelling presentations today." I seriously wonder how much extra he gets paid to ignore his integrity to babysit these morons and give them a passing grade. I hope it's a lot. "The final groups will present at the next class."

We're dismissed and Eric hangs back. "At least we know the bar for a good grade isn't set too high." He watches as the rest of the class files out. "That last one wasn't even coherent."

It seems, like me, Eric realized he's never going to work his way into that group on anything more than a superficial level, and I guess he'd rather get an A on our project than kiss jock ass.

"Yeah we should have this one in the bag," I agree, tucking my stuff into my backpack. "Do you want to practice one more time?"

He makes a face. "Not really."

"Same." I sling the strap over my shoulder. "I'm ready to move on from this class."

"So listen," he says on the way out of the room, "my frat is having a New Year's Eve party after the break if you're back early. I wanted to invite you."

"Are you sure about that? You saw what happened in there. I'm still pretty much a pariah on campus."

"I think everyone, but those Neanderthals have moved past that."

"You think so?"

He nods. "Seriously. No one else cares."

Axel has a game on Saturday and neither of us have been going out much, but it may be fun to blow off some end of semester steam. "Okay, I'll think about it," I say, then add, "you know this is just as friends, right? I'm seeing someone."

"I don't know. I think we're a little more than friends," he says, taking me by surprise. "We're survivors of Communications 204. Never doubt the way it's bonded us."

I laugh. "Seriously. We may need a T-shirt."

"Bring your boyfriend," he says. "Rakestraw, right?"

My heart flip-flops just at hearing his name. "Right."

"Just make sure you wear something red or green–that's the theme."

"Sounds fun. We'll try to make it." I look at my watch. "Shit, I gotta run. I have a shift at work."

Running late is kind of my thing, but I manage to make through the doors right as my shift starts. "Hey," I say to Brian who is already working behind the counter. "Is Abby here?"

"Nope. She had a meeting of some kind so you're in the clear."

"I'm right on time." I take off my jacket and then Axel's hoodie, to reveal my work shirt. "Although, I had to cut through the student center instead of going around it." I grin. "Saved me five minutes."

"Unfortunately, all you're on time for is to go handle a mess someone reported in the spin room." He holds up a bucket filled with cleaners and rags. "Good luck."

I wrinkle my nose. In a gym, a 'mess' could be anything from spilled water to vomit. Especially after a hard class.

Taking the bucket, I head to the back of the gym, to the room used for spin. There's no class right now so the lights are off and I push through the unlocked door. Sometimes people come in here and work on their own, but it's empty.

Or I think it is, until I see the shadow of someone leaning against the instructor's bike.

"Holy shit," I exclaim, heart thudding in my ears. "Brent? What the hell are you doing here?"

"I came to see you."

"I don't know why." I look around the room searching for a mess.

It strikes me then, that there is no mess. This was just a way to get me alone. "We have nothing to talk about."

"I've given you space and time to think about our last conversation." He straightens and walks toward me. "Now that the football season is over, it's time to get serious."

"Look, you had me blacklisted. None of the football, basketball, or baseball teams will acknowledge me. I haven't been to a party on Greek Row in months. And that's fine. I accept it. I've held up to my end of the deal–not going to the police and you need to hold up to yours by leaving me the fuck alone."

His eyebrow arches. "Impressive speech–how long have you been practicing that?"

"God, you're infuriating. None of this is happening, Brent. It's not like you need the money. And I know you were helping CJ out before but come on, you and I both know making money off of me on LonelyFans isn't going to help him in the long run." I take a step back. "I have no fucking clue why you're so obsessed with it."

Then it hits me. Maybe, after all this time I was wrong about how Brent felt about me. I thought he saw me as a piece of trash to be used and tossed away, handed over to his friends, but now... God. What if I was reading this wrong the whole time? Maybe Brent isn't obsessed with exploiting me. Maybe he's just obsessed *with me*.

My reaction is to blurt, "I have a boyfriend."

"Rakestraw?" He cuts his eyes at me. "You realize that out of every man on this campus, he's the one that knew what you were capable of." He crowds me against one of the bikes. "He knows exactly how slutty and desperate you are. You think he didn't want a taste of that for himself?"

"That's not true."

"No?" He scoffs. "How long did it take for you to fuck him? One date?"

The memory of our first night together comes back. The epic fuck-up.

As if he's reading my mind, he chokes out a laugh. "Less? A one-night stand? God, you're more pathetic than I realized." I can't come up with the words to defend myself, so he just continues to pick apart my life. "Let me guess, after that, he agreed to go slow. Take his time with you because of everything you've been through." His grin is wide and mean. "He got you to trust him, didn't he?"

"You don't know anything about my relationship with Axel."

"But that's the thing, Nadia, I do. I know him, because I *am* him, and he's me. We're all the same, testosterone-fueled alpha males who want the one thing we can't have."

"You could have had me," I whisper. "I would have done anything."

I *did* do anything and that's the whole problem.

"You still don't get it, do you?" He leans toward me, mouth close to my ear. "You're the forbidden fruit. The vixen who will play out in our every fantasy. You're the one we want to fuck. To secret away and keep for our own. But you're also the one that won't make it past our PR teams, or get parental approval. They want the girl next door. A woman that knows how to smile and say the right thing to the press. That have perfected how to look on the sidelines, or wearing a pristine white dress as they lock us into marriage. They glow while carrying our babies. Those women convince the world that we're the All-American heroes worthy of the millions they pay us to lead their team–their city–to victory." His fingers graze down my arm as he describes his current girlfriend, Shanna. "But they don't ignite the hunger in us that a woman like you does. They don't make me hard with only a dirty, secret, look. Or the knowledge that you'll let me do whatever I want, whenever I want, for as long as I want. It's not that we don't want you, baby, it's that we want you too fucking much."

Somewhere during his speech I've become frozen. My breath trapped deep in my throat. He takes advantage of my silence and adds, "Before you think that your boyfriend is different, let me explain it to you. There is no future for you with Axel Rakestraw regardless of if he goes to the NHL or heads into the family business." He nods when I startle. "Yeah, I know all about Daddy Rakestraw and his multi-million dollar religious Kingdom. Axel is the heir and those people will *never* accept a piece of trash like you." He presses his hips into me, forcing the hard line of his erection into my lower belly. "You're better off working for me, than being nothing at all."

I recoil at his touch and snap into motion, shoving him back with both hands.

"Talk to me again, I'm going to the police."

The grin he responds with tells me he doesn't believe that I have the guts to do it.

That makes two of us.

20

Axel

"Where is she?" I push past Twyler and enter the Teal House, eyes scanning the small living room.

"In her room." Twyler's little legs follow behind me. "I can't get her to come out."

I rap on the bedroom door. "T, it's me." I try the knob, but it's locked. "Can I come in?"

"No." Her voice is muffled, but I can tell she's crying. "Go away. And tell Twyler to go away too."

Ouch.

"What the hell happened?" I ask Twyler. I'd been sitting in my tattooist's chair, getting a few new pieces of ink, when Twyler texted telling me to get over to her house right away. After a few more back and forths and all I knew was Nadia was upset and locked in her room.

"She came home from work early, obviously freaked out about

something, and ran into her room. She won't talk to me or let me in." She wraps her arms around her upper body. "I'm scared, Ax, this isn't like her."

I run my hand through my hair, agitated and trying to figure out what to do. I'd already tried texting her and now I'm locked out. Logic tells me to give her some space and let her come to me when she's ready.

I'm not really one for logic.

"Did she look hurt?" A million different scenarios ran through my mind on the way over. But one lingered the most and I ask through a clenched jaw, "Drugged or anything?"

"No." Then she reconsiders. "I don't know. She didn't give me much time to notice anything other than her crying." Decision made, I spin and start toward the front door. "You're leaving?"

"No. Just using an alternate entrance." I give her a look that I know I'll pay for later. "Stay here."

I walk around the side of the house, taking the same route I have several times now. I always feel like a creeper coming and going this way but she's the one that kicked me out after our first night together. Her curtains are drawn and part of me hopes the window is locked because my girl needs to stay safe, but when I nudge at the glass, it opens. Not great, but I'll take it.

I climb in and throw my leg over the window sill, knocking something with my foot. "Ow!"

Craning my neck, I see that she's sitting under the window in the small space between the bed and the wall. She's also rubbing her head. "Shit, sorry, T." I come the rest of the way in, taking care not to land on her. "What's going on?"

Without looking at me she says, "She shouldn't have called you."

"She should *always* call me when you're upset. You should too." I squat down in the narrow space. "Talk to me."

"There's nothing to say." She takes a deep breath and pulls her knees up, wrapping her arms around them. "You should go."

"Yeah, that's not going to happen." I sit, or try to. The space is small and my body doesn't want to cooperate, but I wedge myself with my back to the wall, and shove my feet under the bed. "Did I do something? Because sometimes I do stupid shit–"

"It's not you." She shakes her head and tightens her grip around her legs.

"Then talk to me, because I'm about to walk out of here and start breaking jaws until someone tells me why you're so upset."

She exhales, sounding tired. "I saw Brent."

Oh yeah, first jaw on the list.

"Did he touch you?" I touch her chin, focused on her eyes. I look for enlarged pupils–anything out of place. Her eyes are red from crying but otherwise they look clear.

"No. Not really." She turns away. "He just told me the truth."

I can't even imagine the bullshit that guy is spewing. With trepidation, I ask, "What's the truth?"

"That I'm the kind of girl men like him want, but can't have. Not in any official capacity." She looks down, eyelashes wet. "I'm a sidepiece. A mistress at best. Used for pleasure and because we're weak. Apparently, I'm not the kind of girl that they want to marry or have babies with, I'm just there to be used."

That fucker hit her square in her insecurities. The stuff we'd spent so much time working through. In the steadiest voice I can muster, I say, "You know Reynold's is an asshole who gets off on being a dick and you shouldn't listen to a fucking word he says." Then a thought strikes me and a painful sensation spreads through my chest. "Is that what you want from him? Marriage and babies? Do you still want him?"

"God no." She shifts away, closing her eyes and leaning her head against the bed. "It's not that..."

"Then what is this about?" I spread my hand over my chest and rub against the ache. I don't like how this makes me feel. How talking about this sets me on edge, feeling out of control. "Because yeah, hearing him say that has to hurt, but if you're not with him, why the fuck does it matter?"

"He said it's what *all men* like him want." Her eyes open, pained brown meeting mine. "Men like you. Athletes. Leaders."

I understand it now. Brent Reynolds has a death wish.

"Darlin', Reynolds is a selfish prick. He doesn't know shit about me and what I want." I reach for her, sliding my arms around her waist, and pulling her onto my lap. She struggles, but it's weak, and wrap my arms tight around her body, holding her against my chest. Inhaling her scent, I just know I want her close. I want her to feel me, to understand that I'm not letting her go. "He's a bully and it's probably driving him fucking crazy that he can't have you."

"He told me it didn't matter if you go to the NHL or go back home to work for your father. I won't be accepted by either."

I'm going to kill him. I may actually do it, but not until I make it perfectly clear to my girl, that I'm not going anywhere.

"If there's one thing you should know about me by now, is that I don't give a shit about what other people say or think about me. Not outside of my coach, teammates, my sister, and you–but mostly you."

I don't know how to tell her about the war inside of me about my future. Following my dream or fulfilling my obligation to my family. "I don't feel right dragging anyone into the complicated decision I have to make in the next few months, which is why I've been wary to commit longer than the next few months. It's not something either of us should take lightly." I lift her chin, looking her in the eye. "But I need you to understand, that whatever happens in my future, I want you with me."

"Yeah?" A small smile tugs at her lips. "I want to be with you, too."

My heart pounds, harder than skating sprints across the ice. So hard, that it feels like it's lodged in my throat. I push past it and tell her, "I love you."

Her back straightens and she meets me eye to eye. "I love you too, Axel."

I kiss her, more gentle than I want, but I don't want to scare this girl away with how much I want her. Thankfully, Nadia meets me with the same intensity and it's not long before we're both squirming against one another and breathing hard.

"I don't know what the future holds, not yet, but we'll figure it out together, okay?"

"Okay."

I shift her so that I can stand, but then pull her with me up to the bed, lying her flat on her back. I hover over her, skimming my fingers down her face. "And if I haven't made it clear, any man would be goddamn lucky to have you walk down that aisle, gorgeous and ready to take their name." I run my hand down her body, flattening it over her belly. "To have you carry their babies."

I'm talking about myself, but I don't want to scare her off. Not yet. But one day I'm going convince her to marry me and give me a boat load of babies. One day. When we figure this all out. Tonight, I strip her down, pulling off her shirt and leggings. She's splayed before me, a goddamn vision.

"Jesus, you're beautiful," I tell her, grazing my finger over the lacey edge of her bra. She greedily pushes at the hem of my shirt. Lifting it over my head, her hands rake down my chest, stopping when she gets to the plastic bandage.

"This new?" she asks, fingering the edge. "Can I?"

I nod, nose wrinkling as she tugs the tape off my skin. "I was at the tattoo parlor when Twyler texted."

Her fingers carefully remove the adhesive, revealing the fresh tattoo. It's nothing major. Just another moment in time I want to preserve.

"Seriously?" she asks, staring at the ink. It's the number one-ten. "You commemorated the first blow job I gave you?"

"I want to remember every single moment with you." I pull aside the cup of her bra, revealing her nipple and tease it into a taut pebble. "Seeing you on your knees, taking me like that. All of me." I swallow back the emotion. "It was a big moment. That's the moment I knew you trusted me."

Her eyes shine up at me and I know what I see in them. Love. I know it because I feel it coursing through every pump of blood in my heart. I don't waste any more time, getting both of us fully naked, and slotting my cock against the warm, slick, heat between her legs. There's no time for teasing or any kind of foreplay. I just want to be inside. To feel her tighten around me. Thank god she's wet and ready.

Rocking my hips back, I'm about to thrust my way home when there's a knock on the door.

"Nadia," Twyler's voice carries through the door, "is everything okay?"

"Son of a bitch," I mutter, dropping my head to the crook of her shoulder and laugh darkly.

"I'm fine, Twy." Nadia clears her throat. "Axel's here."

My cock expands, nudging into her sweet pussy. It takes every ounce of control that I possess not to claim her when she says that. Unfortunately, Twyler is still outside to ruin the moment.

"Okay," her voice hesitates, then lifts an octave higher. "Tell Axel I'm not okay with him using our windows as an entrance and egress."

Nadia smiles up at me, aware that I'm about to lose my mind and blow my shot all at once.

"Never again," I call out, pushing in an inch deeper. I grunt. "Promise."

"Okay, thanks."

We both wait a beat longer, until it's clear that Twyler has moved away from the door. My cock throbs, and I can't hold back any longer, bringing us closer together by hiking her leg up over my hip and burying myself deep inside.

Perfection.

"Hey," I say, allowing her body a chance to adapt to the feel of me inside, "I love you."

Her fingers push through my hair, and she pulls my face down to hers. "I love you, too."

~

Taking one last look into the bedroom to confirm that Nadia is asleep, I carefully shut the door.

"Sneaking out?"

The voice is soft but deep. Familiar. None of that stops my heart from threatening to jump through my ribcage.

"Jesus Christ, Cap." I exhale slowly, trying to regain my wits as I take in Reese sprawled on the couch. "Scared the fuck out of me."

"Sorry," Reese says, but the smirk tugging at his mouth says otherwise.

"I didn't even know you were here."

"Not surprised," he says, rolling his eyes. "You two sounded... occupied."

It's my turn to smirk. "Jealous?"

"Not in the slightest." His laptop open and a notebook next to him. "I got here an hour or so ago, but I've got a final paper I haven't finished. Once Twy fell asleep, I figured I'd get it down."

I shrug my arms into the jacket I'm carrying. "Hey, next to last semester. We're almost done."

"Well, we've got classes to pass and a championship to win, so we're not done yet." He nods to the jacket. "What's going on?"

"Eh, just something I need to go deal with."

"At two AM?"

I tug up the zipper. "Actually, yeah. Can't wait."

He shuts the laptop, turning his full attention on me. Fuck. Reese is the last one that needs to get nosy about what I'm planning. I should've gone back out the window. "Does this have something to do with why Nadia was so upset earlier?"

I don't like lying to Reese. He's my friend and he's had my back through so much of the shit I've gone through recently. But there's a reason we jokingly call him Captain America. He's a good guy, and what I'm about to go do doesn't fall under his code.

"Brent's still messing with her," I say casually, "and I think it's time someone put a stop to it, once and for all."

"How?" he asks. "By going over to the quarterback's house and picking a fight?"

"You think I shouldn't?" I ask, feeling anger prick under my skin. "Why the hell not?"

"Because your ass just got off probation and he'll waste no time reporting you." His jaw tics. "You've worked too hard to fuck up now."

"Let him tell Coach. Or the cops or the NCAA. I don't give a shit. It'll be worth it to let him know that I'm not going to let him harass my girl." I shake my head. "*Ever again.*"

He sighs and runs both hands through his hair. "I understand the urge, man. I really do, but this isn't your fight, Axel."

I can't believe him. "You're saying you wouldn't do the same for Twyler?"

"Remember what happened when her ex was fucking with her at the bar that night?"

I do remember Reese cornering the pretentious little prick in the back hall of the bar, but I also know he left without laying a finger on him, instead going to find Twyler. The team escorted him out.

"So you're a better man than I am. That's not a surprise."

"I'm not better," he says, his tone darker than I've ever heard it. "I wanted to break his fingers off one by one. The shit he said to her that night was nothing compared to what he'd already done. But what Twyler needed, what *she needs*," he jerks his chin toward Nadia's bedroom door, "is you to be with her. Not kicking some prick's ass."

The two options war in my chest. The urge to show Brent Reynolds what it means to mess with the woman that I love. Or to do like Reese suggests, and get back into bed with her and keep her safe.

"Fuck man," I throw my hands in the air, "when the hell did you get so smart?"

"The day I realized what was really important." He stands, picking up the laptop and tucking it against his side. He walks over to Twyler's bedroom door. "These women don't need a hothead throwing punches. We do that every time we get on the ice–it's literally our job. But keeping calm, showing them we're using our brains instead of our impulses. It's fucking hard. But it's worth it."

He enters Twyler's room, leaving me alone. The move is intentional. He's letting me make the decision, because he knows that if I want to go out and chase Reynolds down, I will.

I also know that he's right.

Unzipping my jacket, I toss it on the back of the chair before going back into Nadia's room and climbing in her bed. Dragging her against my body, I breathe in her sweet scent. She's warm, soft.

But most of all, she's mine.

21

Nadia

WHEN I WALK OUT of my bedroom the next morning, Reese is sitting next to a shirtless Axel on the couch. "Hey," I say to Reese, "I didn't know you spent the night."

"I came over late," he says, picking up the box of Sugar Bomb cereal off the coffee table and refilling his bowl. He's in a pair of sports shorts and one of Twyler's oversized, threadbare New Kings T-shirts. He tilts the box at Axel. "Want more?"

"No, thanks. I think I've hit my sugar quota for the day." Axel's long arm swipes out and hooks around the back of my thighs, pulling me onto his lap. His chest is hard–warm–and I smooth out the edges of the adhesive covering his new tattoo. When he'd told me the real significance behind the number 110–about me trusting him–something unwound around my heart. "Sleep okay?"

"Really good." After the emotional talk Axel and I had, then the 'I love yous' and sex, we stayed up for a while, eating dinner and watching Springfield. Then I crashed. *Hard*. Not waking up again until my alarm went off.

"Excellent." He steals a kiss, brushing his lips over mine. He tastes like the sugar from the cereal. Sweet and delicious. God, I love this man.

Across the room, Twyler stands at the kitchen table, organizing her backpack for the day. She glances over at Axel and rolls her eyes, most likely annoyed at his bare chest. I have no doubt half the reason he's foregoing the shirt is just to get under her skin.

"What's that look for, TG?" Axel asks, running his hand up and down my back.

She doesn't have to answer for me to know. Sitting out here like this, with our boyfriends is a little surreal. A few months ago, Twyler didn't date *anyone*, much less the captain of the hockey team. My hook-ups usually consisted of me sneaking out of the house for a three AM hook-up.

"This," she says, waving her hand in our direction. "It's weird."

"You should be happy your best friend and your boyfriend's best friend are in love." Axel grins while tilting his bowl back and taking a loud slurp of milk. That earns him another annoyed glare. "Hey, now we can double-date."

"Love?" Her big blue eyes bulge and she looks at me and then Reese. "That escalated fast."

"Leave them alone, Sunshine," Reese says, grabbing his empty bowl and carrying it over to the sink. He presses a kiss to the back of her neck. "They're happy."

Everything in my life is upside down. And not in a bad way. It's a very very good way. I mean, Axel Rakestraw, a notorious fuck-boy, told me he loves me. It's this unnatural shift in the force that brings me to announce, "I've made a decision." Inhale, exhale. "I'm ready to go to the police."

Axel sets his bowl on the coffee table and exchanges a look with Twyler and Reese. "To make a report?"

I nod, tucking my hands into the sleeves of Axel's hoodie. "It's time. Past time," I admit. "Yesterday proves it."

"Did something happen?" Twyler asks, walking across the room. "Is that why you were upset last night?"

"Nothing *happened*," I say, emphasizing the word, "but I did run into him yesterday and he's just–"

"A fucking douchebag," Axel supplies, squeezing my thigh.

Reese stretches his arm around Twyler's shoulder and says, "Nadia, you know we've always wanted this to be your decision. Whatever you want to do, we've got your back."

I look at Axel. "You're okay with it?"

"This has nothing to do with me, T. I support you no matter what."

"It's probably too late to do anything, and they'll just say I was a willing participant, but I think it's important to have something on the record." I swallow and a wave of anxiety threatens to strike. "Otherwise he'll never stop."

"I sent a copy of the video to Ruby when it happened," Twyler says. "For safe keeping."

Ruby is Twyler's sister who is a few years older and works down in Tennessee as a teacher. She's the one that alerted Twyler to the fact the video had been recorded and shown live online.

"If you can get it from her that would be good."

Axel's fingers link with mine. "When do you want to go?"

"Soon, before I chicken out."

"You're not chicken," Twyler says.

"She's right," he says, then lifts his chin at Reese. "Tell Coach I won't be there today."

Reese nods. "Sure thing."

"What? No." I shake my head. "I don't want you to miss practice or get in trouble."

He turns my face toward his. "T, this is more important than practice and hockey. Coach'll just have to deal with it." His mouth forms a grim line and his eyes dart over my shoulder to where I know Reese is standing. "You're not the only one that has something to report."

A BODY WRACKING shiver runs through my body. It's not cold in here, and despite the mildly warm cup of coffee the receptionist offered me when we arrived, I can't get warm.

"Here," Axel says, slipping off his jacket.

"You'll get cold."

"Nah," he says, draping it over my shoulders. "I'm hot natured. Especially when I'm pissed." He glances up when the door opens. "Are you sure you want me in here for this?"

I nod, taking his hand. "Please."

The coat is toasty warm, and Axel's scent clings to it, making it feel like a shield. The room is nicer than I expected for the small Wittmore Police Station. The chairs are cushioned and the walls painted a soft blue-gray. A woman enters and introduces herself as Detective Shaw. She's young, with dark hair pulled back in a tight, low ponytail. When she says, "Why don't you start from the beginning," I take a deep breath and begin.

I don't know if it's from keeping the trauma inside for so long, or just the relief of finally making the decision to come forward, but once I start, I can't stop. It's not easy detailing my days as a jersey chaser, but even I can tell that there's a shift—when it stopped being my idea and I became part of someone else's scheme.

"They set up a LonelyFans account?" Detective Shaw asks, taking notes.

"Yes. I have a copy of the video," I tell her, reaching for my phone. Ruby screen recorded it, capturing the name of the account. It hurts to see myself like that, but I can't run from it any longer.

Her eyes flick up from the screen. There's a line creasing her forehead. "Where did this take place?"

"In a house off campus." I look to Axel. "Do you remember the name?"

"Red Rock. Those prefab ones on the back side of the stadium."

Detective Shaw nods and watches the video again. "I'm going to make a copy of this if that's okay? It'll be submitted into evidence." I give my approval and she says, "And there were drugs involved?"

"I think so. I felt like they put something in my food or drink."

Axel squeezes my hand and clears his throat. "Yeah, I have something to add to that."

The edges of the room grow fuzzy as I listen to Axel tell Detective Shaw that he'd been drugged at a party last month. He provides a copy of the lab work, and a statement from the team doctor and Coach Bryant that they think he was either intentionally or inadvertently drugged and he received no consequences.

"Drugged?" I ask, trying to process what he's saying. "It wasn't just THC? You were dosed with rohypnol?"

"That's what the lab tests said." He leans forward. "I own smoking the weed. I remember doing that, but things got hazy after that."

"You barely remembered talking to me that night."

His jaw tenses and he glances at Detective Shaw. "I don't have proof, but I think that drink was for you. One of the last things I remember is interrupting you and Brent and taking your very full cup of punch."

"You said it tasted weird." That night comes rushing back to me. Axel taking my drink. How quickly his words became slurred and how we all thought he was just drunk. "Brent didn't give me that drink though. Some sophomore on the baseball team did."

"Do you have his name?" Detective Shaw asks.

I tell her what I remember and then say, "Why didn't you tell me?"

Axel nervously runs his hand through his hair. "I should have, but you were already going through so much, and I didn't want to pile on. Reese and I made the decision not to tell anyone and to keep an eye on you."

Tears prick at my eyes. I've been holding them back since we got here, but hearing all of this sets them loose. If a guy like Axel, who is strong and powerful, can't be safe, how can anyone else?

"I'm going to give you two a minute alone," Detective Shaw says, picking up her pad and sliding her chair back, "and go check on a few things. I'll be back soon."

I don't look up as she exits the room, and Axel keeps his hand clamped around mine until the door shuts, then he pulls me out of the chair and onto his lap. "Tell me what's going through that head of yours."

"I don't even know where to start." I trace my fingers over the letters on his knuckles. "This is so fucked up. Like, did that kid know he was drugging me? Or did Brent put him up to it? We know he's used others to do his dirty work before." I look up at him. "And is this the reason we started hanging out all the time? Because you were keeping an eye on me?"

"*No*," he says quick and hard. "Fuck no. That was about epic-fuck-ups and you and I made that pact before I found out about the drugs. That first night at the Teal House I had no idea." His hand slides under my hair, cupping the back of my head. "And that's the night I got hooked on you. Keeping an eye on you was just an excuse to be more obvious about it." His green eyes hold mine. "I love you and you're right, all of this is just fucked up, but the best part of this is that I found you."

"I love you too."

The door opens and Detective Shaw walks back in. "Ms. Beckwith, as much as I know you'd rather not, I'd like you to tell me everything that happened again. From the beginning." She sets a recording device on the table. "This time we'll record it."

"You believe me?" I ask, needing some confirmation before I subject myself to the trauma all over again.

"I believe you." She sits and sets a large brown file folder on the table. It's stuffed with papers, and at least five inches thick. "And you're not the only report that we've had."

∼

"HAVE YOU HEARD ANYTHING ELSE?" Twyler asks. We're huddled together in the arena, watching the final game of the season. The Badgers are tied and the stress I used to feel rolling off of Twyler at these games, is now something I feel too.

The last few days have gone by in a rush. I'd worried for so long that by admitting what had happened between me, Brent, and CJ would be this huge bomb in my life. But in reality, nothing was different, other than the relief. We rolled right into final exams. Eric and I gave our presentation earlier that day and got an A. My next to last semester at Wittmore is over.

"No." I watch Axel easily deflect a puck with his shin pad. I glance back, making sure that the other girls aren't in hearing distance. Bridget, Heather, and the other girls are in their usual seats. They're decked out in Badger gear, but this time they're wearing matching Santa hats. "They said they would add this to their evidence and start building a case."

"As much as I want to say I can't believe there are other reports, I'm not surprised."

Detective Shaw didn't give me any names or details on these other reports, just that they existed. The thought makes me sick to my stomach. I can't help but think of the other jersey chasers that would hang around the football players–the sorority girls. Could I have helped someone if I came forward earlier? "They're greedy, entitled men, it's foolish to think that they'd think there were limits on their behavior."

"That's the damn truth," she shakes her head. "Do you think they'll really do anything about it? I mean Brent's one of the top players in the country, he's set to join the draft, and it's not like the NFL has a history of supporting victims of players."

"I'm really not sure. Detective Shaw seemed serious about it." My gaze goes to Axel again. He's focused on the action down rink. "Especially the drug stuff."

Below, Reid slams a defender from the other team against the boards, the puck skittering free. Reese hooks it with the end of his stick and starts into a breakaway.

"Go! Go! Go!" she yells, hands clenched into tight fists. Behind us the girls break into panicked cheers. Reese moves with power and fluidity, drawing out the goalie and waiting until the last second to take a shot so fast it's impossible to know if it made it in or not. The lamp flashes yellow, and a buzzer sounds. Twyler cups her mouth with her hands and cheers, "Yes! Let's go one-five!" Reese lifts his stick and points it in her direction. These two: Relationship goals.

Her smile fades and she rolls her eyes. "I can't believe Reese and Axel kept the fact he was drugged from both of us."

"They were being protective."

"And you're okay with that?" she asks. When I nod, she says, "So, you and Axel still good?"

We're more than good, and how I feel about him is hard for me to articulate. "He apologized, and I understand his reasoning. We barely knew each other and I was still reeling from everything else. I probably would have shut down entirely."

I've never had a man look out for me like Axel does. He takes care of me. It's who he is, deep down, a protector, of the net, his friends, his family, and now me. It's sexy as hell.

"Fair, but I hope you made him grovel for a little bit. I got Reese to watch the special three hour New Kings tour with me the other night for keeping it from me." Twyler's eyes flick across the rink and she frowns. "Wonder who that is?" I follow her gaze to a man who just walked in. He's overdressed in what looks like an expensive overcoat and suit. "Maybe it's someone from the NCAA? Or a scout?"

"No clue," I reply, but if I squint, there's something familiar about him.

Play continues on the ice until the buzzer sounds, announcing the second intermission.

I feel a tap on my shoulder and turn to find Bridget squatting behind us. Her earrings look like jingle bells. "Holy shit. Did you know he was coming?"

"Who?" I frown, glancing at Twyler who shrugs. "Who's he?"

She points across the rink where the zamboni smooths out the ice. "Axel's dad."

22

Axel

IT'S NOT until we skate back onto the ice for the final period that I see him up in the stands. It's such an unfamiliar, surprising sight that I freeze momentarily staring up at him trying to process what he's doing here. I know one thing, it can't be good that Nolan Rakestraw decided to make an appearance.

"Yo! Ax!" Jefferson's voice cuts through my haze. His shoulder bumps into me as he skates past. "Wake up. We've got one more period to go!"

I shake it off and skate to the goal. He'd reached out a few times over the last week, presumably about the draft of my sermon I'd sent him, but my schedule was already chaotic before adding the police report. I didn't have the time or patience to deal with him.

Obviously he's not happy about that.

"Let's wrap this up!" I shout. It takes everything in me not to look up in the stands for my girl, but I've got to stay focused. Get the 'W' and move on. I sure as fuck won't be losing this game now that the Reverend showed up to the first game in four years.

The period moves fast. Erskine U is desperate to even the score. That desperation leads to aggressiveness and sloppy mistakes and more than one fight breaks out. Jefferson gets tossed in sin bin, leaving us without our best defender giving more opportunities than I'd like for them down on my end of the ice. They slap the puck at the goal anytime they get near, praying something gets past. Nothing does.

I guard the fucking goal like my life depends on it.

The clock ticks by, counting down the final seconds, and down by the other goal there's a scrum down by the net, Reid and two defenders fighting for possession, Reese shouting that he's open, when suddenly the puck breaks free, ricocheting off the wall. It slides down the ice and the Erskine forward swoops in behind it, chasing down the breakaway. I crouch, filling as much of the mouth of the goal with my body as possible. My knees are bent, hands and stick ready. I clock his position, the way he holds the stick, the direction of his skates and the angle that he rushes toward me. He takes the shot, and I deflect it, the puck zinging behind the net. I break from the crease, chasing after the puck to gain possession. I should clear the puck off to one of my teammates. I should get back in the goal. But instead, I make eye contact with Reese and give him a nod. Taking a few longer glides away from the net, he and I both wait until the other team descends, then he sprints off, and I snapshot the puck down to the far corner, right into the heel of Reese's blade. It's bold and Coach is likely to kick my ass later but fuck yeah, I'm going to showboat. The Reverend came here to create a spectacle. I'm more than willing to up the ante.

Reese doesn't waste the momentum and takes a quick wrist shot at the goal. The lamplight glares, right as the buzzer signals the end of the game.

"Fuck yes!" I shout, raising the stick over my head. My teammates descend, Jefferson rushing out of the penalty box and Reid, crashing into me so hard I almost fall. I look over his sweaty head and catch sight of my girl. She's grinning wide, eyes shining with pride. This is what it's about.

This is love.

I used to just want to win, to get wasted with my teammates and find a puck bunny to celebrate with, but now all I want is to be with her.

It's no real surprise that when I finally look back to where my father had been sitting, that he's no longer there. The only real question is what he wants and when I'll have to deal with him. Hopefully *after* I celebrate.

"Still undefeated!" Jeff roars when we're back in the locker room, stripped of pads and gear, heading to the shower. "Guess that 'stache really is magical."

"That's what Nadia said," Ripley jokes. "Bazinga!"

"Don't." I give him a hard look and he holds his hands up in surrender. "But yeah," I grin, "I'm not hearing complaints, on or off, the ice."

"Is it true," Murphy asks, "that you got called down to the police station the other day for matching the description of a pervert terrorizing campus?"

It's a joke, but it hits a little too close, and my gaze flicks to Reese's, but his jaw just tightens and he gives a curt head shake.

"They mistook me for someone else, but not because of the 'stache." I smooth out the fuzz over my lip and then grip my junk. "They thought I resembled a guy named Hugh Cocke."

"Rakestraw," Coaches voice carries over the revelry. "A minute."

I slam my locker door shut and follow him into the hall. "I know I took it too far on that last play, but I saw an opportunity and I went for it."

"That's why I have you on the team, because you're willing to take risks." He crosses his arms over his chest. "I hate to break up the celebration in there, because you deserve it, but your father is in my office waiting to talk to you."

"F–" I bite off the word. "Now? In your office?"

"Yep." The annoyed look on his face tells me he's not happy about it either. "I've got shit to do," he says, "so make it fast."

"Yes, sir."

When I reach the office door, I see him standing, facing Coach Bryant's shelf of awards and memorabilia. I don't know if he hears me or smells me first, but he turns, wrinkling his nose. Yeah, I'm still shirtless and probably smell like the inside of a hockey glove, but that's what the Reverend gets for calling me in before I had a chance to shower.

"Axel."

"Reverend," I say, like there's nothing unusual about the situation. I drop into the seat across from the desk and stretch out my legs. "What's up?"

"I'll make this quick," he says, eyes roving over the ink on my torso and arms. "I'm aware that you've been interviewed at the police station involving an incident with a young woman on campus."

How the fuck? I swallow the question. My father has eyes and ears everywhere. I should know that by now. "No good game? No, well played on being undefeated? No congrats on blocking that last goal and getting an assist?"

"Not when I'm trying to handle a PR crisis."

"There is no PR crisis. I made a statement and handed over some relevant evidence to help a friend." Nope, that's not right. I amend, "To help my *girlfriend*."

"You mean the girl, Nadia Beckwith, listed in the report."

"That's exactly who I mean."

"I was afraid it was something like that." He sighs and props himself on the edge of the desk. His dark gray slacks have a perfect crease down the front. "This girl... Axel, she's not acceptable."

"What the hell does that mean?" Anger licks up my spine. "Acceptable?"

"From the report, I know that she's had some kind of run-in with men on campus. I've reviewed her social media, the clothing and behavior she exhibits." He looks down at me. "She's got a reputation for pursuing athletes, so the motives behind her interest in you is questionable at best, but what she really is, for you, is a distraction."

I don't even know where to begin with the absolute nonsense that just came out of his mouth. So I call it for what it is. "Bullshit."

"See? You get defensive when I call you out on truths and it leads to vulgar language."

"You're right," I tell him, happy to double down. "I am fucking defensive, but it's because you're talking shit about my girlfriend."

"I knew you were up here carousing and testing the bounds of my patience. First it was the drugs and probation, now it's this police report and an association with someone who has a questionable past and motives." He exhales slowly. "I gave you four years and more freedom and indulgence than I ever should have allowed. You've got five months before you come back into leadership at Kingdom, where your entire life will be set; financially, professionally, and personally. Now isn't the time to pursue any kind of public relationship, especially with a girl like that."

"Tell me, Rev, what kind of girl do you think she is?"

It's a dare he's more than willing to take. "Loose morals. Sexually promiscuous. Attention seeking, and from what it looks like, gold digging. She's not the kind of woman that you can have standing by your side as you take on your future. She's a liability."

If we weren't in Coach Bryant's office, I'd be in a rage of destruction. But that would only prove my father's point. That I'm not in control. That I'm not thinking clearly. That I don't know what I want. Because for the first time in my life it's perfectly, crystal, clear.

"I know you're used to being surrounded by people that kiss your ass all day long, but that's not happening here." My conviction gets stronger with every word. "I'm not breaking up with her. I love her, and I plan on being with her for a long time."

"Love," he mutters. "I never expected this would be one of your rebellions."

"Getting together with Nadia is the least rebellious thing I've ever done in my life. She's helped me get sober. She's the reason I stopped chasing every female on campus looking to get my dick wet. She's good for me and believe it or not, I'm good for her." The more I talk the more calm I feel. "She's the victim in that police report–we both were–but you can't see that because you're too busy judging and controlling everyone."

"When you minister over a congregation the size of mine, it's important to have a hand in everything." He clears his throat. "Like the draft I received of your sermon. It's sloppy and uninspired."

"That's because I'm not inspired. I can't get up there on that stage and fake it like you do. Pretending to be pious while you're flying around on private planes and living in a multi-million dollar home."

His irritation flares, flipping like a switch. "I give everything to that church and congregation. *Everything*. Don't you dare question my integrity."

"Look, it's working for you–and them. They treat you like a god and you provide them with some kind of guidance and peace. But I think that it makes you crazy that I'm the only one that doesn't fall on my knees." I stand, circling the chair to get some distance. My adrenaline is already running high from the game and I don't want to do something I'll regret. "You're not a god to me. You're my father. I'm not breaking up with Nadia. She's mine and I'm not letting her go."

"I suspected you'd say as much," he says stiffly. "But remember, you're not just walking away from your future, but the family. I know you don't care about me, but this includes your mother and sister. I'll forbid them to see you."

"They're adults." I pinch the bridge of my nose. "You don't control them. See? This is what I'm talking about!"

"Don't I? They're as used to the life I've created as anyone else. The big house, the trips, the celebrity. The mistakes I made with you," his voice is heavy with regret, "are ones I made sure not to repeat with your sister. She'll be married to David soon and he's more than eager to step into the position if you choose to abandon it."

I blink, trying to process what he's saying. "So you already had a back up plan."

"It's been clear to me before the girl came into the picture that you're not dedicated to this path. Having a back up plan is the only way to run a business."

A business. Not a church.

"Fine. Train David to take my place, but Shelby is just a kid. She doesn't need to get married yet. Give her time to grow up."

"And turn out like you?" His head tilts. "Your sister is loyal and ready to devote her life to the Kingdom. She'll be content to be a wife and mother."

"You mean she's ready to devote her life and marriage to you."

"That's your problem, Axel." He shakes his head. "I release you from your obligations and you don't like it. I tell you to get focused and you rebel. Nothing makes you happy."

If anything, leadership, but I'm still worried about Shelby. She's too young for this kind of commitment. She needs to grow up, experience the world, get an education outside of our father's teachings. That will never happen if I walk away. I'm the only thing standing between her and a suffocating life.

"I know this conversation has been heated. You're coming off a big game. Due to that, I'll give you until tomorrow to fully make your decision." He walks to the door. "You know my terms and what I can offer you, but in return I require your full commitment. To your father, both heavenly and on this earth."

He walks out, leaving me feeling like I'm being torn in two. I'd always known my future wasn't with the Kingdom, but being separated from my family? From Shelby?

It's the one thing he knows I won't agree to.

~

UNABLE TO FACE my teammates or the fans waiting outside, Coach Bryant gives me permission to wait them out. When the locker room is finally empty, I hit the shower, ducking under the scalding spray finally allowing my emotions to unleash. I scrub away hot angry tears along with the sweat and grime. My father actually drew a line. My girl or my family. The future he wants for me or the future I want.

But the worst of all, is the way he spoke about Nadia. If I'd ever entertained ideas of bringing her back to Texas with me, those thoughts are gone. She's not safe there. And that's what I promised her with me; a safe space. This is why I never tried to have a real relationship with anyone before. Everything here has always been temporary. My real life is back in Texas–back in the Kingdom.

I was foolish to think I could have both.

Turning off the water, I grab a towel and dry off before wrapping it around my waist. I head into the locker room and stop short. I shouldn't be surprised Reese is still here, dressed in his post game suit and tie, waiting on me.

"Don't you have programs to sign? Fans to suck up to?"

"Eh, the other guys deserve a chance every once in a while." I open my locker and drop my towel, giving him a view of my bare ass. "Jesus. I probably should have waited until you were dressed."

I yank up a pair of boxers and turn to face him. "Better?"

"Infinitely." He leans against the bank of lockers across from mine. "So, your father was here."

I slide into my pants, one leg after the other. "Yep."

"Want to talk about it?"

"Not really."

He doesn't move, just watches as I pull on my undershirt.

"Fine," I mutter, knowing it's futile. Reese is a nosy bitch. "My father has spies everywhere that keep tabs on me. I knew he was aware of my probation. He managed to get that shut down, which is why it never leaked into the media. But he also knows about Nadia's police report, as well as my statements."

"Okay, well, keeping it out of the media isn't the worst thing."

"No, the worst thing is him telling me to stay away from Nadia because she's not an appropriate girl for a man going into church leadership."

"Oh fuck."

"Yeah." I button my shirt, getting riled up again. "He said some really shitty things about her. *Untrue*, shitty things about her reputation and morals. And he gave me an ultimatum. Her or the Kingdom."

"Easy," Reese says. "You pick her."

"I do pick her," I tell him. "Every fucking time, but because I'm dealing with Nolan Rakestraw there's more."

"What else does he want?"

"If I choose Nadia and walk away from the Kingdom, I'm walking away from my entire family. For good."

"Shelby."

"Yep." I throw my tie over my neck. "He had it all planned. He already knew I wasn't sure about going back to work for him, so he had a back up plan." I tell him about David and how my nineteen year old sister is promised to this guy. "She'll be stuck popping out babies and supporting him for the rest of her life. I can't let that happen."

I grab my jacket and my bag and slam the locker door.

"Ax," Reese says, taking a moment to choose his words, "you can't save everyone."

"What? What does that mean?"

"Protecting shit? That's what you do. It's in your nature. The net. Your teammates. Your girl. I know you love your sister, but she's got her own life to live." He frowns. "Does she even want your help?"

"She doesn't know what she wants," I argue. "She thinks she wants what my father wants."

"Dude, listen to yourself. How the hell is that any different from your dad making decisions for her?"

"It just is," I say, refusing to back down. "I just want her to have options."

"I know it's hard to accept, but technically she is an adult. These are her own decisions to make and I know you don't agree with them, but Nadia... she's here. And for some insane reason she wants a tattooed, pierced, reformed fuck-boy as her partner, and fuck man, *you* have options. Incredible ones and they may give you the chance to help out Shelby later–*if* she wants it."

The NHL.

"I told coach I don't want in the draft."

"With an undefeated season and a game like tonight, I promise you it's not too late."

The truth is that I've spent my lifetime running toward a cage, and anything out of it never truly seemed like an option. Maybe I've been as trapped as Shelby. Or maybe I've just been scared.

But regardless, it's time for me to decide what life I want to live, and who I want to live it with.

23

Nadia

I KNOW when he doesn't come out with the others that something's wrong.

Reid strolls out in a purple pinstripe suit and aviators despite the fact it's dark out. When he signs the last program thrust in his direction he walks over to where I'm standing with Twyler.

"You guys coming to the party tonight at the Manor? I'm DJ'ing."

"I told Reese I'd come by for a few minutes. I'm leaving early for Tennessee tomorrow." She looks at her phone. "Where is he anyway?"

"Coach called Ax into his office." His eyes flick up to mine. "I think he's sticking around to find out what's going on." He holds his hand up in a wave. "See you back at the house."

"Do you think he's in trouble?" I ask.

"For that last play? Maybe, but they won, so I can't see Coach Bryant giving him too hard of a time."

I have a nagging feeling it's not Coach Bryant that's holding him up and after waiting another five minutes I tell Twyler, "I'm going to go check on him."

"Are you sure?" she looks uneasily at the arena door. "If Coach Bryant really is mad, you don't want to get in the middle of it."

"I just want to make sure he's okay." I squeeze her hand. "If he or Reese comes out, text me."

"All right, but if Coach Bryant has that vein on his forehead, get out of there." She gives me a stern look. "I mean run, don't walk."

"Gotcha."

I weave through the remaining fans and push through the arena doors. This takes me to the lobby, but I know my way back to the locker rooms after going with Twyler during the game.

The warm heat of the lobby feels good and as I cross the space toward the back staircase, a man approaches, calling my name. It's the first time I've seen Axel's father up close. He's handsome, an older copy of his son with no piercings or tattoos. His hair is closer to gray than blond at this point, but the warm smile is so familiar, it stops me in my tracks. "Miss Beckwith?"

"Yes."

"I'm Nolan Rakestraw. I wanted to see if we could speak for a moment?" He adds, "It involves my son, Axel."

"I was just going to look for him."

"He may be a few minutes longer. That's all this will take." He gestures to a bench near the ticket booth. "Please."

I sit, admittedly both curious and suspicious. There's no way Axel knew his father was coming to the game. I saw it when he noticed him after intermission. He was flustered for a moment–but in true form, got it together quickly.

He sits next to me, legs crossing over one another. "I spoke with Axel after the game, which is why I'm sure he'll need a few extra minutes before he comes out. We had to speak about current events in his life and how these will affect his future."

"Okay."

"Miss Beckwith–"

"You can call me Nadia."

"Nadia, of course." He smiles tightly. "By the time I was Axel's age, I was in college, but already married and preaching at my father's church every Sunday. I had my life planned out and although it was comforting, at times I felt like something was missing–a worldliness I was unable to share with my congregation." He leans back. "I felt like I couldn't always relate to the struggles they came to me with. I felt limited in my knowledge and guidance, and I determined then, that when my son was of age, I'd give him the freedom to explore life a little more so that when he stepped into his role, he would be more prepared to minister to his flock's needs." He nods over at the doors that lead to the ice. "That's why I've always allowed him to pursue sports. Even on a high level. Why I didn't keep him from sowing his oats, from getting an education, from seeing the world. All of this was just experience for what came next; the Kingdom."

"That was very forward thinking of you," I say, because I'm not sure what this is about or what he wants from me. "Axel is a good leader. He's dedicated to his teammates and friends."

"It's my understanding you two have become more serious than his prior relationships."

Heat prickles on my neck. I'm not sure it's because I'm talking to a minister or Axel's father. Maybe both. "We have."

"The one demand I have made of my son in exchange for this freedom is that he return home to minister to the Kingdom when he graduates."

"He's told me and he seems prepared for that."

"Good," he says quietly, then lifts his chin. "Has he told you that to fulfill his duties he'll need to present himself in a certain way–a particular lifestyle?"

"You mean like the tattoos and piercings?"

"As much as I personally dislike them, they're relatable to our younger congregants." He shifts. "No, I mean that Axel will need the right kind of woman to support him for the rest of his life. Someone who can handle the scrutiny of an international congregation. She'll need the background and backbone of a saint."

A wave of anxiety unfurls in my chest. "What are you saying?"

"I'm aware of your history, Nadia. Of the athletes you've spent the last four years persuing. I know about the pornography and the online accounts. This kind of lifestyle, this past, will follow my son around like a cloak of sin." His expression turns grave. "It will follow our entire family around, undoing everything we've worked so hard for."

My jaw drops but before I can formulate any words, to ask him how he knows about the LonelyFans account, or anything else about me, he adds, "The conversation I had with Axel after the game was decisive. He's choosing his family and his future. Regrettably, you will not be a part of that and I'm afraid my son hasn't come out of the locker room yet because he's avoiding having this conversation with you."

"He's breaking up with me?" I ask. "Because I'm not good enough for your family?"

"You're one of God's children, Nadia. He loves you and I'm sure you'll find your own path." He stands. "It just won't be with my son."

My chest feels like it's being crushed by the weight of every stupid thing I've ever done. What Reverend Rakestraw says makes sense. I am a mess. I do have a soiled, dirty past. I'm a liability for a man like Axel–for a family like his. The idea of being with him–being his partner in whatever career he chooses was dumb. I learned that with Brent and all the other athletes I chased.

"What I can do for you, is make this video and report disappear. I can wipe them off the face of the earth and you can pretend they never happened. Neither you or Axel will be tied to this sordid affair and everyone can go back to fulfilling their expectations."

I blink. "Everyone?"

He reaches into his pockets for his gloves. "Yes. It'll be like it never happened."

"But it did happen. Brent and CJ drugged and used me. They filmed me without my consent and sold it online." I stand, the anger bubbling to the surface. "And they drugged your son–who probably saved me from it happening again when he accidentally consumed it instead of me." I push up on my toes in an attempt to look him in the eye. "Do whatever you want to save your son, but leave me out of it. I own my past, flaws and all, and refuse to have it erased. The people that did this to me need to be stopped, and I'm not backing down because it makes you uncomfortable."

"And this," he says, pulling on a glove, "is exactly why you're a liability, and why you'll never be my son's future." He spreads his fingers. "Good luck, Miss Beckwith."

He walks out the arena door, allowing in a gust of cold air. I'm shaken, not from the cold, but from trying to process everything that he just told me–trying to sort out what was real and what was just a twisted threat. I don't know what he said to Axel or what he really thinks, but if he plans on breaking up with me, he sure as hell is going to do it to my face.

~

THE PARTY at the Manor is full blown by the time I arrive. Someone hung colored holiday lights along the porch railing, and a huge blow up reindeer wobbles by the steps. Upbeat Christmas music pours out of the speakers and everyone seems to be in good spirits. Winter break starts in the morning and most everyone will leave campus and head home for the next two weeks. I'm not exactly looking forward to going to Florida. My parents will undoubtedly have questions about how fast I left at Thanksgiving. Will Holt may still be living next door and I'm not interested in ever seeing him again. It sucks. Home used to be a safe space, but not anymore. Axel became that for me, and now I'm not sure if I have that either.

I didn't wait for Axel to come out of the arena, instead texting Twyler that I would meet her here. I needed a minute to recover from the force that is Nolan Rakestraw. I went home to change, taking off Axel's jersey, and wearing my own clothes. Standing outside the Manor, looking at the crowd of people up on the porch and through the lit windows, I realize that for the first time since arriving at Wittmore, I feel like I belong. Not just with Axel, but with his friends.

They see me as more than a jersey chaser or a girl ready to party. No one inside is looking at me for a hook-up, or an easy lay. They've embraced me for who I am, both as Axel's girl, and Twyler's friend.

I'm going to hate giving this up.

I climb the front steps and head into the party.

"Nadia!" Reid appears the instant I cross the threshold, throwing his arms around me. He's had a wardrobe change and is no longer in the purple suit but a flashy cardigan with an argyle pattern and baggy jeans. "You need to go find your man. He looks like someone ran over his kitten."

"He doesn't have a kitten." I've avoided my phone, afraid I'd pick it up. We need to talk face to face.

"Well, if he did," he points to the kitchen where I see Axel standing by the kitchen counter talking to Murphy. "That's exactly what he'd look like."

He's already lost his shirt, and his jeans hang precariously low on his hips. When I finally make it inside, I get a closer look and he doesn't look sad. In fact, he looks like he's doing just fine, with a bottle of Jack in one hand and a joint loose in the fingers of his other.

"Got a light?" he asks Murphy, who frowns as he pats down his pockets. His expression brightens and fishes one out. Axel holds out the bottle to trade, but I snatch the lighter mid-air.

"I'll take that."

"T," he says, tongue swiping out over his piercing. It's not quite the confirmation I need that he's already had some of the whiskey, but he proves it when he grabs for me, drawing me close and slanting his mouth over mine. He tastes like whiskey, and the instant his tongue swipes against mine, I forget why I'm here. I'm dizzy by the time he releases me, his forehead pressed against mine. "Fuck, you taste good."

I, in and exhale, trying to steady myself, but it's really hard when he's looking at me like he wants to devour me.

"You weren't outside the arena after the game," he says, eyes narrowed at my shirt. "And you changed." He fingers the hem of my sweater. "You know I like it when you wear my jersey."

I tilt my head. "You're drunk."

"Not quite." He hands the joint back to Murphy who's smart enough to vanish, leaving us alone. "It's been a shitty night," he admits, rubbing his hand over his bare chest. "I just wanted to feel something."

"I saw your dad was at the game."

His eyebrow quirks, the silver glinting off the light. "Ah, so you were tipped off by the scent of pretentiousness and narcissism."

I laugh, because he's not wrong. But *something* is wrong. I can sense it.

"So that's why you're drinking again," I say, curling my fingers into the belt loops of his jeans, tugging him to me. His pants hang so low, I can see the 'T' inked below his hip. "Because I thought we talked to one another when something goes sideways?"

"For once this isn't an epic fuck-up," he says, pushing my hair off my cheek. "It's more of a royally fucked."

"Come on," I pull him toward the stairs, but they're too crowded with people. Instead, I push open the door that I know goes to a small enclosed porch just off the living room. It's where they stash the stuff they don't want getting broken or stolen during parties. It's dark inside, only lit by the soft glow from the Christmas lights outside. The noises of the party are muffled. I see the old couch pushed up against the brick wall and force him to sit with me. "I have something to say."

He looks up at me with those brilliant green eyes and my heart starts to break. And even though I'm putting up a good front, nothing about this feels safe. It feels like I'm dragging us in front of a firing squad, finger locked on the trigger, ready to pull the first shot.

Maybe this is what happens when you've been hurt so much, that it feels easier to do it yourself.

I take a deep breath and continue. "And you need to let me just get it all out, okay?"

"You're scaring me a little, but okay."

"I know you're going to break up with me." His mouth opens but I give him a look of warning. "I know your dad doesn't want us together. That he thinks I'm not an "appropriate" girl for you now or for the future. And I get it. The way I used to be... it's a mess. I'm a mess. I come with baggage, and history, and flaws. You've always accepted that about me and it's made me a better person." I take a deep breath. "So if you want to break up with me, I understand, we've always kind of been 'for now' and I hate it, but I accept it. But if you're ending this, then you've got to do it to my face, and not leave me wondering what I did wrong like all those other guys did."

Axel's forehead furrows and he says, "You talked to my dad."

"After the game."

"Son of a–" He grimaces. "Yeah, well so did I, and he came to issue me an ultimatum."

"Oh." That's not exactly what I was told.

"He doesn't approve of my lifestyle choices. Or the sermon I wrote for the holidays. Or the fact I made a statement to the police." He toys with the hoop in his bottom lip. "Or, to be totally, painfully, honest, my relationship with you." His eyes cast down. "And if I want access to my family, in any way, I have to give up you and everything else I love."

"Wow." I drop back into the couch, "that's quite thorough."

"That's Nolan Rakestraw. If he's going to go scorched earth he's going to do it fully." He takes my hand. "But here's the thing, darlin', I was willing to give up hockey. Women. Drugs and drinking. I was willing to get up there on that stage at Kingdom and do the little song and dance–out of some genetic obligation–but the one thing I absolutely refuse to give up, is you."

My heart flutters. "You told him that?"

"Unequivocally."

Well. That's not how Reverend Rakestraw presented it to me. "Interesting."

"How's that?"

"He told me that you were breaking up with me."

He laughs darkly. "You gotta give it to him, for someone who bathes in holy water, he sure as hell plays dirty."

I shift to look at him better. "I don't want to be the thing that comes between you and your family."

"*He's* the thing that's come between me and my family. It's just a bullshit excuse to exert his control and I'm done with it."

"Axel–"

He grabs me by the waist, lifting me like a ragdoll until I'm straddling his lap. "I'm not happy about cutting my sister and mother out of my life, but Cap and I talked about it." His jaw tenses. "I can't drown myself while trying to save everyone else–especially if they don't want it."

"So that's that. You're walking away from Nolan Rakestraw and his Kingdom."

"Yeah I guess I am." His hands slide down to cup my ass. "Good thing I've got options."

There's only one real option this man has and it really is a good one. I raise an eyebrow. "You mean the NHL?"

"If they'll take me." His eyes light with an eagerness I've never seen before. "You okay with that?"

"It doesn't matter what I want." I touch his chest, fingers running over the 110 above his heart. "I just want you to be happy."

"I never allowed myself to really believe it. My future was too locked in and obviously it's still a fucking long-shot, but yeah. I think I want it." He tilts his head, looking up at me. "And it does matter what you want, because part of making me happy is knowing you're there, sitting with the rest of the wives, wearing my name and number."

I still. "Did you just say wife?"

"One day." He grins, knowing it's too fast, even for two impulsive people like us. "If I'm going out on my own, chasing this dream, then I'm going to have to have someone by my side to make sure I don't make any epic fuck-ups."

All I ever wanted was to be a WAG but I'd been told over and over I'm not good enough. That girls like me aren't wife material.

"Hey." Axel touches my chin. "Don't freak out on me. Just know that no matter what happens, I want you with me."

"Sounds like you need me."

His hips push up, letting me feel how much he needs me. Wrapping his hand around the back of my neck, he pulls my mouth to his and mutters, "You have no fucking idea."

Our lips meet, and this kiss is different. I feel it in the tremble of his finger tips, and the way my heart skips every other beat. We're not two people running from our problems. We're Axel and Nadia. Two people that know what they want. Each other.

"I love you," he says, "and I want to fuck you so bad right now, but not on this couch. It's filthy."

I laugh, touching my nose to his. "Hey, so what are you doing for Christmas?"

"No clue." His hand thrusts into his hair. "Guess I could tag along with the guys. Reid's mom is always happy to see me."

I nod, then offer, "Want to come to Florida?"

"Florida," he says, a small curve on his lips. "You gonna be wearing one of those sexy bikinis?"

"It's winter, Ax, Florida gets cold too."

"Darlin', I'll always keep you warm." His mouth and hands do the job, stealing another kiss until I'm not just warm, but breathless.

24

Nadia

"Explain the facial hair to me." Kendall, my future sister-in-law, nods to where Jason, my dad, and Axel are breaking-in the new corn hole game my mother bought my dad for Christmas. They're set up in the backyard in the grassy area next to the pool deck. "Not that it detracts from his looks, because he's very good looking, but it doesn't really fit his whole vibe."

"Superstition," I say, watching as he picks up his bean bag and lines it up with his target. "He'll shave it once they lose a game."

"How long has that been?"

"Two months."

We're sitting next to the fire pit, keeping warm while the guys play their game. Mom is inside curled up with a new book she got from my dad. Once the presents are open and the brunch dishes are cleaned up, she declares the rest of the afternoon for herself, and takes a much needed break.

Axel's bean bag lands in the hole and he lifts his arms in victory. I clap and cheer, earning a wink in return.

"It sucks that things aren't great with his family, but he seems comfortable here." She arches an eyebrow. "And he seems super into you."

A warm blush rises on my cheeks. I've had sex and a lot of hook-ups over the years, but never a boyfriend. Especially not one like Axel.

"Axel isn't afraid to show his feelings," I admit, "that's for sure."

Kendall is right, he does seem comfortable here. My mom was surprised, but didn't push back when I told her I was bringing a friend with me for the holidays. Dad definitely did a double take at the tattoos and piercings, and it was weird seeing Axel next to someone like Jason, who isn't out of shape or anything, but definitely doesn't have the physique of a college athlete. I'm used to seeing Axel around his teammates and friends who are all as big as he is. Even with all of that, he won everyone over with that Axel Rakestraw charm and charisma.

"Any word from the police?" she asks. I'd updated her on everything the first night we got back.

I shake my head. "No and I don't know if we ever will. Going after someone like Brent and CJ are more than going after a single person. They've got agents and managers. NCAA reps and people looking out for them with the NFL. They're assets and no one wants to lose that–especially with a player with as much promise as Brent. They'll do whatever they need to do to protect him."

It's that entitlement that allows him to take risks like this in the first place. I hug my knees to my chest, feeling the warm heat from the fire. It's not nearly as cold as it is up north, but just thinking about the case gives me a chill.

The guys finish their game, and clean up the bean bags, while leaving the boards out to play again later. I hear Dad ask Axel as they walk up, "Sure you're not a forward? You've got good aim."

"Nope. Maybe all that time on the ice with Reese rubbed off on me."

Dad ruffles my hair on his way past, and Jason grabs Kendall's hand to help her lift off the chair and they all go inside. Axel sits next to me and throws my legs over his lap and pulls me close. His warm lips press against my temple. "You cold?"

"Nah, not with you next to me."

"You up for a swim?" He saw my father swimming laps this morning, realizing the pool is heated.

"You really want that Florida Christmas Day swim, don't you?"

"I'd rather go skinny dipping, but your family likes me, and I'd like to keep it that way." His mouth moves close to my ear. "But yeah, I mostly want to see you in one of those bikinis that have been taunting me from your ChattySnap page."

I tilt my head to look at him. "We eat dinner at six and I still need to finish the kolaches."

He checks his watch. "It's only two. Think there's enough time?"

The sun is out, and Axel may not be the only one looking to see the other mostly naked. He's been relegated to the pull out couch in my mom's office since we got here, and even though we've spent our days together, there's always family around. Sure, we've managed to sneak off for a few quick make-out sessions, mostly out here in the backyard, but having him close? Feeling his body? I miss him.

"Yeah, I think so. Meet me back down here?"

His smile is worth it, and we part in the kitchen. I go upstairs to change and he heads to the temporary guest room. I cover myself with one of his jerseys and grab a few soft pool towels from the linen closet. When I get back outside he's not there, but I notice the flame is low on the fire pit and drop the towels in a chair, walking to the edge of the patio to grab a few pieces of kindling my dad keeps stacked by the house.

Bending, picking through the wood, I hear, "Red or white?"

I spin, and see Will with his arms draped over the gate separating our properties. He looks like crap. Skin pale, eyes bloodshot. A tendril of smoke wafts from the tip of his cigarette.

"What do you want?" I thought he was spending the holiday out of town with his parents.

"Just wondering if you've got on the red bikini or the white one," he says, eyes roaming over me. "It is Christmas so maybe you went with red, but that new boyfriend of yours probably wants the white."

The way he looks at me makes me feel sick. "You're a creep, you know that?"

He takes a long drag on the cigarette and then exhales. "I've seen you sneaking out here with him." I ignore him, grabbing another piece of wood, but when I look up, I don't miss the mean smirk lifting his bottom lip. "I thought he seemed familiar and I looked him up. Axel Rakestraw, right? He's some kind of super star hockey goalie up there, huh?"

"You stalking me now?"

"Nah, I was just curious if I needed to warn this guy that he's fucking around with a cock-teasing, rape-crying, lying whore?"

My body convulses, anger seizing me, and I drop the wood on the ground. I don't know what I'm going to do to him–but the rage that runs through me terrifies me–but before I can act, strong hands pull me aside, and Axel's broad frame separates us.

"What the fuck did you say to my girl?"

"Hey, just looking out for you, man," Will says with a shrug. Proving that he's either high as fuck or dumb as hell. "She'll let you fuck her six ways to Sunday, and then cry foul."

Whatever he is, Will never sees the punch coming. It's a bone shattering crack that snaps his head and body back. He stumbles, but when he regains his footing he's holding his cheek and cries, "What the hell, man? Are you crazy?"

"Not even close." Axel leaps over the gate and crowds up on Will until his back is against his parent's house, his fists balled. "I know who you are and what you did. Nadia was a kid and you preyed on her."

"She's really got you convinced, huh?" Will says, spitting blood on the ground. "She came on to me. She came to my house. She teased me with her little virgin act, almost begging me to take it and then later, when she had regrets, she called me a rapist."

Axel slams his hands into Will's chest, flattening him against the wall. "You've got a problem, dude. A serious one, but let me tell you one thing, Nadia isn't it. You stole something from her, something she's fought tooth and nail to get back, and like hell I'm going to let you keep messing with her." Axel's chest is pushed out, he looks like he's one second from tearing Will limb from limb. "Understood?"

Will seems to come to his senses and nods. "Yeah, fine. Whatever."

Unsatisfied, Axel's hand clamps down on his shoulder and pushes him toward the fence–toward me. "But first, apologize."

Will licks his bloody lip, and the side of his face has started to swell. "I'm sorry."

"For what?" Axel prompts.

"For calling you a whore," he mumbles. "And saying you're a cock-tease. I admit it. You were easy and a little desperate and I knew I could talk you into just about anything." Will touches his cheek and winces. "I won't talk to you again. Just keep your attack dog off of me."

Axel's green eyes meet mine and the anger and love in them makes my heart flip flop. "That good for you, T?"

I nod. "Yeah, knowing I'll never have to talk to him again is enough."

Will is yanked away from the gate and Axel leans down, whispering something in his ear. Will gives a curt nod and walks off. He goes into the pool house, slamming the door behind him.

"What did you say?" I ask Axel once he's back on our side of the fence.

He wraps his arms around me, pulling me flush against his body. "I told him that if he ever speaks to you again, I'll feed him his teeth one by one and then call the cops on his predatory ass." He tucks a lock of hair behind my ear. "You okay?"

I flatten my hands on his abdomen and kiss the number tattooed over his heart. "Yeah, I think so."

"Good." He frowns, fingers toying with the back of my bikini bottoms. "I guess he kind of ruined the vibe of an afternoon swim."

I look up at him and say, "I think I've got a better idea."

"Okay. The timer is on," I press the button on the oven and call out to my mom. "Can you take them out when it rings?"

"Yes," my mom says, nose still firmly in her book. I'm not sure I believe her. Once she's lost in whatever world she's engrossed in, it's hard to pull her back out.

"The kolaches?" Kendall asks. "I'll get them out."

"Yeah?"

"Yeah. I can't wait to try them." Then she gives me a pointed look. "Take your time."

I grin. "Thank you."

The shower is already running when I get to the bathroom linking my room and Jason's. Steam fills the room, fogging the mirror that Axel stands in front of waiting for me. His knuckles are raw and red, and I take his hand, kissing the bruises.

"Good thing you're cooking for me," he says, reaching for me the moment I've shut and locked the door. A towel sits low on his hips, "Or I would've gone down there and dragged you away."

"You like my kolaches?" I ask, feeling his hands ruck up his jersey, feeling for what's underneath.

"I like everything about you." He peeks at my bathing suit, then quickly shucks the shirt over my head. "Jesus Christ, darlin'."

Will had gotten it all wrong. My bikini isn't white or red. It's custom made, black, with the Wittmore badger logo on each of the triangles covering my breasts. Number 01 is stitched on my hip.

"I take that back," he says, face already between my breasts. "I *love* everything about you." He runs the back of his knuckles over my nipples, drawing them into peaks. "You know how I feel when you're wearing my name and number."

The hard line of his erection pressing against the cotton towel confirms how much he likes it, and I yank it away wanting to see him as much as he wants to see me. His cock bobs thick and ready, an arrow directed at me. I touch him, fingers grazing over the velvety tip.

"Fuck," he mutters, guiding me into the shower. "Let's get you cleaned up for dinner."

The spray is hot, but I like it that way. His hands are greedy, and I like that, too. He takes his time, tugging at the strings of the bikini one by one, revealing my body like he's unwrapping a present. The pieces of cloth drop to the tile and he grabs the bottle of gel, soaping up both of his hands, then running his palms over my tits. His cock rubs between us, hard and insistent.

"Ax," I say, body liquid fire from his touch, "I need you inside me."

"Want to get out?" he breathes, water dripping from his hair. "Get a condom?"

I shake my head. "Nothing between us. I'm on birth control."

His jaw tenses, a new hunger sparked in his eyes. He spins me around, pressing my palms against the tile walls. His hand covers mine, the black letters YOLO, staring back at me. My spine shivers when his other hand grabs my hip and pulls my backside against him. His cock is thick, slippery from the soap, and his knee moves between mine, nudging my thighs apart. I feel him at my entrance. I'm too hot. Too horny, and I back into him. He meets my push with a thrust, stretching me out from this angle. The feel of him bare, is too good, and when he wraps an arm around my stomach and groans in my ear I know he feels it too.

"You just get better," he tells me, voice low as he drags in and out of me at an excruciating pace. "Everything about you." His teeth bare down on my shoulder. "Your body. Your laugh. Your fierceness." His hand drops between my legs and he rubs lazy circles into my clit. "I didn't have to step in today. I know that. You can take care of yourself, but, darlin', all I want is to take care of you." I can't see his face, but I feel the veracity of his words. "I want to slay your dragons, and eat your food, and fuck you senseless."

In one day he'll have done all three, and my mind drifts from how good he feels. How *safe*. This wild man, at first sight dangerous, covered in ink and silver. But he's not a hard man. He *loves* hard and that's what makes him different.

That's what makes him mine.

I let him fuck me, let him draw me to the edge, our bodies frantic as we chase each other toward oblivion. And when we reach it, he wraps his arms around me, shielding me from the water, surrounding me in his warmth. Holding me as we topple one after the other.

"I think I'm ready," I say, the orgasm rocking into gentle waves. I touch the letters on his knuckles.

"Hmmm?" he says, chin on my shoulder. I can feel his heartbeat hammering against my back. "For what?"

"My first tattoo."

"Yeah?" His voice perks up. "What's it going to be?"

"The letters EFU."

"What's that mean?"

"Just something I want to remember." I turn and look at him. "That sometimes an epic fuck-up can be the best thing to happen in your life."

EPILOGUE

The bad news is that the guys lose their first game of the season on December 30th.

The good news is that I get to spend New Years Eve with my freshly shaven, no-more mustached, boyfriend. And damn, he's hot.

The frat house trembles with music, half the guests spilled into the yard. Everyone is happy to be back at school–excited to ring in the new year. I'm just obsessed with Axel's mouth.

"T," he says, breaking away from the kiss, "don't get me wrong, I'm happy for you to shove your tongue down my throat, but if that's all we're going to do maybe we should head back home and we can test how it feels everywhere else."

"Tempting." I sigh, trying not to think about Axel's face between my legs. "But I told Twyler we'd meet them here." I run my thumb over his smooth upper lip. "It just feels so weird."

"Maybe I should have ditched the 'stache months ago."

"I told you women were repelled by that thing," Reid says, giving me a questioning look. He'd tagged along with us when we left the manor in a black sweater and dark plaid pants.

"It was sexy," I affirm. "But this is sexier. Don't do it again."

Reid snorts and Axel glares at him, "Why are you even here? We're here because Nadia's project partner invited us. Did anyone even invite you?"

"I'm invited everywhere," he says with absolute conviction. "And it's New Year's Eve and I'm single for the first time in a while."

"Oh, so the thing with Darla is over?"

"Completely." He shrugs like getting out of a long term relationship isn't a big deal. "I'm thinking about entering my slut phase. No more monogamy."

"Maybe you should take a break," I suggest. "It worked for us."

"Yeah," he says, scrunching his nose, "but that feels like I'm limiting myself. I said monogamy, not celibacy." With that, he vanishes through the front door and into the crowd.

"You think he'll go full fuck-boy?" I ask.

"He talks a big game, but Reid's been a one woman man since I met him. He'll be back in a relationship before the end of the month."

His phone buzzes and I can tell by the expression on his face it's not who he wants to hear from.

"No word from Shelby?"

"Just Reese. They're inside."

Axel still hasn't spoken to his father since the night he showed up at his game. He said he told him everything he needed to that night and there was nothing left to say. But he's been trying to reach out to Shelby with no luck.

"Hopefully you'll hear something soon."

Tucking his phone in his pocket, Axel takes my hand and leads us into the party. Bright colored lights reflect off a disco ball hanging from the chandelier in the foyer and a makeshift photo booth is tucked under the stairs. Sorority girls in nearly identical outfits cluster underneath glittery New Year decorations, taking selfies to post on their social media.

Axel catches me watching them. "What? You want a picture?"

I shake my head. "I used to be jealous of those girls, or I thought I was."

He grabs my face and kisses me, and yep, I'm good.

It only takes a few minutes to realize that I may have been the one with the official invite to the party, but Axel has friends in every group on campus, and they all come up to say hello, commenting on the game or his cleanly shaven face. During it all, he keeps me tucked into his side, his thumb rubbing little circles on the tattoo I got the day after Christmas on the inside of my wrist.

"Nadia!" I hear. "You made it."

I twist out of Axel's grip and see Eric walking over. He's got a cup in his hand. We haven't spoken since we found out we got an 'A' on our project and texted each other over the break.

"Looks like a good turn out," I say.

"People are always looking for an excuse to get back on campus after a long break." Axel stayed with my family for two days after Christmas, then he flew back for practice with the team and the game. Will seemed to believe Axel's threat about his teeth because I didn't see him again. "We figured we'd provide everyone with the opportunity."

"Hey, man," Axel says, shaking Eric's hand. "Thanks for the invite."

"There are drinks in the kitchen and on the back deck. Ball drop will be on the front lawn at midnight." He explains how a few of his frat brothers are engineering majors and worked up something for the drop. "I think your friends are in the back playing Quarters."

Axel groans, running his hand through his hair. When Eric makes a questioning face, I say, "Twyler is a Quarters pro. She always wins."

"A fucking ringer," Axel adds. "You'll either lose your money, dignity, or shirt by the time she's done with you."

"Thanks for the tip," Eric says, noticing a couple of girls across the room, gathered around one phone. "See you guys later, Happy New Year."

Leaving us alone, Axel says, "I'm not in the mood to get my ass kicked by Twyler tonight, especially if I'm not drunk." Neither of us have started drinking again, but he did bring a bottle of champagne secure in the bag hanging over his shoulder. He grins down at me. "Want to make out instead?"

"Honestly? Yeah."

He takes my hand and leads me down the hall, testing door knobs along the way. He finds one that's unlocked. It looks like it's a study room, and he's about to pull me inside when Twyler shouts my name, "Nadia, wait."

"TG," Axel says, looking at Reese walking up behind his girlfriend. "This better be good."

"Did you see it?" she asks, looking between us.

I frown. "See what?"

She opens up her phone and pulls up a text thread between her and the other physical therapy interns on campus. One is from the football intern. It's a link.

"It's Brent and CJ." The video pops up and starts playing. It's from a phone and the footage is shaky, but clear enough to see the outside of a club in town and a crowd gathering at the entrance. Suddenly the crowd parts, and Brent comes out first, handcuffed and escorted by the police. CJ follows. The caption underneath says, "Wittmore Football Players arrested on New Year's Eve."

"Does it say why?" I ask, opening the comments.

"Not yet," Twyler says. "Mostly rumors and speculation, but there are a lot of people who seem to suspect it's about drugs or assault."

"Are there any names in there?" I ask. Axel's arm wraps around my waist. "Did they name me?"

Twyler scrolls down the page. "No. Not yet, at least."

My best friend looks up at me and I feel the hot tears building in my eyes. All the emotions hit me at once; relieved. Exhausted. Scared. Twyler senses it and throws her arms around me. "I'm proud of you," she says. "I know it wasn't easy."

"Thanks for pushing me to report them."

Reese squeezes my shoulder and I give him a hug, too. Without Reese and Axel coming with Twyler that night, I don't know what would have happened.

Axel spins me around, and cups my cheeks in his hands. "Talk to me, darlin'."

I take a deep breath and say, "They believed us."

"They believed *you*."

I smile and he says, "Oh shit."

"What?"

He opens his bag and pulls out the bottle of champagne.

"What are you doing?" I ask. "That's for midnight."

"This is for a celebration," he says, lifting the bottle and peeling off the foil wrapper. "And there's no celebration bigger than this."

The cork pops, spilling champagne all over the frat's hardwood floors. He grins and hands me the bottle. "Happy New Year, Nadia."

Not T–for Trouble. Or darlin' because he likes to mess with me. Nadia. Because Axel Rakestraw knows the one thing I need more than anything else.

To be seen.

AFTERWORD

Wondering what happened between Axel and Nadia on the night of their one night stand? Check out this exclusive BONUS SCENE where you can see exactly how big of a f-up it was!

∼

Thank you to everyone for reading Guarded by the Goalie. If you missed book 1 of the series, Faking it with the Forward, you can find the link here!

Book 3 of the series, *Daring the Defender*, following Axel's sister Shelby and Reid will be released next year and is available on preorder.

***

If you're looking for a community that loves reading join us over at Monarch's for some fun.

ACKNOWLEDGMENTS

Thank you for reading Axel and Nadia's story. They kind of crawled into my heart during Faking It with the Forward and their story started unraveling. The response to Faking It was so much bigger than I expected and I honestly needed to clean the dark cobwebs out of my head from writing the Princes, and figured, eh, I'm sure some people will read it. A lot of you read it, and that makes me so happy.

As many of you may know, the Lawson timeline is tough right now and writing keeps me sane during the ups and downs. Being able to have a project to work on at all times really helps.

I wanted to write a quick thank you to Danielle for my lovely covers. They look SO GOOD when we add the foil. Beth for assisting me with plot help early on, Mariana for coming in with a red pen and catching the pesky typos and errors. Sara for always being an enthusiastic supporter. Sam for indulging me in the time I need to tinker with sweet boys and get it out here instead of accidentally making a Royal be too nice, too soon. And of course everyone else who reviews, posts clever edits on socials and is just supportive of my career. It's been a hard few years and all the extras help!

I'm definitely planning on the third book in this series. The publish date will be pushed pretty far out. I'll get to it when I have time in my ROFU schedule and the rest of life!

Thanks again,
Angel

Printed in Great Britain
by Amazon